THE ROAD TO INDEPENDENCE?

CONTEMPORARY WORLDS explores the present and recent past. Books in the series take a distinctive theme, geo-political entity or cultural group and explore their developments over a period ranging usually over the last fifty years. The impact of current events and developments are accounted for by rapid but clear interpretation in order to unveil the cultural, political, religious and technological forces that are reshaping today's worlds.

SERIES EDITOR
Jeremy Black

In the same series

Britain since the Seventies
Jeremy Black

Sky Wars: A History of Military Aerospace Power
David Gates

War since 1945
Jeremy Black

The Global Economic System since 1945
Larry Allen

A Region in Turmoil:
South Asian Conflicts since 1947
Rob Johnson

Altered States:
America since the Sixties
Jeremy Black

The Contemporary Caribbean
Olwyn M. Blouet

Oil, Islam and Conflict:
Central Asia since 1945
Rob Johnson

Uncertain Identity:
International Migration since 1945
W. M. Spellman

THE ROAD TO INDEPENDENCE?

Scotland Since the Sixties

MURRAY PITTOCK

REAKTION BOOKS

For Neil MacCormick

Published by Reaktion Books Ltd
33 Great Sutton Street
London EC1V 0DX
www.reaktionbooks.co.uk

First published 2008, reprinted 2008

Copyright © Murray Pittock 2008

All rights reserved
No part of this publication may be reproduced, stored in a retrieval system, or
transmitted, in any form or by any means, electronic, mechanical, photocopying,
recording or otherwise, without the prior permission of the publishers.

Printed and bound in Great Britain
by CPI/Antony Rowe, Chippenham, Wiltshire

British Library Cataloguing in Publication Data
Pittock, Murray
    The road to independence?: Scotland since the sixties. – (Contemporary worlds)
    1. Nationalism – Scotland 2. Scotland – History – 20th century 3. Scotland –
    History – 21st century 4. Scotland – Social conditions – 20th century
    5. Scotland – Social conditions – 21st century 6. Scotland – Politics and
    government – 20th century 7. Scotland – Politics and government –
    21st century 8. Scotland – Economic conditions – 20th century
    9. Scotland – Economic conditions – 21st century
    I. Title
    941.1'085

ISBN: 978 1 86189 365 9

Contents

Introduction

Why Scotland?

Separate histories of Scotland are fine for Scots. That is the general consensus. Scottish history is a big subject in Scotland: famously, Tom Devine's 1999 study *The Scottish Nation 1700–2000* briefly outsold J. K. Rowling in its home country. But across the UK in general, Scottish history occupies a rather strange no-man's land between the local and national. The BBC and the commercial terrestrial companies broadcast English history UK-wide: but Scottish history programmes, even major series such as Magnus Magnusson's *Tales of a Grandfather* for Radio Scotland in 1998, Fiona Watson's 2000 television history, *In Search of Scotland*, or even – puzzlingly – Charles Kennedy's 2007 programme on the Union, *A Chip on Each Shoulder*, are almost never networked. Scottish history describes itself as national, but is often identified by non-Scots as local. The importance of the Union of Scotland and England in government rhetoric is accompanied by news coverage which barely alludes to Scotland.

There is a double-mindedness in all this: a curious ambivalence, which is the manifest correlative in social and media behaviour to the use of 'Britain' and 'England' as almost unconscious synonyms in normal speech. When it comes to formal descriptions of Scotland itself within Great Britain, a complementary kind of ambivalence reigns. Scotland is routinely referred to as a 'region', a term that seems never to have been used of the country before World War II:[1] yet when it comes to sporting events – and indeed other events where Scotland competes internationally – it is one of the 'Six Nations' or the 'Home Nations'. The very currency bears the Scottish thistle on the 5p and (in combination with the English rose) the 20p coins, and the unitary Anglo-Scots Britishness of the Royal Family was stressed between 1937 and 1967 through the issue of separate Scottish and English shillings, while Scottish pound coins were issued long before Scottish pound notes had begun their slow extinction within Scotland itself. The Scottish Lion sits in the quarters of the Royal Arms: when displayed in Scotland, it occupies two quarters. Iconographically and culturally, Scotland is a national entity in a British union: socially and politically, this is less certain. British values and society are still often seen as unproblematically unitary or equally diverse by commentators: in either case, homogeneous.

Much has changed since earlier epochs of the Union: when, indeed, Scotland was more often regarded as 'national', not least through the great and distinct visibility of its native aristocracy and university-educated middle class. It was not until the second half of the nineteenth century that England had more universities than Scotland, and not until 1945 that the prestige of the Scottish ancient universities began to wane against the new major English city universities like Bristol or Manchester, as an examination of the backgrounds of senior British politicians and officials bears out. If we wind the clock back to 1875, the British ruling class was dominated by Oxford and Cambridge, it is true: but the products of Edinburgh, Glasgow and Trinity College, Dublin were also prominent. One of the things that has really changed since the nineteenth century is that the United Kingdom elite is drawn far more from those educated in the English provinces, and that the chief losers in this process have been the products of Scottish universities (quite a number of whom were in fact English in the era when Dissenters were still effectively excluded from Oxford and Cambridge). Despite plays like The History Boys, Oxbridge influence is also declining: but the sense in which Victorian elites represented the different nations of a united kingdom has been lost. In the Victorian era, the perceived bias of Indian Civil Service exams against Scottish graduates on their introduction was a national issue, debated in the Commons. This in itself was a product of the expectations of Scots as a group for a share – a disproportionate share in terms of population – in the fruits and spoils of the British Empire. Among the dimensions of this was the key role of Scots (and indeed Irish) in the armed forces in the imperial age.

Even before Dublin became the capital of an independent Ireland in 1922, this situation was changing. The greater importance of the English regions in the composition of elites through the development of secondary and tertiary education in the provinces arguably led to a defensive action on behalf of 'BBC English', 'Received Pronunciation' in the 1930s, and then to a decline of the value set on conformity to the metropolitan standard, a decline from conformity accelerated by the BBC itself from the 1960s on. At the same time, the twenty years from 1947 saw the steady dissolution of the British Empire: it was, as I argue in chapter Two, no coincidence that the Scottish National Party's by-election victory at Hamilton and the first surge of Scottish nationalism which accompanied it, happened at the end of this process. Scottish engineers, doctors, merchants and financiers no longer had access to overtly imperial opportunities and markets: the age of Sir Thomas Lipton (1850–1931), of Dr William Jardine (1784–1843) and James Matheson (1796–1878), of George Burns and Robert Napier's Cunard line, was passing. As the British Army declined in importance with the withdrawal west of Suez, there was no longer the same opportunity for figures like Sir Ralph Abercromby (1734–1801), Sir John Moore (1761–1809) and even Douglas, Earl Haig (1861–1928) to shine in command: as late as 1928, the Chief of the Imperial and Indian General Staffs were both Scots.[2] Irish Protestants like Wellington, Wolseley and Kitchener had all served as commanders of the British Army in the nineteenth century, when it was often half-manned by Scots or Irish troops: now the situation was very different. The sensitivity over the continuing amalgamation of the Scottish regiments since the 1960s needs to be seen in this context of an ever-diminishing role for Scots in the British Army. In the last years of Tony Blair's premiership, it has been a significant question whether or not a Scot – leaving aside the vexed question of Blair's own nationality – can be again Prime Minister of the United Kingdom. Between 1945 and 2007, only Alec Douglas-Home's brief tenure in 1963–4 can really be counted; but between 1900 and 1945 the Scots Arthur Balfour, Sir Henry Campbell-Bannerman and Ramsay MacDonald were all at some time Prime Minister; Bonar Law might also be included. The complaint that Scots have too much influence in British government is not infrequently raised: be that as it may, the situation was probably more pronounced in the past. If one counts Gladstone, born in England of two Scottish parents, with a life-long Scottish connexion and a detectable intonation in the surviving recording of his voice, then a tabloid conspiracy theory can be hatched: for it was Gladstone's legislation that made Home Rule for Ireland inevitable (though he could not directly engineer it) and who took the first steps towards Scottish devolution. This is fantasy, no doubt. But the reality was that if we count Gladstone a Briton rather than a Scot, it is on the basis not of his Englishness, but his mixed background and consequent breadth of knowledge and sympathy (north-east Scotland, Liverpool, Oxford, London) within Great Britain. In that sense, he was a not untypical member of the nineteenth-century British elite.

In Gladstone's era, governments attempted relatively little in terms of domestic policy compared with governments since 1945: one reason why the Grand Old Man could still be Prime Minister in his mid-eighties. In more recent years, a much greater tendency for central legislation and thus for the operation of a central British governmental policy has meant that sensitivity to the internal conditions of the sepa-rate nations of the British Isles has become more important than ever at a time when their influence is arguably declining within the elites (non-governmental as well as governmental) responsible for develop-ing, promoting and implementing policy on a UK basis. Policy and institution-led homogenization of Britishness arguably does disser-vice to the English regions also. An obvious case of this is the dominance of London within the English electronic (and print, though that is for commercial rather than government reasons) media, where a regional accent is taken as a suitable synecdoche for a regional culture, without any need for further attention to origins. There is a study to be carried out here on the erasure of locality through the preservation of accent. How often will the BBC cover a major art exhi-bition in Leeds or Liverpool, however many northerners it hires to cover culture and current affairs? The construction of regional news bulletins and regional coverage more generally reinforces an impression that the provinces are locales for comedy, murder, disaster and human interest stories, not for politics, culture and society. Almost the only extensive current affairs reporting in the UK from outside the metropolis has come from coverage of Northern Ireland, for obvious – now diminishing – reasons. The absence of networked coverage of Scotland or Wales since 1999, however, is increasingly doing disservice to the new British polity which has been evolving since then: how often do BBC news bulletins now add the obligatory 'in England' or 'in England and Wales' to describe health or education policy changes, without ever letting the networked audience know what is going on in Scotland? Scotland may be termed a 'region', but it itself is composed of several regions; it has (unlike anywhere else in the UK) a separate print and to an extent electronic media, which has never ceased to run national Scottish questions and a Scottish agenda, and in which much of the devolution debate took place, long before the 1997 referendum; moreover, since 1999, it has had a parliament enacting substantial legislation on domestic affairs. The 2001 Graduate Endowment and Student Support and Regulation of Care Acts are only two areas where policy has diverged from England in a major way; more recently, the discussions leading up to the banning of smoking in public places confirmed that the Irish Dáil was a greater inspiration to Scottish domestic policy than Westminster. Tentative overseas ventures such as Tartan Week in the United States and the Holyrood-Malawi collaboration indicate an interest in foreign policy, even from the Scottish Labour Party, of which their UK counterparts are apprehensive. Certainly, UK ministers seem to take the opportunity to keep Holyrood in its place when possible, even at the cost of risking stoking nationalism: for example, in the exclusion of Scottish ministers from critical roles in EU negotiations, even in areas such as fisheries, where Scotland has 70 per cent of UK activity.[3] Centralized British policy, in media and government, appears in an increasingly tense relationship with the emerging Scottish political agenda.

This is a good reason to write Scottish history for everyone, not just Scots. The Union between Scotland and England has changed very markedly since its inception. Great Britain (the 'Great' indicated the

Union, for 'Britain' has its origins in the name of the Roman province, which ended at Hadrian's Wall), later the United Kingdom of Great Britain and Ireland, later still the United Kingdom of Great Britain and Northern Ireland, has always been a state based on a series of unions, rather than one having its basis on a common nationality: it is thus closely related to the distinction between a 'union state' and 'unitary state'.[4] 'British values' themselves form a concept that has shifted from Protestantism, racism and the stiff upper lip to multicultural tolerance and emotional self-revelation within the space of 50 years, a much greater shift in so-called national 'values' than has occurred in, for example, the United States, despite milestones like the end of segregation. 'British values' have shifted radically over time; but the British state itself can be traced most consistently not through these, but the sequence of unions through which it has evolved as a constitutional entity, and the way the relationships created by these unions have developed and shifted in practice. The Union with Wales in 1536–42 ratified an earlier conquest and was the least problematic; that with Ireland in 1801 foundered rapidly, not least because of the long delay in introducing Catholic Emancipation that followed it; that with Scotland in 1707 was always the most incomplete, since it guaranteed substantial independence for Scottish society and its institutions – the domestic public sphere – in an age when British governments sought to do far less in policy terms than they attempt today. Lindsay Paterson has explored this state of structural semi-independence in *The Autonomy of Modern Scotland* (1994), where he points out that while countries such as the Czech lands had 'nationally representative bodies' in the nineteenth century, they had nothing like the freedom Scotland enjoyed in law, local government, culture or education: 'Scotland had freedom mainly because the UK state let civil society function autonomously'.[5]

Throughout the long eighteenth century, Scotland was managed for the British Government by a major nobleman or politician – by Argyll, by Islay, by Dundas. When the country caused trouble, as in 1715–16 and (particularly) 1745–6, the British government intervened; when it didn't, it was largely left alone. Marginally greater centralization in the nineteenth century was balanced for much of the time by the huge opportunities for Scots in the British Empire: even so, the election of five crofting MPs, the reintroduction of the Scottish Secretaryship and the founding of the National Association for the Vindication of Scottish Rights (1853) and the Scottish Home Rule Association (1886) all evidenced a perceived need in at least some to ensure adequate recognition for Scotland as equal partners in the Union. A key difference among campaigners for Scottish home rule compared with their Irish equivalents, though, was their largely unquestioned support for the British Empire, which continued up to the 1940s: it simply offered Scotland too many benefits to be ignored. Only a handful of extreme nationalists, such as Theodore Napier and Wendy Wood, saw the Scottish situation in colonial terms, and the comparison with the Irish position made in the 1920s and '30s by writers like Hugh MacDiarmid (1892–1978), Neil Gunn (1891–1973) and Fionn MacColla (1906–1975) did not gain general acceptance. Scottishness at home remained bound up with Britishness overseas.

At the same time, Scotland's industrial power at the beginning of the First World War led to overcapacity developing in the cause of the war effort which helped to unbalance the economy, particularly in the longer term, and was itself combined with disproportionate losses: 15 per cent of Edinburgh and Glasgow graduates and 20 per cent of British war dead in 1914–18 were Scots, and 26 per cent of all enlisted Scots died. Before 1914 Scotland was a major economic power, producing 120 per cent of average UK output per capita, a relative position of strength which dwindled steadily as the century progressed. In 1914 the Scottish unemployment rate was 20 per cent of London's; in 1923 it was 125 per cent of the UK average: between 1924 and 1937 UK GDP rose at 2.2 per cent per annum, but Scotland's by only 0.4 per cent, and the country continues to trail the UK GDP growth average, though not so markedly, to this day. Scottish universities, already under new competition from the provincial English redbricks, actually lost 5 per cent of their student numbers between 1924 and 1937, at a time when the expansion of higher education across the UK was gathering pace. Scotland's population growth slowed to a standstill. Between 1911 and 1980, almost a quarter of those born in Scotland emigrated. In 1911, Scotland's population was 86 per cent of Sweden's; in 2006, it was 57 per cent. On independence in 1922, Ireland's population was no more than 60 per cent of Scotland's: in 2006, despite having suffering the long economic isolation of the De Valera era, it was nearly 90 per cent. Such statistics indicate the contraction of Scotland's position from economic powerhouse of imperial industry to marginal – and increasingly regional – economy. The development of political nationalism against such a background is not surprising;[6] what is perhaps more surprising is the length of time it took to make an impact, which can to some extent be put down to the abilities of the Labour Party in particular in managing domestic decline through the machinery of British subsidy externally, while presenting itself internally as a patriotic Scottish party.

At first, decline was slow: a quarter of the world's shipping was still built on the Clyde in 1929. Nonetheless, some pressure for change was felt: the foundation of the National Party of Scotland in 1928 (from 1934 the Scottish National Party, following its merger with the short-lived Scottish Party) was followed in 1937 by the movement of the Scottish Office to Edinburgh. Cultural developments at the time included the foundation of the National Trust for Scotland (1931) and The Saltire Society (1936). In 1941, during World War II, Tom Johnston, the Labour Secretary of State in Churchill's coalition government, set up a Scottish Council of State and allowed 'for meetings of the Scottish Grand Committee to take place in Scotland'. This was an innovation which did not survive the war, reappearing only as one of the 'too little, too late' measures adopted by the Conservative government in the 1990s, in succession to their even more abortive 1980s plan for a Scottish Select Committee, which was abandoned when in 1987 the Tories lost too many MPs to be able to staff it.[7] In 1945 Dr Robert McIntyre was briefly returned as Scottish National Party MP for Motherwell at a by-election, a seat he lost within weeks as the ensuing general election ended the wartime pact under which the major parties did not stand against each other. The incoming Labour Government established a Scottish Council for Development and Industry and a Scottish Tourist Board in 1946; in 1948 a White Paper on Scottish Affairs was published, which suggested 'a degree of administrative devolution for parliamentary business, economic affairs, the machinery of government and nationalized industries'. The Tories proposed their own measures, and on returning to power devolved planning authority on roads and bridges to the Scottish Office. Bill Miller has argued that this 'build-up of the Scottish Office' was 'a Danegeld' which stimulated 'the appetite for self-government', a long and gradual road, along which the removal of the Stone of Destiny from Westminster by a group of students in 1950, and John McCormick's infinitely more substantial Scottish Covenant movement of 1949–52 were milestones.[8]

In other words, the nature of the Union and the relationship taking place between Scotland and England within it was changing throughout the twentieth century, often through a series of incremental and to English eyes (and some Scottish) almost invisible changes. Why then begin this history in 1960?

Arguments can no doubt be made for different dates. But the 1960s was the decade when a number of the processes set in train by the Labour victory of 1945, by the general centralization of British policy under both parties, and by the divestment of Empire, came to a head. The Scottish National Party had existed for 30 years, and (with the exception of the Motherwell by-election held in unrepresentative political conditions) had failed to win anything more notable than the Rectorship election at the University of Glasgow. In the 1960s, it started to win – and, arguably even more importantly – to drive the agenda of the Unionist parties. In part this could be argued to be the result of three different kinds of change which came to a head in this decade, all of which will be explored in more detail as this study progresses, and all of which arguably changed some of the fundamentals of the bargain of Union more than all the incremental alterations which had preceded them.

First, the Union was always and crucially about Scottish access to imperial markets, with all that went with it: massive opportunities for educated Scots and Scottish soldiers abroad, in a culture which had a long history of successful European diaspora and a robust domestic higher education system to draw on in giving it a critical advantage within Great Britain. In the 1960s, these opportunities finally vanished: between 1960 and 1967, almost 25 colonies became independent, including Somalia and Cyprus (1960), Tanzania, Sierra Leone and Kuwait (1961), Jamaica and Uganda (1962), Kenya, Borneo, Malaysia and Singapore (1963), Malta, Malawi and Zambia (1964) and Lesotho, Botswana and Guyana (1966), to say nothing of the departure of apartheid South Africa from the Commonwealth in 1961 or the unilateral declaration of independence by a white supremacist Rhodesia in 1965. Secondly, the Union preserved, to an extent perhaps unrealized in postwar British government circles, a protected domestic public sphere as the counterpart to equality of imperial opportunity, which advantaged Scots at home by leaving them effective control of their professions: the law, education, finance, the Kirk. In its turn, this domestic public sphere reinforced Scottish ability to compete in imperial markets by fostering professional networks entirely composed of Scots, and reducing (though by no means eliminating) London's pulling power. Edinburgh had many times the proportion of professionals in its population that Birmingham or Manchester enjoyed in the early nineteenth century,[9] while perceived attacks on the judiciary in 1785 and on the Scottish banks' autonomy in 1826 elicited ferocious responses from leading literary figures (Boswell and Scott) precisely because the autonomy of the Scottish domestic public sphere depended on its institutions, and on their control by and for Scots.

The creation of a unified British social and economic policy on an unprecedented scale after 1945, combined with the greater mobility attendant on the early stages of modern globalization and the decline of the influence of the Kirk on domestic social mores, undermined the domestic bargain of Union as surely as withdrawal from Empire undermined the imperial bargain. The nationalization policies of the 1945–51 Labour Government had the effect of centralizing at a rapid pace the control of industries in which Scotland had long been a leader (e.g. railways, mining) in the south-east; the creation of the National Health Service in 1948 and the nationalization of the Bank of England in 1946 alike served to set a unitary British policy agenda increasingly determined from London. No longer was the capital an economic magnet only; it was now also a social master. Monolithic industries helped complete the move to monolithic unions, and 'the 200 independent Scottish trade unions' there had been in 1900 disappeared one by one, with 60 per cent going by the twenties and virtually all by the sixties. Unified British policies helped to create a more unified labour market, and the protectionist power of Scottish civil society eroded, despite the importance intermittently placed on 'Scottish needs and the Scottish point of view' in government reports such as the 1954 Royal Commission on Scottish Affairs.[10] Pressure on the real distinctiveness of the 'Scottish point of view' was now coming from many quarters, with an increasingly British policy being created in education through comprehensivization and centralized funding policies for universities. Some of the Scottish universities held out against the new central UCCA admissions system until the 1980s, and when Edinburgh became the first to enter in 1962, there were student riots. By the late 1960s, the Scottish Universities' Council on Entrance (SUCE), which had once set 'going rates' for entry to all Scottish universities, was no longer effectively able to guarantee the participation of all its members. In 1971, the Scottish Union of Students collapsed, and students in Scotland had the choice of joining the British centralist NUS (National Union of Students), or of not affiliating, which a number of universities – most consistently Glasgow – chose to do. In 1962 the old Scottish Leaving Certificate (ironically similar to the now popular International Baccalaureate) was abolished in schools. Its replacement included an exam, the O-grade, transparently based on the English O-level, and although the attempt to introduce an A-grade was resisted, the Higher – since the 1880s the gold standard of Scottish education – has been under intermittent assault ever since.

The 1960s, then, saw the intensification of a process begun some fifteen years earlier, but which took its time in coming to fruition. The third major change which became apparent in that decade was the scale of the decline of Scottish economic power. After 1945 for a brief period 'the traditional industries thrived' as 'competition from the ravaged economies of Europe and the Far East had been temporarily suspended'. In 1950 the Clyde 'launched a third of the world's shipping tonnage', a greater proportion than twenty years earlier; by 1960, the year of the celebratory but also elegiac film, Seaward, the Great Ships, it was 5 per cent. By 1968–9 both yards and tonnage were down by almost half from the 1961 figure. Other opportunities faded more quickly, not least in agriculture; in the 1950s, 500,000 emigrated, 250,000 to England. Nationalized industries frequently removed economic competitiveness through lack of restructuring, and their prioritization of social over economic mission: in 1955–65, the National Coal Board's deficit in Scotland was £136M, over 90 per cent of all UK losses. Attempting a corrective, regional industrial policy brought motor plants such as Linwood and Bathgate and a steel strip mill to Ravenscraig under the 1959–64 Tory government, but these could not offset the increasingly evident pace of decline in domestic heavy industry: in fact the idea that Ravenscraig steel would supply Bathgate and Linwood and thus make them viable was little better than a pyramid scheme, where individual operations of doubtful viability were expected to succeed through an artificial structure of supply designed to foment demand. Labour's victory in 1964 was followed by disillusionment, as regional disparities within Scotland (here was one of the problems in viewing Scotland itself as an undifferentiated 'region') and rising unemployment were increasingly evident. The response of the Secretary of State, Willie Ross, was a National Plan for Scotland, which, ironically, confirmed the centralist nature of British policy by implementing 'planning on a far more rigorous basis than in any of the English regions'.[11] The creation of a Highlands and Islands Development Board (HIDB) offered recognition to the realities of internal regions in Scotland, but its official status was almost immediately undercut by the allocation of Scotland's only completely new university of the 1960s to Stirling rather than Inverness. Calling centralized planning Scottish rather than British didn't make it any more efficient, and the 1967 devaluation of the pound called in question the economic prestige of the British state itself in the very year that British troops withdrew from commitments east of Suez, the symbolic end of Empire. In November, Winnie Ewing overturned a vast Labour majority to win Hamilton for the nationalists.

The 1960s, then, were a watershed for the impact of postwar British government policy on Scotland. International pressures from both the United States and colonized peoples themselves were leading to the end of Empire: but domestic policy too was undermining the basis of the Union, almost certainly without its authors realizing that this would be its effect. The failure to create a 'home fit for heroes' after the First World War put pressure on the 1945 Labour Government to deliver across Great Britain: and if it sought to perpetuate wartime solidarities by strategies such as prolonging rationing artificially, it did so out of a conviction that the decline in nominal wages followed by slump of 1918–32 should not be repeated, and that there should be 'fair shares for all'. Yet the centralization of British policy as it intensified from 1945 was no emergency measure: it continued as successive governments of whatever stamp proved reluctant to withdraw from powers and responsibilities acquired by their predecessors, and indeed, sought to extend these as a measure of their own success. Such developments have no doubt in the long term been corrosive in terms of civic solidarity and political trust across the UK: in Scotland, they had the by-product of damaging the Union settlement, which depended on the local autonomy and domestic management of Scottish affairs. This was the serious ambivalence at the heart of British government policy: that it could not altogether discern whether Scotland was a 'nation' or a 'region', and when treating it as the latter, effectively discarded the terms of Union with the former. In the context of the end of imperial opportunity, this was a devastating combination which helped to feed the growth of a Scottish national consciousness for which Britishness was not, as before, a concentric identity, but – potentially at least – an oppositional one.

These are the reasons for beginning a history of modern Scotland in 1960. But before turning to a summary of the way in which this book's argument will develop, two questions need to be asked. First, do the trajectories of other comparable nationalisms in Europe parallel the Scottish case, or does it remain truly distinctive? Secondly, what was it that made Scotland a nation at all, with a desire as well as an ability to survive within the Union, and in late years to demonstrate dissatisfaction with its position within the UK? To some extent, these are related questions, because the distinctively semi-autonomous position of Scotland within the Union was one which allowed concentric Scottish and British identities to be acceptable to Scots from the middle of the eighteenth to the middle of the twentieth century.

Nationalism can be found in the armed resistance of Jacobite Scotland to the Union between 1707 and 1746, but its great age in European terms came when Scotland was entering into the heyday of its role in the British Empire, in the aftermath of the French Revolution and the destabilizing impact of the Napoleonic Wars on the great empires of the early modern period. The Spanish and Portuguese empires lost control of Latin America, while Czech, Finnish, Greek, Hungarian, Norwegian and Slovenian nationalism all became much more visible in the nineteenth century, at a time when Scotland's nationality abroad was largely represented by Scottish associations, Caledonian societies, and the sometimes distinctive outlook of its imperial servants. Many of these countries drew on Scottish writers, such as Macpherson, Byron and Scott, in defence of the revival of their distinctive languages and cultures; in Chile, Brazil, Greece and Venezuela, Scottish soldiers and seamen of fortune contributed greatly to the wars of national liberation.

Perhaps the most obviously comparable cases with Scotland's from this period are those of Ireland and Catalonia. Norway, in some respects very close to the Scottish position by virtue of its parliamentary union with Sweden, was not part of a great empire, nor was Sweden's independent position remotely comparable to what England's would become in point of power, wealth and influence. Irish nationalism became a major force in response to the climate created by the American and French Revolutions, but it was the Union of 1801 that enhanced its long-term chances of success, because of the delay in Catholic Emancipation, the unequal and ignorant treatment of Ireland manifest in the response to the Famine, and the failure to address historic questions of landlordism. The Union ensured that Irish policy would be made in London, but such policy was made in a climate of ignorance and neglect of local conditions, which, moreover, perpetuated the very Protestant bigotry which the Union in part might have been held to address. Home Rule was withheld by successive Westminster Parliaments, despite the presence of a majority of pro Home Rule MPs from Ireland from the 1880s. In the early twentieth century, the position became dangerous, as Orangeism and elements in the Conservative Party countenanced illegality to preserve the Union. When the British Government turned a blind eye to the arming of the Ulster Volunteers in 1913, it appeared to many nationalists that the armed Irish Volunteers were the only effective resistance to protect Irish interests. The outcome was the unnecessary brutality of 1916, 1918–23 and beyond. Centralized British policy which did not allow for local conditions (the *laissez-faire* approach to the Famine which did not appreciate that landlord power in Ireland prevented a free market there was a fatal error) combined with denial of democratic Irish wishes over many years led to extremism, in the first place fostered by senior British politicians, in the second a cause of war in Ireland itself. Ireland had never enjoyed the fruits of Empire as Scotland did (though many individual Irish, particularly Pro-testants, had successful imperial careers); the Union had not created true equality of treatment, and democracy had been overruled, first by Parliament, then – shamefully – by the complicity of democratic politicians in the threat of Unionist force, and worse than complicity, since Sir Edward Carson, who threatened illegal force in Ulster, was rewarded with the Cabinet post of Attorney-General in the wartime government.[12] Irish nationalism was stronger than Scottish: but there are historic parallels in the failure of centralized British policy to deal with local conditions, albeit that Scottish discontent is a faint echo of Ireland's.

The Kingdom of Spain had originally been a regnal union, like that of Scotland and England in 1603. Its constituent kingdoms kept a significant degree of local autonomy internally, while externally project-ing an imperial Catholic Spanish unity under the joint crowns of Aragon (united with Catalonia in 1137 and subsequently ruled from it) and Castile. In 1714–16 the multi-kingdom monarchy came to an end with a centralization of royal power in Madrid and 'the practical dis-appearance of the Catalan aristocracy'. A century later Spain's weak performance in the Napoleonic Wars led to the loss of much of its over-seas empire: at almost exactly the same time, there was a renewal in internal nationalism. As Lindsay Paterson notes, Catalan and Norwegian nationalism was to an extent a response to the declining power of Spain and Sweden as well as to changing internal social structures. In the 1830s Catalonia, the most prosperous part of the Kingdom of Aragon, and one with a distinctive language and culture, underwent a nationalist 'Renaissance'.[13] After the Spanish monarchy came to a temporary end in 1931, the regaining of Catalan autonomy was one of the triggers for the Spanish Civil War, where the Republic was supported by Basque and Catalan nationalists, and the (Spanish) Nationalists sought to regain the old Church and Crown unity of imperial Spain. After General Franco's death in 1975 Catalonia regained its autonomy, becoming officially a nation within Spain in 2006. Nationalists won 46 per cent of the vote at the 2006 election, but many of these wish only to expand Catalan autonomy rather than achieve outright independence. Catalonia is similar to the Scottish situation in elements of its historic position and in the fact that a weakened external empire was the catalyst for a reviving internal nationalism, but there are important differences. Catalan nationalism has been more ethnically particularist, though there are signs that this is changing (the idea of a single Catalan Volk dates from the nineteenth century), and the borders of Catalonia include part of what is now French territory in the eastern Pyrenees, where (in keeping with French centralism) there is no political and little cultural acknowledgement of Catalan difference. The Spanish state is more mature than the British one in allowing autonomy to Catalonia's political parties; on the other hand, outright independence is more of a minority pursuit in Catalonia. Significantly too, neither Ireland nor Catalonia (save as the dominant part of Aragon) were fully independent early modern states, with separate legal, financial, educational and political systems (as well as overseas colonies, as in Nova Scotia and New Jersey, though Catalonia had 'a powerful Mediterranean empire' in the Middle Ages).[14] In these respects, Scotland was different, and again closer to the Norwegian model.

Ethnic and linguistic divisions count for more in Continental European nationalisms in general than they do in Scotland. In Corsica, where France has been slowly pressurized to consider increasing local autonomy, the violence directed against outsiders and in particular those of North African origin, has made Corsican nationalism relatively easy to isolate and demonize. Relatively few Corsicans want outright independence, despite feeling overwhelmingly Corsican rather than French; even the modest 2003 plebiscite to extend the powers of the regional authority was voted down. Here, extremism is a sign of nationalist weakness as much as central neglect.

In Bavaria, by contrast, despite strong feelings of cultural, religious and to an extent linguistic distinctiveness, pan-German ethnicity is strong. Bavaria was not incorporated into the German Empire until well into the nineteenth century, and retained its own monarchy until 1918, but there is (in common with other German *Länder*) little appetite for 'freedom'. The pro-independence Bavaria Party has had no deputies since 1962: Bavaria is a distinct society, but still a German one. The federal German constitution allows considerable powers to its distinct entities (and indeed, some less distinct ones), including the ability to project an image abroad, and Bavaria has a distinct right-wing party in the CSU. Germanicity is still ultimately very important, especially where the constituent parts of the federal republic have their own wide powers. The enormous desire to reintegrate (and the enormous cost of reintegrating) East Germany, a separate state for 45 years, in the 1990s, is evidence enough that ultimately Germans are Germans before they are Saxons or Bavarians. This is not true of Spain, nor of Great Britain.

Comparison of Scottish with other European nationalisms tends to confirm some similarities: declining empires and centralizing policies reinvigorate or alienate the component parts of multinational states: centralized Canadian conscription was a flashpoint for modern Quebecois nationalism, for instance, as it was in Ireland in World War I. Scottishness was not absent in the heyday of the British Empire: it was just less visible. On the other hand, there are differences: the language issue, strong in Corsica, Catalonia (and indeed Wales) is much weaker in Scotland, despite the presence of Gaelic and Scots. It may be that this is connected to the lesser importance of ethnic nationalism, as opposed to a nationalism based on a distinct culture and institutions, in Scotland. This is addressed in more detail below: it may make Scottish nationalism weaker, but it certainly makes it more inclusive, than nationalisms based on group or race identity politics. Institutions do make a difference in other ways: strong recognition of federal powers, as in Germany, can help to increase, rather than diminish, German solidarity. Even where there are markedly different languages and ethnicities, as in Switzerland, local self-determination can act as a strong bond within a larger polity: 'ethnonationalism within language communities is discouraged by primary powers being vested in the cantons'.[15] While the UK has always been by contrast a multinational union state, failure to accept Irish autonomy almost certainly led to Irish independence. Although the world moves on, the British state still has – as this book argues – a problem with its own centralizing tendencies, and an inability to recognize that it is a multinational, not a unitary British, state.

Scotland has always been a hybrid society of different cultural groups, and provides a poor basis for any ethnic nationalism. There has never been a time when one language was spoken across the whole of the country's modern territory. Yet the disparate peoples who occupied it confirmed the relative territorial integrity of Scotland at an early period – and again, as in the Catalan situation, fixed borders are often absent in other European nationalisms. There were two main reasons for this. The first was Hadrian's Wall ('north of Hadrian's Wall' is still a frequently used, if inaccurate, synonym for 'Scotland' in England). The Roman province of Britannia (later the basis for the term 'Britain') was south of the Wall, and a different Romano-British culture developed there. Secondly, Scotland itself was almost divided in two by the Forth-Clyde line, and early mapmakers exaggerated the extent to which this split the whole island; as it was, before the drainage of the moss land at Stirling in the eighteenth century, Scotland north of Forth-Clyde *was* almost a peninsula. The boundaries of modern Scotland were largely determined by conflict between Forth-Clyde and Hadrian's Wall, and ended up roughly halfway between them. When Scotland fought on or north of Forth-Clyde, victory – aided often by landscape, with high ground and/or boggy ground proving critical at Dunnichen/ Nechtansmere (685), Stirling Bridge (1297) and Bannockburn (1314) – more commonly resulted than was the case south of it.

The struggle to establish a boundary between the geographic barrier at Forth-Clyde and the cultural barrier of Hadrian's Wall was one of the key determinants of Scotland's consistent boundaries over time (compared with, say, Poland) and also the importance of these boundaries as a primary determinant of Scottishness. Scottishness was at first territorial: hence the King of Scots was sovereign of a number of different peoples. Subsequently, as the unifying force of the monarchy became increasingly linked both to national self-defence and national institutions, these also became important in defining nationality. As Anthony Smith points out, a historic territory, common history, public culture, legal jurisdiction and economy are five of the key bases for nationality.[16] By 1018 Scotland effectively had the first; by 1300 (ahead of England) it was conscious of the second; the third was clear in the Middle Ages, and was – as we have seen – protected by the Union; the fourth and fifth likewise. Developments such as the Benedictine house in Dunfermline (1070), Kelso Abbey (1128), the royal burghs (1120s), the Grammar (now High) School of Glasgow (1124), the Cathedral and University of St Andrews (1160/1410) and the Court of Session (1532), bespoke the complexity and continuing development of the country's national institutions.

These institutions were themselves based on a hybrid political structure. Scotland's society was originally organized along 'Irish' lines with a high king and under-kings at different levels (the most senior of the latter being the 'mormaers'). From the twelfth century at least, this hybridized with an Anglo-Norman model, but one which did not significantly disrupt the importance of regional power-bases and family connexions. The Chiefs of the Name combined the two, sometimes in their very title (Duke of Gordon). Those who depended on these chiefs (who often bore conventional feudal title, as barons, lords of parliament or earls, later viscounts, marquises and dukes), often took their name or responded to it. The 'clan system' (a nine-teenth-century term) is a misleading summary of some elements of this practice.

Distinctive social structures linked to the monarchy were important; so was the separateness of the Scottish Church, which, like the monarchy, struggled for its sovereign independence against English claims for centuries. Kings bent on unifying Scotland in the early period (Aedán MacGabráin, Oengus mac Forguso) had (or were reputed to have) a strong relationship with the Church, which in its relations with the monarchy provided a unifying principle: 'St Andrew be leader of the compatriot Scots'. In 909, according to the Annals of Ulster, the

Albanaich united as one people under the 'miracle-working standard' of Columba, while the canonization of St Margaret in the thirteenth century reinforced the connexion between Church and Crown.

The plurality of peoples in Scotland (and even their distinctive legal practices) was recognized in early charters. By 1300, the idea of loyalty to the Crown or to the Realm was arguably paramount over any 'blood and soil' markers of nationality: for example, Scots with primary interests in England or who had not supported Bruce could be viewed as 'English' aliens, whatever their 'ethnic' status.[17] The unity of Church and State as the foundation for Scottish identity developed significantly in this period and, from 1300, a historiography evolved which saw the Kingdom of Scots and its institutions as locked in a struggle for liberty against all comers. The development of other institutions (e.g. the law) in the Stewart period provided a broadening basis for a Scottish identity. This identity was disrupted by the Reformation, some of whose more extreme adherents sought a Year Zero which would discard the Scottish past altogether as priest-ridden and idolatrous.

Although some of the Scots elite had previously sought a Union with England, the Union which came about in 1707 largely occurred because of English fears that an independent Scotland might restore the Stewarts and open a second front in any war with France. As I have indicated above, the Union bargain served Scotland well at times, between 1760 and 1914 in particular. A separate public sphere survived, in part through the very institutions whose preservation was guaranteed by the Union. Local control of the professions continued, and Scottish clubs and societies had a distinctive cast in the age of Enlightenment, which itself flourished in the more politically secure and religiously moderate culture that Scotland had acquired by 1760, though it would be a mistake to suppose that the Union brought the Enlightenment about, as many of its roots were clearly present in the more troubled seventeenth century. Scottish music hybridized with classical music to create new forms, and distinctive Scottish modes in literature, architecture and other forms of culture continued to develop. Scotland also (despite the internationalization of Britishness through the Empire and the frequent acceptance by Scots abroad of the soubriquet 'English') survived as an overseas nationality in the diasporic establishment of new Caledonian and Scottish societies across the Empire after the Union. The creation of Scottish societies abroad was a political act after 1707, however muted: it was one of the major routes by which the Scottish domestic public sphere made itself visible and advantaged its members.

Such was the nature of Scottishness under the Union, supported by institutions, networks, a domestic public sphere and a territory still defined by the jurisdiction of its own laws, where the Kirk and the Faculty of Advocates acted as quasi-parliamentary organizations of national expression and survival. This was the Scotland of 1800 and of 1900, even to an extent that of 1945, though without denying the many changes that had taken place in the Union's long development. It was no longer the Scotland of the 1960s. The challenge of the contemporary age for Scotland and Scottishness was – and remains – a challenge to the integrity of Great Britain, and this is one of the themes of this history, and the reason for its starting date.

In the chapters that follow these difficulties will be addressed: but I also intend to give a flavour of the whole breadth and nature of Scottish culture, politics and society since 1960, to which there is much more than can be captured by any constitutional debate. In particular, this history will aim not simply to cover Scottish contemporary history as a subdivision of that of the United Kingdom as a whole, but to reach out to the broader market which this book will occupy by examining Scottish difference and distinctiveness, the reasons for it, its develop-ment and possible future: in short, why Scotland should be a subject for network coverage, not devolved discussion, for it is in everyone's interests that Scotland should be better understood. I will begin in 'Contacts and Corporatism', by outlining the main economic and historical developments in Scotland in the period, before turning in Chapter Two to the nature, history and rise of the Scottish National Party: then the argument will turn aside from politics to focus on Scotland's six main cities in Chapter Three. Chapter Four looks at the development of Scottish culture and the extent to which there is a sepa-rate cultural agenda in Scotland from the rest of the UK; Chapter Five, 'Who are the New Scots?', explores the impact of immigrant communities on Scotland, and of Scottish immigration abroad. The last chapter, 'Devolving or Declining?', addresses the effect of the 1999 devolution settlement on both Scotland and Great Britain as a whole, concluding with an evaluation of the results of the 2007 Scottish elections, and leaves the reader with a number of questions to consider in predicting the nature of future developments.

Chapter 1

Contacts and Corporatism: Scotland Since 1945

In the 1945 General Election, the Labour Party was returned to power with a substantial majority, and a lead of almost 200 seats over the Conservative opposition: Labour support in Scotland was broadly in line with the UK figure. Although the party's Scottish manifesto had made Home Rule for Scotland its 'second priority after the defeat of Japan',[1] Labour's domestic goals – as their election propaganda showed – were in reality far more geared to the perpetuation in peacetime of the common purpose of 1939–45. The Second World War had been a conflict which had pressed the British Empire more closely than the First, and the threat to the state itself was such that even those of the population not directly engaged were called on to accommodate evacuees, give up their houses for military billeting, or – as happened in many well-to-do middle class areas – volunteer their railings and decorative ironwork for the war effort. It was very much an atmosphere of 'from each according to his ability to each according to his needs', and this sense of the war as Socialism in action was rather enhanced than damaged by Churchill's own Christian-derived rhetoric of the sacrifices the few were making for the many. This sense of being 'all in it together' was one that Labour sought to perpetuate beyond the date of Victory in Europe; and the combination of skilful propaganda, Labour's own solid performance in the wartime coalition, and a general disinclination on the part of the electorate to risk the disappointment that followed the promise of a 'home fit for heroes' in 1918, combined with Tory complacency to produce a historic victory.

Once in power – for the first time in history with an overall major-ity – Labour naturally turned to wartime means to implement peacetime goals. Central planning and the continuation of rationing served to promote the sense of social solidarity and to normalize government procedures of direction, allocation and confiscation designed for emergency. A wave of nationalizations both gained government control of the commanding heights of the economy and also ensured that that economy would be directed from the south-east of England. Between 1946 and 1951, the Bank of England, coal, railways, road transport, telecommunications, gas and electricity supply and iron and steel all came under the control of government, which itself set up a National Health Service in 1948. Nationalization implied stan-dardization – fair shares for all again – and this can be clearly seen in contemporary posters advertising the change. For example, the Electrical Trades Union in their 'As A Housewife I say . . . Switch Over / Nationalise the Electricity Supply Industry' poster stressed 'one rate that all can afford to pay' for electricity used, 'Supply to Remotest Parts' and 'standard sizes and voltage' for appliances: the promise of univer-sal and homogeneous provision.[2] Unions of course were one of the major beneficiaries of nationalization, which concentrated their bargaining power, rendered it monopolistic, and brought them close to the ear of government. Huge numbers of workers became govern-ment employees for the first time under Attlee's administration.

Standardization was found not only in economic organization, but also in industrial production, where centralized supply benefited from economies of scale and helped to make a political case for consistency and uniformity as financial as well as moral benefits. Regulation also extended the powers of government. The greater share of state activity in the economy (by 1983, the Scottish Office was spending 'about four times the expenditure of the Home Office, and twice that of the Department of Education and Science'),[3] acted together with capitalist tendencies towards monopoly and the weakness of many businesses in the immediate postwar environment to accelerate business homo-geneity through the decline of local firms, as many companies were taken over. In this, as in other areas such as public housebuilding, where the Conservative Government returned to power in 1951 they trumped Labour: it was the Tories who set up a Ministry of Housing.[4] The 1945–51 government thus set a precedent which long outlived it. Governmental centralism helped to establish a governmental and indeed cultural prejudice in favour of large organizations which replicated the standardization of public ownership in the private sector. The development of vast conglomerates in key manufacturing areas like the British Leyland Motor Corporation (a 1968 development driven by the Labour Government's Industrial Reorganization Committee, chaired by Tony Benn) and the Rootes Group in the expanding car market, helped to promote homogenization far outside the confines of the state. At one point, the historic Brown's Lane Jaguar factory was dubbed 'Large Car Plant Number Two' by its BLMC masters, for all the world as if it had been a tractor assembly plant in Minsk. The brand erosion which resulted from this and similar practices contributed to the catastrophic decline of the British car industry, accelerated by mediocre management and militant unions who – possibly encouraged by the extent of government intervention – treated vulnerable private sector companies as if they were monopolistic suppliers. Between 1960 and 1976, Alvis, Armstrong-Siddeley, Austin-Healey, Bond, Hillman, Humber, Riley, Singer, Standard and Wolseley all disappeared as brands, while Sunbeam lingered only as a model title, Triumph and MG had had no new models for a decade or more, and quality control at Jaguar had sunk to the lowest common denominator. In the end, the destruction of the domestic British car industry (in contrast to its successful retention in France, Germany and Italy) owed much to the way in which it cloned itself as a nationalized industry long before it came to need the assistance of the state because it had done so.

In Scotland, the Scottish Office, in the wake of the 1960 Local Employment Act, began an 'Inquiry into the Scottish Economy' which gave rise to the 1961 Toothill Report, and a new phase of planning. The Linwood plant, among those set up to compensate the country for the increasing centralization of heavy industry, was reliant on manufacturing the Hillman Imp, which was neither replaced nor upgraded between 1963 and 1976. After it disappeared, the factory staggered on making other outmoded models until the end came in 1981. Linwood's fate epitomized the double bind of a centralizing industrial policy. Nationalization and commercial centralization alike drew power to the centre: but when regional policy used taxpayers' money to undo the ills which to an extent taxpayers' money had been used to create, it repatriated the assembly jobs which produced favourable media coverage, not the research and development capacity which was expensive, took longer to develop and replace, and which created fewer headline jobs. Yet without R & D, the long-term future for plants like Linwood was bleak, and clumsy central initiatives like the 'National Engineering Laboratory at East Kilbride' (1947) did not rectify the situation. Political imperatives were always short-term, and it would matter little to Macmillan's government that Thatcher's would let Linwood close. But what would matter to Scotland was the fact that R & D spend fell against the UK average to stand at only 45 per cent of it overall by 1997. Within even this poor figure, manufacturing (30 per cent), chemicals, aerospace and transport (10 per cent or below UK levels) stood out.[5]

Fifty years earlier, things had looked much rosier; 'from the vantage point of the late 1940s it appeared that Scottish industry had a bright future', as Richard Saville remarks: but this postwar dividend depended on the short-term effects of the ravages of war elsewhere in the world. Government policy was highly interventionist: it was influenced by pre-war reports stressing Scotland's weakness in electrical engineering and vehicle and aircraft manufacture, and the rectification of these was among the planning priorities of government, determined as it was not to let Scotland suffer the disproportionate pain (one shared by areas of the north of England) it had experienced in the slump conditions of the 1930s, which had themselves called forth early government planning quangoes such as the Scottish Development Council of 1931 and the beginnings of regional planning policy in the Special Areas Act (1934, 1937). These developments were, however, dwarfed by the British centralism brought about by World War II.

Postwar regional planning within Scotland (as in other areas of the UK) was initially driven by the 1945 Distribution of Industry Act and the 'system of Industrial Development Certificates established under the 1947 Town and Country Planning Act' – which led to the creation of industrial estates created by governmental 'non-profit making' companies. As well as neglecting the effects of governmental central-izing in other spheres on the long-term capacity of a peripheral economy, these policies tended to be 'broad brush' and to neglect investment and development of existing strengths in favour of diversification so that Scotland would be more in line with the general UK model: the Clyde Valley Plan of 1946 was an example of this, not only with regard to the nature of industry in the area, but also in respect of the fact that it 'argued the consistent line of the English town planning format . . . and applied this to the Clyde'. Directly and indir-ectly, the Clyde Plan led to the setting up of five New Towns in Scotland to accommodate 'overspill' from Glasgow. The term was too frequently used in planning circles, and on occasion those who left Glasgow in the 1960s and '70s still use the term ironically to refer to themselves: 'overspill' symbolized the growing gap between central planning and the lives of individuals, whose initially positive experi-ence of replacing tenements with council houses faded as time went on. The New Towns met with mixed success: Cumbernauld, twice winner (2001, 2005) of the 'Plook on a Plinth' award for bad architec-ture and with a town centre nominated for demolition in a Channel 4 programme, is frequently reviled: its wages may be higher than aver-age, but its house prices are lower. Almost none of the five New Towns (with the eventual exception of Livingston) expanded to their planned potential, and few see them as desirable places to live, despite the fact that over many years 'they have received favourable treatment in the allocation of public investment and have enjoyed additional advan-tages compared with other areas of Scotland in the attraction of incoming industry'. The development of the last, Stonehouse, was abandoned in 1976.

More successful was the development of a hydro-electric industry (championed by Tom Johnston, Secretary of State for Scotland in the war years) which drew on the distinctiveness of local conditions, and which provided the first step towards Scotland's current position as a potential leader in renewable energy. In 1975 the setting up of the Scottish Development Agency (SDA) was a response to claims for a share of North Sea Oil revenue, which the July 1974 White Paper on North Sea Oil deemed inadvisable. One benefit of the devolutionary atmosphere that obtained after the 1974 elections was that there was – at first at least – 'no real parallel' with some of the SDA's activities outwith Scotland. The modelling of the SDA on the Irish Industrial Development Authority, combined with its role as a consciously national agency, served to make it arguably more effective than previous governmental development initiatives which were more centrally driven and attempted, even via regional policy, to homogenize one economic model throughout the UK.[6]

It is true that the 1961 Toothill Report had sought, through the identification of 'growth points', to fine-tune regional distinctions within Scotland, but the 'broad Scottish Development Area' introduced by the incoming Labour Government in 1964 restored centralist and homogenizing policies. Despite the development of a Highlands and Islands Development Board (1965) and regional development areas, the linkage of 'employment growth to social expenditure' was a premiss whose remit militated against constructive engagement with local difference. The creation of an expensive infrastructure would itself create lasting employment opportunities: all enterprise would come through central government action. Within a very short space of time, it was fairly clear to many that this policy, which boasted plans for an ambitious growth rate of nearly 4 per cent, was not working. Moreover, planning priorities within Scotland were 'from the start distorted' by the areas of devolved policy within the Scottish Office, which themselves had a bias towards infrastructure, Glasgow, where only 9 per cent of the population had cars in 1966, gained a gigantic new urban motorway network, which was underused for many years: there was little sign it boosted economic growth in the short term.

If government action in Scotland was a mixed blessing, there were other problems also. Scottish businesses lacking an established market position in new areas or 'first mover' advantage became more vulnerable to takeover from outside, and to competition from incoming industry: between 1937 and 1950 some 235 firms from the rest of the UK 'were established in Scotland', thus diluting the local control so central to Scottish Unionism, with its historic stress (see Introduction) on local autonomy and a separate domestic public sphere, driven by education, finance and the professions. In 1950 'only 4 per cent of

Scottish manufacturing employment was provided in overseas-owned plants', a proportion which had risen five-fold by 1985. Inevitably, the power of incoming capital helped to increase the pressure on the Scottish economy as much as political centralization was already doing. Regional policy initiatives, deriving from the Local Employment and Industrial Development Acts (1960,1966), like 'the pulp mill at Fort William, motor vehicle assembly plan at Bathgate and the aluminium smelter at Invergordon' were all, like Linwood, transient headline-grabbing initiatives doomed to closure in the long run. Increasing population loss underlined the reality of endemic weakness and decline: between 1861 and 1951, net migration was 43 per cent of the natural increase in population; in 1951–81, it was 102 per cent.[7]

After 1945, at first Scottish GDP kept pace with the UK rate of growth, but by the late 1950s, it once again began to lag: it was, however, already far behind the superior (119 per cent) level of output per capita at which it had stood before World War I, though there were arguably signs of decline even then. By 1960, it was 87.5 per cent of the UK figure, and falling in relative terms year on year. It was not until the impetus caused by the discovery of North Sea Oil at the end of the decade that matters improved, leading Scotland to recover to around the UK rate of growth in the 1970s, a time when regional industrial policy became devolved to the Secretary of State in the shape of the SDA and other initiatives. Regional incentives undoubtedly created jobs in Scotland in the 1960s and '70s: but these jobs did little to address the deeper structural imbalances caused by the overall context of government policy and the weakness of domestic business which once had spanned the globe. By the end of the 1970s, Scotland was probably a net contributor to the European Community budget, despite the limited EC assistance it received; it was certainly contributing to the UK budget in the shape of North Sea Oil. Of the UK parties, only the Liberals (briefly) suggested that North Sea Oil revenues might to an extent be ringfenced for Scotland's benefit. As it was, after the initial surge of employment which helped increase Scotland's GDP to 97 per cent of the UK level per capita by 1980, no further relative improvement was made, although around £170 billion in oil revenues had flowed into the UK exchequer in total by 2006.[8]

The major heavy industries of Scotland may have been signs of a lack of economic diversification, but they were culturally very important. Coal, steel and shipbuilding contributed more per capita in Scotland than elsewhere in the UK: these industries also had a tendency to be geographically concentrated in the Central Belt of the country, and within that predominantly the west. Scotland, with around 9 per cent of the UK population, produced 12 per cent of UK coal in 1947 (down to 6.6 per cent in 1982, though still uneconomically high), 15 per cent of UK steel in 1945 (down to 8 per cent by 1978), 47 per cent of UK shipbuilding in 1938 (down to under 30 per cent by the 1970s). These industries were strongly bound to a nexus of cultural self-representation in west central Scotland which stressed the masculinity, skill, hardness, endurance, decency, solidarity and egalitarianism of the Scot, and presented a heroic and unbudgeable manliness as the core of Scottish identity. This portrayal of the country as gritty, male and working class was regionally limited: but then 49 per cent of the population of Scotland lived in Strathclyde as late as 1971 and, within that region, Glasgow had since the Victorian era seen itself as a kind of gigantic city state that at once epitomized and transcended the identity of the country in which it was located. The self-proclaimed Second City of the Empire, host of one of the last Empire Exhibitions of 1938, was in its own mind both the guarantor of Scotland's status as junior partner in the British Empire and a leading player beyond Scotland in that empire. The loss of Empire and the decline of the native industries on which the manliness of Glasgow rested hit it doubly hard, and it is arguable that the rise of Glasgow as a cultural location for a sociopathic manliness from the razor-gang novel *No Mean City* to the era of *Taggart*, was to some extent a compensation in the city's own self-image for the decline of more legitimate expressions of its cultural masculinity.[9]

If Glasgow excelled in heavy industry, then Edinburgh was the chief home of those cultural institutions which had been protected by the Union, and which contributed to the preservation of a separate national public sphere in Scotland which had helped to bring so many opportunities to the country in the imperial age. Most of these were professions rather than industries: globally, banking and financial services were the most important. Here too there were problems, however, as 'from the late 1950s onwards financial institutions were widening the scope of their activities . . . and the area of competitive overlap between what were formerly quite distinct organisations had extended greatly . . . the Scottish clearing banks saw their traditional market invaded by English and overseas banks . . . and above all by the building societies'. A sequence of mergers in the 1950s had already more than halved the number of banks that existed at the beginning of that decade. In the 1960s the building societies, invisible at the start of the decade (there were always relatively few building societies hailing from Scotland: in 1979 all but two were operating from a single office), grew to have deposits amounting to almost 40 per cent of the Scottish clearing banks' figure (60 per cent by 1982).[10] In 1981 the relative decline of the Scottish banks reached its first major crisis point with the attempted takeover of Royal Bank of Scotland by the Hong Kong and Shanghai Bank (now HSBC). As Scotland experienced closure after closure (Linwood disappeared that year), the proposed takeover seemed a sign of irretrievable decline. It was greeted with furious political opposition, which in the end helped to prevail. In 1999 the Royal Bank prospered by completing an audacious takeover of NatWest, to render it a global player: its unsuccessful rival in that bid battle, Bank of Scotland, feared becoming a takeover victim itself and rushed – perhaps unnecessarily quickly – into the arms of a merger with the Halifax Building Society, which kept the beautiful headquarters in Edinburgh but otherwise largely colonized BoS with its own culture. Thus the building society movement, invisible in Scotland when this history begins, had by the end of the century effectively swallowed the country's oldest bank, founded by act of the Estates (the Scottish Parliament) in 1695.

Due to their role in issuing their own distinctive notes, in supplying finance to Scottish businesses for centuries, in their innovation in the creation of financial instruments, and their widespread branch presence throughout Scotland, the banks were an important reference point for Scottish identity. Visible evidence of success of the country's autonomous institutions after 1707, they also provided careers for middle-class Scots in which they could excel without leaving Scotland. If they emerged with mixed fortunes from the pressures of centralization and globalization in the later twentieth century, the insurance industry and other financial services were not so fortunate. Mergers with English offices began in the 1950s and, although even in 1980, 16 per cent of British life business was written in Scotland and General Accident in Perth was the largest general insurer in the UK, the consolidations of the 1990s almost entirely wiped out the industry's HQ capacity in Scotland in all areas. In the 1960s Scottish stock exchanges (in common with local ones elsewhere in the UK) began to stop trading: but the foundation of a national Scottish Stock Exchange in 1964 was overtaken by a general UK-wide merger into London functions in 1973. By contrast with the banks, complaints and anxiety about these developments in Scotland were far more muted: despite the catastrophic fate of the country's insurance industry, it was quite simply far less important as a measure of national existence and prestige. Similarly, the relative success of the investment trust industry (40 per cent of UK investment trust assets in 1982,[11] and, despite takeovers, still a substantial figure) had little resonance in determining attitudes to industrial decline in Scottish society: the relative triumphs of the (largely Edinburgh-based) investment industry have not been seen until recently as a significant Scottish success – culturally, it clearly plays a weaker role than the City of London does in English consciousness of self-worth. For most of the period since 1960, such consciousness in Scotland rested first and foremost on the industries which had been the sinews of Empire, secondarily on the financial system which supplied domestic and business capital and thirdly on the traditional professions secured by the Union settlement. Here the decline of the Kirk (the Church of Scotland, see below) was a major factor.

The period from 1960 to 2000 witnessed major erosion in the breadth of the Scottish banking industry, and the near-collapse of domestic control in insurance and distilling. The Kirk was in decline as was all the heavy industry which had not been already appropriated by nationalization. The professions became more vulnerable to centralizing policy, including, of course, that brought about by the National Health Service. External investment brought most new jobs, but these were often public sector (or public sector at one remove via industrial policy), or lacked headquarters or research status. Attempts to dub

Scotland's vulnerable central belt electronics industry, largely composed of secondary or tertiary multinational outposts, as 'Silicon Glen' were exposed for the hype they were when the downturn in the global technology economy saw thousands of jobs lost at these marginal and expensive plants. By the end of the 1990s the opening of a new call centre was a major employment event, as Scottish society desperately tried to convince itself of its continuing economic significance. One of the key problems was the extent to which – in what once had been one of the most entrepreneurial societies on the planet – it was assumed that employment would be imported into Scotland rather than created there.

This was due in large part to two factors. The first was the nature of the close network of Scottish society itself, what Tom Nairn has labelled the 'pickle-jar', an identity structure within which certain inherited elements have matured too much and for far too long in their own company'.[12] The autonomy of the professions and much of the institutional economy of Scotland (e.g. the banks) was seen as guaranteed by the Union, a kind of middle-class home rule.

This produced certain kinds of behaviour: for example, senior legal figures in Scotland who were deep-dyed Conservatives and who apparently loathed nationalism in all its forms, not infrequently became furious critics of the British state at that moment, and that moment only, when some unwelcome and apparently alien measure was intruded on Scots Law. They had their nation, and it was their profession. As long as a relatively closed commercial, professional and industrial economy could operate in Scotland and throughout the wider imperial markets acquired in 1707, local networks could succour, not hinder, enterprise.

This balance between domestic autonomy and imperial partnership was undercut by centralizing British policy on the one hand, and the withdrawal from Empire on the other. These were issues of unique importance to Scotland; a third, the globalization of capital flows and investment, was a more general problem. However, Scottish society, with its inward networks now unbalanced by the loss of a global stage (and the EEC/EU never convincingly replaced the British Empire in this, not least because it didn't speak English) and under attack from within by a centralizing Britishness, found it difficult to identify and address the third challenge of globalization.

In addition – and this will be dealt with in more detail in chapter Two – from the 1960s public sector expenditure in Scotland was geared to preserve the damaged Union compact by ensuring that strategic resources and developments went Scotland's way. Even the Barnett formula, developed in 1978 on the eve of what was expected to be Scottish devolution, provided for the convergence of Scottish and English public expenditure only at a very slow rate. In the 1980s the Conservative Government was unwilling to import the whole panoply of Thatcherism into Scotland, in part because of fears of the political consequences (which for the Conservatives were in any case serious enough). Ironically, criticism from England which points out perceived excessive public expenditure in Scotland is attacking the very policy framework designed to keep Scotland in the Union. However – and this is implied by the business formation figures adduced below – the effect of heavy public expenditure in Scotland has been, many argue, to create a dependency culture. The attempts since 1999 by entrepreneurs like Sir Tom Hunter (who, fittingly enough, became Scotland's first billionaire in 2007) to re-energize this dimension of Scottish society are themselves a sign of the validity of this diagnosis.[13]

The oil and financial industries (and later, the establishment of the Scottish Parliament) made the greatest difference to changing patterns of comparative regional wealth distribution within Scotland in the period under discussion. In 1968 the poorest region was the Borders, with average male earnings 16 per cent below the Scottish average. The south-west and the Highlands were both over 10 per cent below, with Glasgow and Edinburgh on the average. By 1977 Grampian was 14 per cent above the average (largely thanks to oil and its secondary effects), Lothian 2 per cent above; in 1995 Grampian was 36 per cent above average, with the Highlands 16 per cent and the Borders 11 per cent below. Lothian was 11 per cent, but Edinburgh city was 50 per cent above the average. The massive and disproportionate effects of Scotland's success in oil and financial services had helped to skew the economy on a regional basis with far greater disparity than had been the case 50 years earlier: by 2007 salaries in major accountancy firms in Scotland were matching those in the Home Counties. Half a century of central planning had not changed anything when the picture is examined on this scale. Those areas which had received the most government direction were also the areas of lowest business formation. The proportion of VAT-registered businesses per 10,000 population in 1996 was over 400 in Aberdeenshire, 250 in Edinburgh city, 175 in Glasgow, and around 125–130 in North Lanarkshire and West Dunbartonshire. More recently, Glasgow has been performing a little better, very necessary for the overall economy given that 63 per cent of the country's population live in the greater urban area of its two biggest cities, with 2 million in the Glasgow travel to work area alone.[14]

Despite the major shifts towards policy centralization in the postwar era, and the consequent erosion of Scottish autonomy, Scottish professional society continued to retain elements of its historically close networks: though these, increasingly on the defensive in a union settlement which had been greatly altered by changing political conditions, seem to have become less effective than in the past. Nonetheless, in Scotland, as in other small countries, anyone who 'matters' is likely to know someone else who does. In greater Glasgow in particular, and in certain sectors of Edinburgh and Aberdeen society also, there is a self-perpetuating professional and commercial middle class, who are likely to have attended the same schools and universities. Participation in higher education in Scotland has always been higher than was the case south of the border (17 as against 10 per cent in 1979 for example, while in the late 1990s Scotland reached the 50 per cent target desired for England by Tony Blair). The age of their universities, their structural importance to Scottish society's sense of itself and the different school examination system mean that few of those domiciled in Scotland leave it for higher education – almost always below 10 per cent of leavers in any given year.[15]

As pointed out above, a significant proportion of the Scottish self-image, particularly in the west of the country, was bound up in the collectivist masculine pursuits of heavy industry, while the protected and autonomous professions and organizations of post-Union Scotland formed another significant dimension in Scottish identity, arguably strongest in Edinburgh (and the basis of its 'bourgeois' as opposed to Glasgow's 'working-class' self-image, only slightly borne out by statistics) but found throughout the country. But as well as the slippery questions of identity, it is important to explore what areas of Scottish experience were clearly and definitively different from the UK norm, how these may have affected the performance and life of Scottish culture since 1960, and whether they have increased or decreased in importance during that period. Some of these, such as culture, politics and the development of a diverse society, will be discussed in the chapters that follow. As a sample of some other areas of Scottish difference, housing, football, the media and religion are discussed below.

For a long time, the proportion of public sector housing, and the consequent lack of private home ownership in Scotland was a significant feature of cultural difference. As Richard Finlay suggests, low rents made council housing 'a cultural preference rather than an economic necessity for many Scots'. In 1981 55 per cent of Scottish households 'lived in public rental housing compared with 32 per cent in the rest of Britain'. Not only, however, has this difference largely disappeared in the era of council house sales (by 1996 the figures were 30 per cent and 19 per cent), but it was also of quite recent appearance. Some 75 per cent of Scottish house completions between 1950 and 1980 were public sector developments, which in turn built on the 67 per cent public sector share of completions in the inter-war period, when the equivalent proportion in England and Wales was 25 per cent. This process began as a conscious effort to improve the notoriously poor housing stock in certain areas. If local authority housing levels were for a time a signifier of Scottish difference, it was one created by central British government policy, and one which moreover witnessed a strong move away from Scottish architectural tradition, particularly as represented in the urban tenement. Moreover, the vast provision of subsidized public sector housing was another central policy feature which arguably weakened the economy, as lack of investment 'in private housing has meant that the nation has been poorer in the long run'.[16]

If one walks round the streets of French towns with many intact old buildings, one can come across the familiar pattern: a set of bells beside a common entrance, a chilly and sometimes dank stone stair behind leading to a multitude of front doors. In this arrangement, high population density can be achieved in limited space: moreover, the tenement (of which the oldest surviving are in Edinburgh) was not the preserve of the humbler members of society. When the middle-class suburb of Hyndland was built in Glasgow in the early 1900s, it was still to a tenement design, and the model continued to dominate Scottish housing stock in the main cities (with the partial exception of Aberdeen) until the local authority boom began in 1919. Since that boom ended in 1980, private sector supply in Scotland has largely followed (with the odd exception) a unitary UK model. A younger generation of Scottish buyers has turned more towards small family houses than large tenement flats (some of which have the floorspace to accommodate the rooms of two English 1930s detached houses), but living on a stair retains a strong following in Scotland at high levels of the market: it is easy (2007) to pay £400,000 to £500,000 for a nineteenth-century flat in Glasgow or Edinburgh.

If most of the public sphere of Scottish life depended on professions, business, institutions and culture which reached back at least to the eighteenth century, and in most cases beyond the Union, among the most crucial of more recent developments reinforcing a distinct Scottish experience was football. Other Scottish sports serve as displaced expressions of nationhood on the international stage, but none with such vigour and persistence: the cry of 'Gi'e us an Assembly, and we'll gi'e ye back your Wembley' after the breaking of the Wembley goalposts in 1977 following Scotland's 2–1 win over England was only one sign of a symbiosis between nationality and football which was also manifest in the unpleasant anti-Englishness which accompanied the 2006 World Cup, doubtless stoked by articles such as 'Want something to do during the World Cup? LET'S INVADE ENGLAND' in one redtop newspaper.

The creation of a separate Scottish cup competition in 1874 was followed by a Scottish League Championship in 1890, only two years after the inaugural Football League. The development of a national football league helped stifle the rising popularity of cricket in particular in Scotland. By the beginning of the twentieth century, nationalist activists like Theodore Napier were noting the symbolic importance of the sport to Scottish nationality; while at the same time, its dual role as a representation of Irish politics by other means was becoming enshrined in the development of two giant teams, Rangers and Celtic, the 'Old Firm', who came to dominate the domestic game while reprising Protestant–Catholic tensions from the north of Ireland, much more enduring among their supporters than was the case elsewhere in Scotland for teams like Hibernian and Dundee Harp (now Dundee United), originally formed on similar lines. As early as 1909, the Scottish FA withheld the cup after the replayed Old Firm final ended in rioting, in the midst of six sequential Celtic league titles. Of the first 50 Scottish league titles, 44 were won by Rangers (one shared) or Celtic, and since 1960, the only other champions have been Hearts (1960), Dundee (1962), Kilmarnock (1965), Aberdeen under Alex Ferguson (1980, 1984, 1985) and Dundee United (1983). This is not a new development – between 1904 and 1932 there were no champions outwith the Old Firm – but what has changed is the balance of the fan base. The shrinking of the top Scottish league from eighteen to ten in 1975 has never been fully reversed (an expansion to twelve now seems settled) despite widespread doubts about the structure, largely because the opportunity to play each other four times in a season rather than twice in a bigger league means more Old Firm gates for the members of the lucky top division. Inevitably, the middle tier of Scottish provincial clubs unable to guarantee top tier football under the new arrangements – Ayr United, Morton, Airdrie, St Johnstone, even Dundee – have suffered progressive attrition in resources since the 1970s, although the position of league teams from smaller communities – Cowdenbeath, Forfar, Stranraer – remains largely unchanged. Moreover, the Old Firm gates have got bigger and bigger. In 1975 the average combined Rangers/Celtic home gate was 45,000, and the combined Aberdeen/Hearts (the next largest clubs) c. 25,000. In 2005–6, the Old Firm home gate averaged 107,000, and that of the two next largest clubs, Hearts and Hibs, 30,000 combined. Rangers and Celtic are in or on the fringes of the top twenty clubs in Europe by turnover despite the absence of domestic TV income: with it, they would be in the top ten. Within a league where the average home gate of most top division teams is on a par with English League One at best, they are bloated giants who in recent years have shown ever more consciousness of the problems attendant on a domestic environment which deprives them of tv income and sends them on a round of unappetizing visits to teams of very modest abilities who are talked up by the media to conceal the lack of competition, and because of the enduring national pride which surrounds Scottish football. Scottish domestic football is ranked tenth in Europe in 2006, ahead of countries like the Czech Republic, Turkey and Poland: but take away Old Firm performances in European competition, and the rest present a sorry state, a change from the 1960s, when strength in depth was evident. Scotland is a football-mad country (2.1 per cent of the population view club football, as against 1.4 per cent in England and less – often much less – everywhere else), but on any given weekend 44 per cent of all attendance at home games for Scotland's 40 clubs is at Ibrox or Celtic Park, a disproportion which deepens Glasgow's (resented) sense of itself as a synecdoche for the whole nation, in football as in other fields.[17]

The symbiosis between Scottish football and the Scottish media has been very important: before devolution, and to some extent after it, football was the chief marker of independent nationality in the Scottish press. One of the key distinctions between Scottish society and the rest of the UK was that Scotland had its own national press, and this press was reinforced by the public institutions of Scottish life, from education to football. At the quality end of the market, Scotland had a national press very unlike England's, and more like that – as Michael Fry has argued – of Germany or the United States: major papers with national news coverage based in large city areas. *The Scotsman*, *The (Glasgow) Herald* and *The Press and Journal* (Aberdeen) all to varying degrees filled roles which regional newspapers in England would not address (the Dundee *Courier* has arguably always been more of a regionally based paper). The *Scotsman* and *Herald* covered national and international news from a Scottish perspective inflected towards the culture and interests of their own cities, though not dominated by them; the *Press and Journal* undertook the same task less convincingly: its primary role was rather supra-regional, to cover the interests of all northern Scotland from Montrose to Shetland, and with that purpose in mind it produced a separate Highland edition.

The entrenched position of the Scottish press used to be very powerful. In Margaret Oliphant's 1896 story, 'The Library Window', *The Times* does not arrive in Scotland until the evening, and it remained true in the 1960s that the English papers (*The Guardian* in particular) might not be in the newsagents until the afternoon, even in a large city. The Scottish press had at that time, however, a predominantly British outlook, and it was not until the 1970s that it began to reflect a separate Scottish cultural and political agenda, which in its turn led to the development of the first broadsheet Sundays in the 1980s: the *Sunday Standard* (1981–3), *Scotland on Sunday* (1989–) and *The Sunday Herald* (1999–). By the 1980s, the London papers were arriving earlier and with better distribution: nonetheless, Scotland remained dominated by its own press. The outstanding example was *The Sunday Post*, which at its peak circulation of 1.14 million, was read by 79 per cent of Scots, though its mixture of sentiment, religiosity, homely advice, stories and cartoons (most famously Oor Wullie and The Broons) was a declining asset after 1980, and the paper proved incapable of reinventing itself, though circulation was still 470,000 as late as 1999. Elsewhere the *Daily Record* had a circulation of 651,000 in 1999, 550,000 in 2002, collapsing to 380,000 by the end of 2006, with its counterpart, *The Sunday Mail*, selling up to three-quarters of a million. In 1999 *The Times* had 28,000 Scottish sales, *The Telegraph* 24,000, *The Guardian* 14,000 and *The Independent* 7,500; by contrast, *The Herald* had 101,000, *The Scotsman* 78,000 and the *Press and Journal* 102,000.

Globalization of course furnished its own pressures: in the limited marketplace enjoyed by the Scottish papers, it was difficult to invest, expand the paper or generate major advertising or promotional revenue: also, in a small and highly competitive market, the falling market share experienced by newspapers in general was harder to absorb. Loss-leading price-cutting campaigns won both *The Times* and (especially) *The Sun* market share. *The Scottish Sun* was also helped by being the first paper (in 1992) to come out in favour of the Nationalists at an election, and won market share at the expense of the (sometimes rather truculently) Labourist *Record*, which some nationalists loathed enough never to buy. By the time *The Scottish Sun* switched back to Labour for 1997 it had done plenty of damage to its rival, which used to sell almost 1 million copies daily, and the Mirror Group's decision to allow *The Daily Mirror* to compete with *The Record* in Scotland may not have helped.

Paradoxically, devolution damaged the Scottish press further. The London newspapers, particularly *The Times*, responded to increasing awareness of the importance of the Scottish dimension within Scotland through separate editions and better news coverage, while *The Guardian* deserves special credit for being almost the only media outlet to run Scottish news to an English readership. At the same time, *The Scotsman*, which had long supported devolution, under its new right-wing ownership ran a savage, small-minded and pointlessly rebarbative campaign against the Scottish Parliament and all its works, which, combined with a rapid turnover of staff and acts of genius such as using the education supplement to attack the teaching profession who bought it, succeeded in achieving a circulation of 54,000 by the end of 2006, a year in which – following takeover by the Johnston Press – the paper's situation stabilized. In 2007, in an interesting volte-face, it supported an SNP-led coalition, as did three of the Sunday papers, breaking ranks in favour of the Nationalists for the first time. An attempt to launch a new business paper for Scotland, *business a.m.*, collapsed after a couple of years when circulation failed to reach 20,000, though it did at least provoke the *Financial Times* into giving some unwonted attention to Scottish business. But the positional strength of the Scottish press in a fragmenting and highly competitive media market continues to give cause for concern. In 1981 the *Herald* and *Scotsman* combined sold 215,000; in 1999, 179,000; in 2002, 171,000; in 2006, around 125,000, with the Glasgow paper down 40 per cent in 25 years and its Edinburgh rival down 45 per cent. Meanwhile *The Times* has almost maintained its 1999 position. *The Herald*'s online site may be at least part of the shape of the future of Scottish newspapers, and rumours of a possible *Herald–Scotsman* merger occasionally circulate, though the gap in quality between the two papers has become very marked since 1995. As far as the quality market goes, *The Scotsman* has – largely through its own actions – totally eroded the natural ascendancy it enjoyed in 1960. What is very clear is that the old saturation coverage has gone: in 1981, 52 per cent of Scots adults read *The Record*, a position which gave the newspaper a social – and political – influence it appears to have lost for good.[18]

The Scottish press has nonetheless remained the major forum for discussing the distinctive culture, politics and society of Scotland. Scottish broadcasting was either established or franchised by centralized British policy, and as a result it has been far less satisfactory in covering the changes of the last 40 years. Its major show successes (networked outside Scotland), such as *Taggart* (stv) and *Rab C. Nesbitt* (bbc) have largely been content to reprise stereotypes of the music hall Scot and Glasgow as a violent 'No Mean City': Scottish broadcasting is centred in Glasgow, and relatively little in the way of Scottish voices or outlook appear on it which are not Glaswegian in fact or form. Football, humour, sentiment or violence sums up the bulk of Scottish television, with some fine history programmes – almost never networked – the leaven in the lump. Much bbc production in Scotland – e.g. *Film 2007* and bbc3/4 productions – may benefit the internal bbc economy in Scotland, but does not contain ascertainably Scottish material, while BBC Scotland as a whole is continuing to lose ground in overall bbc commissioning within the uk, with a drop from £60m to £39m in commissions between 2004 and 2007. Increasingly, the view is being heard (and not only in nationalist circles) that Scotland needs properly devolved broadcasting (it is reserved to Westminster under the current arrangements), amid a climate of deepening suspicion that the Scottish electronic media have been allowed to deteriorate since devolution.[19] There are severe budgetary constraints: only *c.* 3 per cent of bbc programmes are made in Scotland in exchange for 10 per cent of licence fees, and there is also quite clearly an unwillingness to use Scottish coverage to address serious issues or major concerns (with the exception of the tokenistic *Newsnight Scotland*). Holyrood's business is reported on non-networked output, it is true, but not usually in the main bulletins, which offer changes to government policy 'in England and Wales', usually without addressing what the differences in Scotland are or might be: hence Scottish viewers of the main evening news who don't pick up *Good Morning Scotland*, *Newsnight Scotland* or the early evening bulletins remain ignorant of Holyrood's actions, while all other British viewers tend to be in the dark about them on a permanent basis.

Radio Scotland, established in 1978, used to discuss the broader-based issues of Scottish society, but since devolution in 1999 it has become – either by accident or design – more and more like a local radio station and less and less like a combination (in differing proportions) of Radios 4, 5 and 2, which is the position which it largely fulfilled in the years before devolution. Radio Scotland in fact suffered from the ambivalence concerning Scotland's status in the postwar UK highlighted in the Introduction: it is – in BBC parlance which well reflects the ambivalence of central government policy since 1945 – a 'national region'. The lack of devolution in broadcasting policy puts Scottish public life and culture at risk of lacking any forum for its expression, especially as the global media market itself tends to centralize, and the English media becomes less global and more Anglocentric, with ITV1 and C4 showing barely 25 hours a year of factual programming from developing countries, for example. Even the BBC's planned increase in Scottish, Welsh and Northern Irish coverage from 12 per cent to 17 per cent by 2010 has not been without controversy: Scottish Enterprise's apparent desire to attract English production companies to Scotland to help meet this target in preference to local talent has fed complaints in Scotland that the industry is being starved of the projects it needs to reach the critical mass necessary to retain the best employees. There are, however, some local successes such as Tartan TV, an Aberdeen company which makes Scottish shows for expatriates: its current agreements with public sector broadcasters give it potential reach into 46 million US homes.[20]

Administrative devolution in combination with governmental centralism paradoxically produced a number of 'national' organizations at a time when Scotland was coming to be classified as a region outwith its borders. Scottish Television (1955) and Scottish Opera (1960) were examples of regional policy in commercial and public sector spheres leading to the creation of new 'national' organizations, though in Scottish Television's case, Grampian was a regional rival within Scotland, and Border – always unsatisfactorily – straddled

Scotland and England. Although never as strongly as in Wales, Gaelic broadcasting gradually became an issue in Scotland in the context of the increasing emergence of the language in the 1960s, with the establishment of the Historical Dictionary of Scots Gaelic (1966) and the Gaelic Books Council (1969). The stabilization of Gaelic's position in society was itself only one facet of the wide-ranging renewal of Scottish cultural life in the 1960s and the ensuing decades, which stretched from folk music to literature, and which will be dealt with in more depth in chapter Four.

Part of the growing interest in the country's national history and culture seems to have been possible because of the relative decline of the Presbyterian ascendancy, particularly in its Orange manifestation. The legacy of the Scottish Reformation had always made Scotland uneasy with aspects of its own past, not least its historic links with Catholic Ireland: folk music, for example, is still distrusted in Orange areas of western Scotland for its apparent Irish links, while in their turn Scottish ceilidhs in areas of significant Irish immigration often present a hybridized programme of Scottish and Irish dances. Scotland's close historic, linguistic and ethno-cultural ties to Ireland (outwith the north-eastern counties) were long suppressed or ignored during the years of Presbyterian ascendancy: in 1923 the Church and Nation committee of the Kirk of Scotland even published an infamously racist report on Irish immigration, implicitly rebuked in John Buchan's novel Witch Wood (1927) which shows the anti-Irish brutality of Presbyterian Scotland in earlier times. Combating the Kirk's reservations about aspects of Scotland's native and hybrid cultures had been going on for centuries: in the 1960s, it began to be clear that the power, dignity, restraint and repression of Calvinist culture in Scotland was failing. In Aberdeen at the beginning of the 1960s, Christmas Day was a normal working day for many; by the time a Free Kirk headmaster had a Christmas tree at his school chopped down in the 1970s, his action was widely regarded as both newsworthy and ridiculous, and when the Lord Chancellor, Lord Mackay, was ostracized by his own even more extreme Free Presbyterian sect (which subdivided as a result, a talent for which Scottish Presbyterianism has few rivals) for attending a Requiem Mass as a matter of official courtesy, such behaviour had become ludicrous. Deep distaste for Catholicism, once a staple diet even among moderate Anglicans, was beginning to be a lost cause in Scotland, though among traditional and relatively immobile sectors of society such bigotry remains a force, particularly in the west central belt. In 1960 'almost 70 per cent of Scots over 14 were claimed as church members, compared with around 23 per cent in England', but this dominant position was rapidly eroding. By 2002, a poll indicated that 47 per cent of Scots regarded themselves as belonging to the established Kirk, though in point of fact only some 16 per cent do.

To some extent, the decline of Presbyterianism in Scotland was simply a function of a general increase in western European secularism, and it is undeniable that Scotland has become more secular, though at a slower rate than England, where only half the proportion of the population go to church. What has been distinctive, however, is the development, following John Paul II's visit of 1982, and the general decline in rampant anti-Catholicism in Scotland, of the Catholic Church's role (despite declining congregations) as the major clerical voice in Scotland. Throughout the 1990s the voice of the Scottish bishops was increasingly heard on matters of public morality and social solidarity, in a country more open to Catholic social teaching on the Continental model – if not always Catholic moral teaching – than its southern neighbour. When the most senior bishop, Thomas Winning (1925–2001), Archbishop of Glasgow, was installed as a Cardinal in 1994, it was seen as a dignity of national significance, much more so perhaps than had been the case when his predecessor, Joseph Gray, had become Scotland's first Cardinal since the Reformation in 1969. The much stronger opposition to abortion in Scotland compared with the rest of the UK led to unsuccessful pressure for it to become a devolved issue, and in 2007 the Holyrood administration apparently assured to the Catholic Church that it would be exempted from gay adoption legislation: if this was the case, Westminster ignored the assurance. If Presbyterianism has declined in importance in Scottish life since 1960, Catholicism has become relatively more powerful, and has – in recent years at least – become closely associated with an open and positive – if coded and cautious – attitude towards Scottish independence, both in its bishops' letters and in the pronouncements of some of its senior clerics: in 2007, Cardinal O'Brien was the first name outside politics to appear on the BBC website congratulating Alex Salmond on being elected First Minister. Increasingly, instead of being viewed as alien and Irish (even by the nationalists – only 7–8 per cent of Catholics voted nationalist in the 1970s), the decline of the Union institutions – including the Kirk – has opened a role for the Irish example in Scotland: in 1992 a *Universe* poll suggested 35 per cent SNP support among Catholics, though the actual figure at the election of that year appears to be lower than this.[21] The Catholic Church has – despite increasing secularism in general – benefited from Presbyterianism's decline: it is also the only faith community in Scotland able to challenge the Church of Scotland in numbers and significance. The Episcopal Church, the Scottish branch of the Anglican Communion, has only 35–40,000 members, and all other Christian denominations have fewer, as do all other faiths with the exception of Islam (up to 50,000 in 2007). By contrast, there are some 800,000 baptized Catholics in Scotland, though fewer than half of these are practising.

Scotland, then, has changed substantially since 1945, more particularly from 1960. While there are many British elements in its society and institutions, many of these are of relatively recent date, and the product, directly or indirectly, of British government policy. At the same time, social organization, the pattern of industry, housing, religion and education differ significantly in Scotland: importantly, even where this difference is small, Scots often consider it to be large. School-level education in Scotland in the state sector is now almost completely the legacy of the Crosland/Williams British Labour era: no specialist schools to speak of, and a standardized comprehensive system. With regard to international comparators in Maths and Science, Scottish pupils are often weak, and not infrequently now underperform English ones. Despite the erosion of the education system on which the reputation of Scottish education was built, however, the myth remains. Pre-Thatcher British government policy has been internalized to some degree as representative of traditional egalitarian Scottish values, and education is not the only area where British policies of the 1960s have been adopted as 'Scottish' in contradistinction to new policies emanating from London. Not all central policy-driven institutions fare alike: only some 57 per cent of those domiciled in Scotland view the BBC as a Scottish institution, compared to over 90 per cent for the NHS; but one of the interesting features of contemporary Scottish identity is that, together with more traditional expressions of nationality, a significant part of what people identify as Scottish is the product of the centralist British political system between 1945 and 1979. After that date, centralist policies, whether Tory or Labour, have received less consent, let alone adoption. In part, this may be a reaction against Thatcherism which is spending itself and will in the end disappear. In the 2007 election campaign, this agenda of Butskellite Scottishness was in clear decline in a number of areas, with enterprise, changes in education policy and other fields all showing the onset of new thinking.

In the next chapter I will be exploring the development and rise of Scottish Nationalism since 1960, and also the very significant shifts in Scottish identity more broadly conceived which have taken place after that date: these will be considered in the context of other European nationalisms. What is very clear is the extent to which general political behaviour began to shift in the crucial decade of the sixties. In the first five or even six postwar general elections, Scottish voting patterns echoed those of the UK at large, more than they had done in fact in the second half of the nineteenth century. The Conservative Party won half the popular vote in 1955 and 1959, and could even win seats like Glasgow Govan which were in shipyard territory, clearly to some extent on the back of the Orange vote, which remained sporadically strong until the 1970s, being, as David Ellis and others have argued, a key component in Unionism.[22] Senior Catholic policemen were, for example, as unfamiliar in Glasgow as in the Royal Ulster Constabulary at the end of the 1960s. If there was any distinction in Scottish electoral behaviour in this period, it was probably to be found in the slightly higher support enjoyed by the Liberal Party, particularly in the Highlands, due to historic questions dating back to the era of the Clearances: but the difference was in any event marginal across Scotland's 71 seats.

Then in the 1966 General Election major slippage occurred in Conservative support, and the Tories fell to twenty seats, though still securing 38 per cent of the vote. At the same time, the SNP gained 5 per cent: their first significant inroad at a General Election. In 1970, the Conservatives only moved up by three seats in Scotland, out of a total of 77 British gains; in October 1974 the Nationalists overtook the Tories in the share of the popular vote for the first time, and although that position was not recaptured at a general election until 1992, the resilience of the Labour Party and the permanent boost to the Liberal vote resulting from the SDP-Liberal Alliance in the 1980s kept the Conservatives under perpetual pressure. Jeremy Thorpe's Liberals had achieved around 18–19 per cent of the UK vote in 1974, and the advent of the Alliance and (after 1987) the merged Liberal Democrats led to a slight increase in the vote to around 21–22 per cent at general elections. In Scotland, by contrast, the Liberal vote did not rise by so much in the 1960s and early '70s, standing at 8 per cent as opposed to 18 per cent UK-wide in October 1974, but made significant strides after the Alliance was created in 1981, at the expense of the Tories and SNP rather than Labour.[23] The position reached in 1997, when Scotland did not elect a single Conservative MP for the first time in history, was one which had been brewing for the previous quarter of a century. The decline of the Conservative Party as much as the rise of the SNP, was the defining marker in the shifting sands of Scottish political identity since the 1960s, a situation I will examine in more detail in the next chapter.

Chapter 2

Scottish Politics and Identity

In 1960 the Scottish National Party was largely the weak and marginal organization it had been since its foundation through a merger of the Scottish Party and the National Party of Scotland in 1934. Not the least of its problems arose from the endemic division between and within these two wings of the party, which endured for many years. The NPS, founded in 1928, was more focused on outright self-government, and its ex-Scottish Home Rule Association members thought that the Labour Party had neglected the Scottish question since 1923 (when the first minority Labour administration held power at Westminster). This view of Labour's betrayal of the Home Rule cause is arguably in part responsible for the visceral hatred between the SNP and Labour.

The NPS also had a 'Gaelic revolutionary wing' of cultural nationalists like the novelist Neil Gunn, who identified the Scottish and Irish causes long before it became fashionable to do so, but these were a small minority: some (not Gunn!) may have been ex-members of the Irish Volunteers. The Scottish Party (founded in 1932) by contrast, was more right-wing, more overtly interested in the British Empire (though only the radical wing of the NPS showed any interest in postcolonial readings of the Scottish situation), and more likely to regard a form of devolution as an acceptable final outcome for Scotland. Although the merger of the two parties blurred this distinction for a while, it threatened to divide the nascent SNP for many years. Its distant echoes could still be heard in the differences between 'gradualists' and 'fundamentalists' in the 1990s.

Tensions arose in World War II. Some, largely though not all extreme, nationalists became conscientious objectors, refusing to fight in 'England's war'; the mainstream supported the war as fought in defence of the rights of small nations. In 1942 some of the moderates under John MacCormick (1904–61) split from the SNP to pursue a weaker Home Rule agenda ('the ultimate goal of a free Scotland in a Federal United Kingdom' in MacCormick's words): by 1946 they claimed 5,000 members. MacCormick, the most talented politician the early SNP possessed, had argued for a 'Scottish National Convention' for Home Rule as early as 1930, making a major early effort to secure cross-party agreement on constitutional change. The Scottish Plebiscite Society, founded in 1946, ran a number of local Home Rule plebiscites, with encouraging results. In 1947 a Scottish National Assembly was set up and a Claim of Right put forward to the United Nations, and in 1949 a discussion held by the Scottish Covenant Association at the Inchrie Hotel in Aberfoyle (now the Covenanter's Inn) led to the launch of the 1949–52 National Covenant for Scottish Home Rule, which attracted some 2 million signatures, but was brushed aside by Westminster on the grounds that only general elections counted.[1]

Much of this pan-Scottish activity was due to MacCormick's efforts in trying to build a consensus that went far beyond the SNP: his tireless activity led even to a legal challenge to Royal titles in 1953, which on appeal before the Lord President, Lord Cooper, gained a partial recognition of the principle of Scottish popular sovereignty as against the unlimited sovereignty of Parliament, and in the circles of academic law at least, stirred up some controversy as to the exact legal status of the 'Treaty' or 'Act' of Union. The Union Articles include some (as well as those which reserve right of 'subsequent modification' to Westminster) that 'emphatically exclude alteration by declaration that the provisions shall be fundamental and unalterable in all time coming': that is, they imply limits on the sovereignty of Parliament.[2] However, the failure of MacCormick's efforts in bridge-building to yield results meant that the SNP, chronically weak as it was during the 1950s and early '60s, turned away from the pursuit of common ground with pro-Home Rule activists in the British political parties. This lasting distrust helped to lead to the failure of a proposed SNP–Liberal electoral pact in 1964 and 1968, and to SNP withdrawal from the Constitutional Convention in 1989. It must be said that the SNP view in such situations had some justification, for although the ranks of Home Rulers contained many quasi-nationalists, they also contained many who saw devolution as a political convenience or a way of strengthening the Union which the SNP wished to end. The exact tactical position of the SNP in the various devolution debates will be brought out below.

In any case, by the late 1960s the SNP's apparently impossibilist position, unalloyed with Liberal federalism, was driving the political agenda. The 5 per cent of the vote achieved in 1966 was succeeded by Winnie Ewing's historic win at Hamilton on 2 November 1967, which the Scots Independent saw as a victory for fundamentalist nationalism as against pacts of convenience:

We decided years ago that 'going it alone' was the only way to secure freedom. Our experience of alliances, arrangements, compromises and pacts . . . proved finally that no friends unwilling to put Scotland first . . . were to be trusted when the political battle was joined.[3]

At first, everything went well. Nationalist support rocketed to over 30 per cent in the polls, which also showed majorities in favour of Home Rule and significant minorities of a quarter favouring independence (though one rogue poll put support for independence at 80 per cent!). In May 1968 the SNP gained around 30 per cent of the vote where they contested the local elections and won 108 councillors. Nationalist membership rocketed, and the Labour Government's response was rapid. In January 1968 the 'first sub-committee of any House of Commons committee sat in Edinburgh', and transport was devolved that year to Scottish Office control. Edward Heath, leader of the Tory opposition, stressed the need for Scottish Home Rule in his Declaration of Perth, and 'set up a Scottish Constitutional Committee under Sir Alec Douglas-Home' while, on 15 April 1969, Harold Wilson, the Prime Minister, decided to buy time for the government by setting up 'a Royal Commission under Lord Crowther to consider the

Constitution'.[4] Both major British political parties seemed to be responding to the Nationalist wave.

However, it was beginning to become clear that some of the councillors elected in the unexpected surge of 1968 were not fully prepared for their roles as elected representatives. In the June 1970 General Election, although the Nationalists took an unprecedented 11 per cent of the vote, it was a long way short of their hopes, and the only compensation for the loss of Hamilton was victory for Donald Stewart in the Western Isles. Welcome as that victory was, the Western Isles was a much more peripheral constituency than Hamilton, an industrial town in the Glasgow orbit and at the heartland of west central Scotland. As time was to tell all too clearly, the Nationalists would have much greater success hanging on to relatively remote constituencies low in industrial, professional or financial activity than they would in securing established footholds in the population centres.

In the early 1970s, however, the economic case for independence seemed to be immensely strengthened by the realization of the scale of oil reserves in the North Sea, and the SNP accordingly launched the 'It's Scotland's Oil' campaign in 1973. In 1970 Lord Kilbrandon replaced Crowther as head of the Royal Commission; its Conservative rival, Home's Constitutional Committee, reported that year, recommending a Convention to 'consider the second reading, committee, and report stages of Scottish bills'. This was constitutional tinkering, and the Conservatives did not even implement it, though one might have thought the limited and dependent remit of Home's 'Assembly' plan might have appealed to them in the 1980s. When the Kilbrandon report came out on Halloween 1973, it recommended the establishment of Scottish and Welsh assemblies (though the signatories 'disagreed on whether it [the Scottish assembly] should have legislative, executive, or advisory powers'). There was moreover a dissenting minute signed by two members of the Commission which suggested that the establishment of assemblies in Scotland and Wales would be flawed without decentralization to the English regions and a more federal plan of government. Eight days after the report was published, Margo MacDonald snatched Glasgow Govan for the SNP, whose fortunes were clearly rising again, in part no doubt in protest against the Tory government, in part due to perceived Westminster inactivity on Scottish affairs. In December 1972 the veteran nationalist Wendy Wood (1892–1981) had 'commenced a hunger strike to the death for Scottish Home Rule' in protest at Tory inaction, and was only appeased by Government promises of a Green Paper 'after the Royal Commission had reported'. Despite this promise, Wood's fears were justified: it is clear that Whitehall departments argued vigorously behind the scenes against Kilbrandon's conclusions when they were published, ironically in large part because of a 'centralist myth' of universality and standardization which was the legacy of government since 1945. Ignorant of existing – and historical – Scottish diversity, the idea that common levels of British provision would be jeopardized by the policies of a Scottish Assembly was repeatedly deployed by London commentators.[5]

At the February 1974 General Election, the SNP won 22 per cent of the vote and seven seats. Although they were markedly less successful in the local elections of that year, they surged to 30 per cent of the vote and eleven seats in October, in an election that returned a Labour Government by the narrowest of majorities. The strength of the Nationalist vote, and their second place in 36 further seats, most of them Labour's, was a very clear threat to a weak government, which consequently, after initial reluctance, moved towards legislation based on the 1974–5 White Paper that followed the Kilbrandon Report. The English press widely viewed devolution as inevitable, and there was a real fear, as the SNP continued to rise in the polls to a high of 36 per cent, that independence was a threat. The constitutional atmosphere was more febrile than it was to be again until the mid–late 1990s. Labour Party support continued to wither in Scotland and, in 1976, Jim Sillars, the MP for South Ayrshire, left to found an independent Scottish Labour Party. Much beloved by sectors of academic and cultural opinion in Scotland, the SLP, lacking any serious popular organization or support beyond Sillars's personal vote, predictably collapsed at the polls in 1979, but its short-term impact was profound. Following its defection and Tory by-election victories, the Labour Government had to rely on Liberal support to prevent a 1977 General Election which might have – they feared – delivered further sweeping gains for the SNP.

Who were these Scottish Nationalists, and why did they suddenly, after so many years in the doldrums, make such an impact on British politics in such a short time? The SNP claimed a big membership – over 100,000 – at the end of the 1960s, though it is not clear how reliable such figures are (there is a long history of suspect political party memberships in Scotland, dating back at least to the alleged 30,000 members that the Glasgow Unionist Association alone [!] was reported to have in 1931).[6] The SNP was, however, clearly popular among younger voters (37 per cent in May 1974), and in the 1960s and '70s the populations of the New Towns, separated from their previous communities or brought up outwith them, and often aspirational lower-middle class voters who might have been Thatcherites in England, showed a propensity to support the Nationalists. SNP support was well spread socially: in 1974, professionals (the group least likely to support the party) were still 70 per cent as likely to support it as its strongest supporters from the lower middle class (c_1). By 1979 professional support for the SNP was diminishing, and by 1983 the party's left wing stance meant that although voters in social classes D and E were almost as likely to support it as in 1979, its vote had halved in the key aspirational c_1/c_2 constituency, and was only 8 per cent among professionals. By 1987, however, as SNP support waned among the poorer and less educated members of society by comparison with 1983, it doubled among ABC1 voters: Jim Sillars might have reflected in the aftermath of his Govan victory in 1988 that the SNP had now become a middle-class party. Quite significant changes in the profile of SNP support continued, with the vote among the unskilled working class for the nationalists (27 per cent) double the professional vote in 1992, while in 2001, the SNP, having moved away from the Left, seemed to have returned to their 1970s position, with equal support across all classes (19 per cent) except the petty bourgeoisie – that old C1 area of strength – where they scored 32 per cent.[7]

Throughout the 1970s the SNP was a major electoral threat only in rural and semi-rural areas, a pattern largely repeated up to very recent times, when the SNP has shown signs of being able to win urban seats, at least for Holyrood. Dundee East was the only truly urban Nationalist seat in 1974: elsewhere, gains came in places like East Dunbartonshire (a marginal victory by 22 in a three-way fight), Galloway, Perth and East Perthshire, South Angus, Argyll, the Western Isles and the rural and small town north-east. The majority of these were ex-Tory seats, and there is no doubt that in 1974 the SNP was viewed as the only credible alternative to the Conservatives in the majority of the seats it won, for the Liberal vote was low and geographically concentrated and Labour had no chance in such constituencies. When an alternative anti-Tory party established itself in these seats (as the SDP-Liberal Alliance/Liberal Democrats did in Argyll and Gordon in the 1980s), the SNP typically lost hope of regaining the seat (the 2007 Holyrood election was to be the first at which the SNP inflicted significant electoral damage on the Liberal Democrats).

In other words, the Nationalists were far more vulnerable, limited and strategic in their appeal than the Labour Party feared in 1974–9: only three or at most four of their seats were credible Labour targets, and in the course of events a revival for the Tories under a Labour Government would spell an automatic swing against SNP incumbents in Tory target seats. In addition, the SNP had numerous weaknesses among its membership and candidates. It did not have a strong leadership structure: although Billy Wolfe replaced Arthur Donaldson at the top in 1969, neither were or ever became MPs, and thus could exercise little discipline over the parliamentary group. Powers of central control over the party were limited, and hence senior figures could not impose party discipline on often-incompetent branches, composed of political ingenues who had come late to nationalism, and who were often over-optimistic, with a politics of resentment and dispossession characteristic of the hard left rather than a party of the provincial lower middle class, which was where the SNP's greatest strength lay. The SNP lacked an intellectual wing, and it was often incoherent ideologically: though it is doubtful whether this did it much electoral damage, even though critics focused on this incoherence after 1979. Middle-aged men in kilts turned up to its functions and conferences; hobbyists and the small-minded prevailed in many places in its ranks; its association with Protestantism (evident as late as 1982 during the Falklands War) lost it Catholic votes: in the 1974 General Elections, 79 per cent of Catholics voted Labour, and only 7–8 per cent for the SNP.[8] In the late

1960s, its weakness in depth was revealed when despite its colossal advertised membership it elected many incompetent councillors. The standard of SNP candidates often damaged it electorally, even – sometimes especially – when they were successful. Yet this in itself may have been a reflection of poor central control rather than lack of talent. Centrally imposed candidates cause complaints, but leaving activists to choose leads to some extraordinary decisions caused by small group dynamics which have little to do with competence or electability, being too often reflective of the envies, fears and loyalties of a closely knit group who have worked hard for a cause without necessarily knowing what is needed to make it successful. The SNP long suffered from this problem, most recently in the 2003 election lists for the Scottish Parliament, which saw some of its leading intellectual figures voted down by activists out of apparent envy and resentment; by contrast, the involvement of all party members in the process for ranking candidates in 2007 raised the calibre of those elected. Things were worse in the 1970s: no one in the SNP had any experience in government and precious few had any of senior administrative and management roles outside. Sudden success combined with inexperience and lack of discipline – even among its MPs, who were generally themselves of a good standard – presaged disaster even in the hour of success. A nationalist party has to overcome major opposition, and for this it needs to be attractive to major talent. Beside Davitt, Parnell, Collins or De Valera, the Scottish Nationalists of the 1970s looked small. Gordon Wilson, the MP for Dundee East, was perhaps their most gifted politician in Westminster, though since the SNP was in decline for reasons beyond his control for most of the era of his leadership, he has tended to be underestimated. George Reid and Margeret Bain (later Ewing) were also impressive figures, as were others among the parliamentary contingent, while Winnie Ewing, who had failed to take Moray and Nairn in 1974, was nominated in 1976 to the new European Parliament, retaining her seat at its first elections in 1979.

It was not surprising that a protest movement with negligible electoral support was ineffective when suddenly catapulted into popular success: but why did this success happen in the first place? What drove the SNP bandwagon forward? Oil was not the reason, for the party's first major surge had come in 1967–8, and the long-term effects of the 'Scotland's Oil' campaign were negligible: moreover, in later years, despite the SNP's often accurate predictions of the scale of the revenues and the opportunities they could create, the vast bulk of them were spent outwith Scotland with little or no protest from the Scottish public. The lack of the long-term effectiveness of the oil campaigns is best summed up in the words of a Nationalist commentator who could write as late as 2007 'I have yet to meet an independista who switched from being a unionist because of Scotland's oil'.[9] The other parties paid no electoral price for minimizing the North Sea's economic potential and ridiculing the SNP. The reasons for the success of the Nationalists must be sought elsewhere. One might think that the resurgence of third-party politics heralded by the Liberal by-election victory at Orpington in 1962 surely has some role to play: in large areas of Scotland, the Liberals were quite simply not credible as a protest vote party, and so the vote may have gone to the Nationalists. But were they any more credible? The problem remains. Nonetheless, the success of the Alliance/Lib Dems after 1981 in establishing strong positions in former Nationalist constituencies leads to the inescapable conclusion that some, at least, of the SNP vote in the decade following 1968 was a protest vote; and this conclusion is supported by the fact that support for an independent Scotland in the polls was on the whole both steadier and lower than the Nationalist vote. Interestingly, however, the evidence seems to be that support for Home Rule short of independence increased. In 1965 there was around 44 per cent support for some kind of Scottish assembly/parliament; in 1974 support for independence was 14 to 20 per cent. In 1977 18–24 per cent supported independence in the polls, while the total support for constitutional change of some kind varied between 66 and 81 per cent: within that, there was little enthusiasm for a weak assembly.[10]

The idea that the decline of the British Empire was key to the rise of the SNP has been around for some time, and as outlined in the Introduction, there are some important points in its favour. But surely also key was the apparent decline in Scottish autonomy in a wide number of fields, both domestic and international. The sudden rise of the SNP can be mapped almost exactly on to the acceleration of the decolonization process abroad and the apogee of central planning operating in a context of decline at home, combined with significant anglicizing policy moves in areas such as education. This process was early diagnosed by John MacCormick, who argued that the centralization of government policy was 'the new and spurious and artificial nationalism of Greater London' which 'requires a counterpoise if what we all unconsciously recognize as British is to survive'. MacCormick was prescient; but one thing which was not predicted was the way in which the decline of autonomous institutions in Scotland damaged the Conservative Party, which before 1960 had become 'identified with key aspects of Scottish national institutions'.[11] Subsequently, the Conservative Party's support in Scotland for the centralizing British policies inaugurated by Labour in 1945–51 caused long-term erosion of their position as the patriotic Scottish party which they had appeared to many to be, and gave the SNP an electoral opportunity at Tory expense boosted from time to time by discontented Labour voters and a new and aspirational electorate. The double compact of the 1707 Union – domestic Scottish autonomy and access to a global British marketplace – was in double jeopardy. There were – and are – many cross-Border ties and families, and the United Kingdom had become more of a love match than the marriage of convenience (one arranged by an elite, and very unpopular in Scotland) it had once been: but strong elements of the marriage of convenience remained. Downgraded, albeit ambivalently, to the status of a region, no longer a partner in Empire or dominant in international trade and mercantilism, provincialized by centralist policy, commercial globalization and loss of competitiveness in key industries, Scotland's status was in decline on almost every front. The SNP gave Scots an opportunity to demonstrate that they were a separate country without ever committing them to doing more than using it as a protest vehicle to show just this. Before the crisis of the 1960s, SNP support was low and erratic: since 1967, the SNP has never ceased to be a major political party in Scotland.

When the first signs of Nationalist success became manifest in the late 1960s, those members of the Labour Cabinet who did not dismiss it as a transient electoral spasm, or one to be addressed with that cure-all, 'socialist policies', instantly identified centralism as one dimension of the problem. SNP success was 'evidence that the balance of central and local government had to be recast'. There were a number of options: assimilation, which was part of the reason for protest in the first place, and thus unlikely to work without repression, which was pretty well unthinkable; ridicule and neglect, which was in part adopted and has been included in British government policy ever since; or an accommodation, 'which could be concessional (higher public spending, a bias to Scotland in new projects, protection for Scotland from certain aspects of UK policies, and so on) or involve structural change, such as Home Rule'. Always when in government, and often out of it, both main British parties pursued a similar policy from 1968 onwards: neglect and ridicule for the SNP, combined with 'concessional accommodation' on particular economic grievances which helped to keep Scottish expectations of public service high, and helped to keep Scotland dependent on British public expenditure. After 1970, the Conservatives continued to take on nationalism through higher public spending. Richard Finlay has argued that the Scottish electorate saw a Nationalist vote as a means of unlocking Westminster's bounty through financial concessions, 'a desire to protest at the failure of the London government to meet the aspirations of the Scottish post-war consensus'.[12]

Is this explanation enough? Was the SNP just a tartan lever on a British fruit machine? Unquestionably, the first SNP surge was in significant part driven by a 'remember Scotland' rather than 'free Scotland' agenda. The electorate of 1968–74 was beginning to be disenchanted with two-party politics throughout Great Britain, and in Scotland this disenchantment was linked to questions of national status, autonomy and opportunity, all of which rendered a Nationalist vote appropriate as a protest. At the same time, although October 1974 is still sometimes described as a high-water mark for the SNP's electoral fortunes (it wasn't: the SNP took 33 per cent in the 1994 European elections, which it roughly matched again in 2007), the reality (as we shall see in discussion of identity) is that Scotland was more British in the 1970s than it subsequently became. Yet from 1974–9, and again from 1987 it was the SNP who forced the pace. For most of the last 35 years,

Unionism in Scotland has defined itself reactively: disparaging the Nationalist leadership, ridiculing Nationalist economics, all the time itself drifting gently towards a more nationalist reading of Scotland. The only party which has not really done this, the Conservatives, has suffered severely: but by the late 1980s Labour and the Liberal Democrats were both defining themselves in quasi-nationalist terms in Scotland. If the SNP was merely a vehicle for cynical protest designed to extract public funds from Westminster, such changes would not have occurred.

A number of features of the political climate bear this out. For one thing, demand for constitutional change, though often weaker than immediate anxieties over inflation, unemployment and the health service, remained relatively high on any measure from the 1970s on, and has, intriguingly, shown little sign of disappearance after devolution in 1999. For another, there was a clear shift after 1987 from even devolutionists towards an assertion of Scottish sovereignty in its own right rather than seeing it as being a matter entirely in Westminster's gift. Naturally, this sovereignty rhetoric – evident in the 1988 Claim of Right which led to the Constitutional Convention – was toned down by the Labour Party once it had returned to power in 1997, but it never disappeared. After 1983 Labour politicians began to talk of Scotland's 'democratic deficit' and the 'Doomsday scenario' of a Tory London administration in a tiny minority in Scotland; Donald Dewar, the Shadow Secretary of State for Scotland, even proposed the phrase 'independence in the UK' to describe Labour's plans for a devolutionary settlement. In 1992 there were suggestions of civil disobedience from Labour sources (following SNP commitments to the same approach in 1981 and 1988) while, in 1995, in a public debate with the Nationalist leader Alex Salmond, George Robertson, then Shadow Secretary of State, declined to answer whether he preferred independence to the status quo as a second choice behind devolution.[13]

These were major shifts, in themselves indicative of Labour Party fears of the reality of nationalist sentiment, and we will return to them. The extent to which they represented a significant change is very evident in comparing them to the 1970s, when a large proportion of the Scottish Labour Party wanted nothing to do with devolution, which also enjoyed widespread doubt and hostility throughout the whole of British Labour. After the October 1974 election, when Nationalist success speeded legislation ultimately based on the Kilbrandon Report, the Scotland and Wales Bill progressed slowly through Parliament, being divided into two separate bills in 1977. Liberal desire to amend the bill to include proportional voting and tax powers delayed its progress, but lukewarm Labour support made this impossible, and in the end also made a referendum necessary, as 'there can be little doubt that, in free votes, the Scotland and Wales bills would not have passed the Commons'.[14] The Scotland Act was eventually passed in 1978. It proposed a 142-seat Assembly elected by first past the post (the Westminster voting system), with a First Secretary leading the administration, which would take over most Scottish Office functions, though the Secretary of State would retain the final say in Scottish business, and 'Scotland would continue to send 71 MPS to Westminster'. The division of powers was a mess:

Housing was devolved, but mortgages – and so private housing policy – withheld.

Education went north, but not universities; infrastructure planning – including the new SDA – but not economic planning; transport, but not railways; law, but not courts or judges; local government, but not police. The Secretary of State still retained substantial powers: over agriculture, fisheries, most of law and order, electricity, large areas of economic policy. He stayed in the Cabinet, but also had quasi-Viceregal powers . . .[15]

The Assembly would be empowered to introduce legislation, but this was to be in the guise not of 'Acts', but 'Measures'. Westminster terminology, powers and officers were unequivocally supreme.

A reading of the Hansard of the day is instructive: MPS (not least Labour MPS) used the amount of time spent on Scottish and Welsh business (which was clearly resented) to sound off over a whole host of ethnic, religious and linguistic prejudices against the 'Celtic Fringe'. Backbench unrest led to the Cunningham amendment on 25 January (ironically enough, Burns Night) 1978, which established that 40 per cent of the electoral roll would have to vote 'Yes' for the Assembly; Jo Grimond also sought to remove Orkney and Shetland from the devolutionary process in the event of a No vote. The electoral roll was in those days very unreliable, with a lot of dual counting of particularly younger voters, for it had not caught up with the growing mobility of modernity. Some allowance was made for this, but almost certainly not enough. It was the case, however, that the Cunningham Amendment was 'advisory and not mandatory'. The Secretary of State would have to 'lay a repeal order before Parliament' if the threshold was not met, but Parliament might choose not to repeal the legislation in the event of a close result. Given its record in the debates on the bill, however, it seems unlikely that Parliament would not have repealed the Scotland Act in 1979. Callaghan's offer of talks, rejected by the SNP after the 40 per cent threshold was not met, was almost certainly a delaying tactic only.[16]

The SNP were, unwillingly, forced into accepting the compromised support for devolution offered by Parliament in 1977–8, as there was no alternative save to seek to bring down the government. A 'Yes for Scotland' campaign was launched in January 1978, under Lord Kilbrandon's chairmanship: in terms of activist support, it was dominated by the Nationalists. Unhelpfully, an alternative anti-SNP Alliance for an Assembly was established in the autumn, and there were separate Yes campaigns linked to individual political parties; meanwhile the No campaign (also divided into separate campaigning organizations) was well-funded, well-organized, and played relentlessly on fears of constitutional change and further economic decline. Labour MPs ran their own No campaign, with no ascertainable efforts by government to curtail them in doing so: the Government did not support the Yes campaign with funds, as it had in the 1975 EEC Referendum. Devolution was also compromised by the 1973 Conservative establishment of regional and district councils in preference to unitary local authorities: this change, implemented in 1975, weakened the democratic case for the Assembly (which would be a third tier of government within Scotland), and also promoted concerns that it would simply be a larger version of the vast Strathclyde Region, which contained half the population. The idea of being dominated (under a first past the post electoral system) by west of Scotland Labourites was unpopular in the north and east, and almost certainly cost devolution votes, even though in the end only Dumfries and Galloway, the Borders and Orkney and Shetland showed significant majorities against.[17]

Instead of seeming fresh and new, the long drawn-out discussions of the Bill rendered devolution just another tired Westminster product, a compromise with inadequate powers, and one moreover only half-heartedly backed by a declining and failing government. Efforts were made by the No campaign to attract waverers or weak Yes voters by stressing that the vote was not a vote on the principle of Home Rule, but on the particular legislation at hand, which was widely perceived as inadequate. There were also signs of decline in the SNP vote, with the Nationalists scoring only 24 per cent and 21 per cent respectively in the 1977 and 1978 local elections. Although the SNP's local vote was not necessarily as yet a good or settled indicator of their support in General Elections, Donald Dewar's victory over Keith Bovey in the April 1978 Garscadden by-election was seen by many as confirmation of Nationalist decline, evident in opinion polls from the second half of 1977. When the referendum came, on 1 March 1979, Scotland voted Yes by 52–48, with 33 per cent of the electorate in favour on the basis of a 64 per cent turnout. It was not enough, and it came as a sad surprise to campaigners who had, even a weak earlier, expected 55–60 per cent on polling evidence: only Fife, among all the Scottish regions, reached this level of support. There were some signs that Alec Douglas-Home's late intervention, which promised a better solution from an incoming Tory Government (now widely expected) for those who voted No severely weakened the Conservative Yes vote in the run-up to polling day.[18]

Although Scotland had voted Yes (Wales voted No by around four to one) there was little appetite to contest the 40 per cent hurdle in the aftermath of the result. The Labour Party was divided and unenthusiastic, and a UK General Election was close; the Conservatives had no interest in supporting the legislation; the Liberals, who claimed to be consistent advocates of constitutional change, were, as often, posted missing when there was a real opportunity for it; the Nationalists were facing electoral defeat, a fact which they embraced like 'turkeys voting for Christmas', as the Prime Minister, James Callaghan, put it. When it became clear that the Labour Government would not readily implement devolution on the basis of the referendum result alone, the Nationalists united with the Tories in a no confidence vote which narrowly succeeded in precipitating a General Election. Buoyed up by the No vote and by the winds of political change, the Conservatives moved up from 25 per cent to 31 per cent of the Scottish vote, and from sixteen to 22 seats, in what was to be their best performance since 1970. The big losers were the SNP, who scored 17 per cent of the vote and lost nine of their eleven seats, holding only Dundee East and Western Isles, where Donald Stewart was entrenched for life: an electoral behaviour more common than not in these small, scattered, northern constituencies. There was a tiny overall swing to Labour in Scotland, and they took Cathcart from the Tories, a major prize since the sitting MP, Teddy Taylor, was widely tipped to be Secretary of State in a Tory government.

The 1979 election was traumatic for the SNP, though their vote, severely damaged as it was, had suffered far less than their parliamentary representation. Even the 19 per cent scored in the June European elections, and the return of Winnie Ewing to Strasbourg, did nothing for morale. From the Nationalist point of view, the upholders of Scottish freedom had been wiped out, largely by Tory Unionists, while the dithering Labour Party, which had botched the devolution agenda, got off scot-free. It seemed that whatever the Labour Party did, the Scots would have confidence in them, and that the Nationalists were being blamed for the failure of legislation which, far from initiating, they had been forced to accept faut de mieux. What – it seemed to some – did the Scots want?

To some it seemed that if the Scots kept on voting Labour when the rest of the UK swung to the Tories it could mean only one thing: Scots were Socialists. The SNP's rather muddy ideology in the 1970s came in for sharp criticism, and the 79 Group was founded within the party to promote a definitively left-wing stance. It contained many able figures: Alex Salmond, Roseanna Cunningham and Stephen Maxwell among them, and after Jim Sillars joined the SNP, it and its allies (for it also attracted limited cross-party support) grew yet stronger. Arguably, the high point of the 79 Group and its allies came at the 1981 conference in Aberdeen, which committed an independent Scotland to withdrawal from NATO (a policy which still stands in 2007), and (following a storming speech from Sillars) to civil disobedience as a general policy. The SNP would outflank Labour on the left, and the electorate would flock to it as a Socialist and Scottish alternative: that was the 79 Group strategy, which held it almost as an article of faith that such a renewed and ideologically focused SNP would displace Labour in the Central Belt, thus putting itself on the cusp of victory. Sillars had little time for a strategy aimed primarily at regaining the rural and semi-rural Tory constituencies the SNP had lost in 1979; rather, the focus was on victory in seats they had never won, an extraordinary political goal for a severely defeated political party to set itself, almost as if Labour had decided to target Tunbridge Wells in preference to Bury.

The 79 Group on the Left was far more influential than Siol nan Gaidheal (Seed of the Gaels) on the Right, but it too was a group born (in 1978) out of dissatisfaction with the perceived compromises of the SNP in 1974–9. SNG was not as ideologically focused as the 79ers: but it was also something of a rebuke to the respectable, bourgeois national-ist politics of the 1970s. The SNP had allowed itself to be integrated into the British political system in becoming complicit in devolutionary legislation: but, as SNG predecessors such as Wendy Wood's Patriots and the 1320 Club had believed, compromise with the British state brought no benefits. The compromise and the complicity had – in the view of some – been almost fatal. Like the 79 Group, SNG had belief in direct action. Politically, they were not particularly effective: but their Celticist banners and quasi-paramilitary kit were highly visible signs of potentially extreme politics.

In the 1960s, '70s and '80s, the SNP were intermittently smeared for their alleged sympathy for quasi-paramilitary and terrorist groups, such as the 'Tartan Army' and 'Border Clan', who attempted to attack pylons and pipelines: this kind of activity had been highlighted in Douglas Hurd's and Andrew Osmond's *Scotch on the Rocks* (1971), drama-tized by the BBC in 1973. Some of these groups were probably riddled with *agents provocateurs*; the odd one was genuine, though all seemed incompetent. They were no help to the cause they claimed to support, and the presence of paramilitary uniform at events like the 1980 Bannockburn Rally was politically embarrassing. Siol nan Gaidheal were not an organization of this kind, though they no doubt contained some who might harbour such sympathies, including the reputed Arm nan Gaidheal group. However, the SNG's dress sense challenged the limits of the 1936 Public Order Act, and rallies of up to 500 (for example at Ayr in 1980) or the burning of the Union flag at St Andrews Castle in late 1982 (cited by Scott and Macleay), presented nationalism as a threatening force on the streets rather than a douce alternative politics. Siol were expelled from the SNP in 1982, and folded in 1985, though a different organization with the same name subsequently reformed.[19]

Through all this, the Nationalist vote fell. From 16 per cent in the 1980 local elections, to 13 per cent in the 1982 regionals, to 12 per cent in the 1983 General Election and 1984 local elections. An attempted break-in at the Royal High School buildings in Edinburgh, putative home of the lost Assembly, was the highlight of the civil disobedience campaign, which only succeeded in putting the Nationalists into disrepute. In 1982, in an effort to stop the rot, the 79 Group and SNG were proscribed from the party at the Ayr conference. Gordon Wilson, who had taken over the unwelcome task of leading the SNP in 1979, had a very different attitude to politics. Both groups had been shown to be ineffective, but the influence of 79 Group policy on targeting the Central Belt in preference to the north was to be felt long after 1982, and received a new lease of life when Jim Sillars won Govan in 1988, only to begin to be finally discredited after the 1992 General Election, when Sillars lost his seat while clearly expecting a major Nationalist advance which did not materialize.

The fact was that the analysis of the 1979 election result on which this case rested was flawed. It was very doubtful that the miniscule positive swing (on one calculation) to Labour in 1979 was the result of Socialism: rather, only the Labour Party could effectively protect Scotland against a Tory government. Moreover, the polls in the UK in 1979 did not rule out the possibility of a very narrow Labour victory, or at least a hung parliament, so sticking with Labour was not irrational. In addition, the Scottish electorate was usually too sanguine about Labour's UK chances: in 1987 according to the polls a significant number of Scots expected a Labour victory in a General Election which returned the Tories with a 100-seat majority. At the same time, Scottish

Conservatism was, if weaker than in the 1950s, by no means in irretrievable decline, and a recovery in the Conservative vote was sufficient to oust the SNP in seat after seat, many of which they held with small majorities in any case. The SNP suffered in 1979, as it always suffered, when both major parties were strong – worse, when they were strong in different geographical areas. There was limited evidence of tactical voting, except in Dundee East, where Tories appear to have voted Nationalist to keep Labour out.

The SNP critically underestimated the electoral damage it would receive for bringing down a Labour Government. Unlike SNP activists and core voters, many of whom regarded 'The Great British Labour Party' as a hated Unionist rival, just as bad as the Tories, many of the electorate saw Labour as a party with Scotland's interests at heart, even if it did not always successfully defend them. Although a General Election was only a few months away in the normal course of events, by bringing Labour down on a no confidence motion the SNP had both precipitated that election and the circumstances which made it more likely Labour would lose it. The 79 Group was assuredly right in thinking that the SNP could not afford to be seen as the midwives of a Tory government, but were wrong in other aspects of their analysis.

For one thing, the Labour Party, particularly at local level, controlled a major patronage network. It was impossible to outbid the Labour Party on the left, because (i) the electorate did not vote for them out of conviction socialism; (ii) they were seen as the natural political agents of public expenditure, social solidarity and resource allocation, most particularly in the SNP target area of the Central Belt, and (iii) they were in an unassailable position of patronage with regard to (ii) through their local authority powerbases, even when out of power at Westminster. In any case, there was a (iv): the Conservative Party, particularly while George Younger was Secretary of State (1979–86) followed an ameliorating policy in Scotland which preserved high levels of public expenditure. Inevitably, these were often distributed through channels controlled by the Labour Party. Labour had an entrenched position as the defenders of Scotland, more particularly as the defenders of public expenditure in Scotland. They were the proven establishment: why vote for a more extreme anti-establishment imitation, with a doubtful record and no experience in office?

Thus the 79 Group strategy was based on a fundamental misunderstanding of the strength and dynamic of the Labour vote. They chose the most difficult electoral target and the wrong way of approaching it. On the positive side, though, Sillars brought from the SLP a supportive attitude to the European Union which was to help broaden SNP appeal by the end of the 1980s, and he also showed some welcome awareness of the importance of being more engaged with the Catholic community, one of the bastions of the Labour vote in west central Scotland. The legacy of the social changes of the 1960s, and Labour's increasingly liberal social agenda after 1981 in Scotland, also helped to detach Catholics from the Labour Party.

Nationalist strategy errors in the years following 1979 were similar to those occurring in the Labour Party itself, particularly in England, where there was a major – and electorally fruitless – shift to the Left. This in its turn also hindered the SNP rather than helping it. Not only were the SNP unable to offer a moderate left-of-centre alternative to Labour in the early 1980s, they were also vulnerable to the rise of the SDP, formed by four former Labour cabinet ministers in 1981, which entered into successful electoral alliance with the Liberals, merging with them after the 1987 election. Whereas in the long run in England, the Liberal Democrats (as they eventually became) did not retain much more support than the old Liberals had done, although electoral circumstances brought them many more seats, in Scotland, there was a substantial and lasting change of fortunes for this centre party. In 1982, Roy Jenkins, the SDP leader and former Labour heavyweight, won Glasgow Hillhead at a by-election, retaining it at the next year's General Election. Although many Labour MPs defected to the new SDP between 1981 and 1983, all of them bar one lost their seats as a consequence: that one was Robert Maclennan, MP for Caithness and Sutherland; moreover, in neighbouring Ross and Cromarty, Charles Kennedy, a 23-year-old student fighting his first seat for the SDP, won against the sitting Tory in a constituency in which the Liberals had finished fourth in 1979. The new electoral alliance helped to transform Liberal prospects in Tory or Tory–SNP areas such as Aberdeenshire, Argyll and North-East

Fife, and the SNP were displaced from marginals in which they would have expected to have been the major contenders. Neither in Inverurie nor Oban, still less in St Andrews, were the Red Clydeside antics of the 1980s SNP a votewinner. The rise of the Alliance/Liberal Democrats in Scotland was the greatest electoral challenge posed to the SNP in the 1980s: it was one they entirely failed to meet, a strategic mistake which proved almost irreversible in its effects.

Nonetheless, as the SNP moved towards a version of their older, more moderate, campaigning platform in the mid-1980s, there were signs of some improvement in support, with 18 per cent in the 1986 regional elections. In the 1987 General Election there was a mighty effort in Scotland to vote out the Conservative Government, which was combined for the first time with widespread evidence of tactical voting. Labour won 50 seats, as the over-optimistic electorate believed that UK Labour victory was possible: in the end, Scotland supplied almost a quarter of all Labour seats. At the same time, where it was clear that Labour could not win, other parties benefited from the anti-Tory vote, with the SNP (on 14 per cent of the vote nationally) gaining Moray, Banff and Buchan and Angus, but losing both Dundee East and Western Isles to Labour. The Tories lost more than half their seats.

However, in the context of the British political system, the Labour Party proved unable to do what they had been elected to do – namely, to protect Scotland from the Tories, and the 1987–9 period thus proved critical in the development of a new phase of Nationalist politics, as indeed, in the development of the idea of devolution which was finally to be implemented. The introduction of the Poll Tax in Scotland by the Conservatives in 1989, a year ahead of its introduction in England, was – to an extent at least – in response to demand from their own activists. The new tax (to which everyone was theoretically liable at the same level in lieu of the old property tax of rates, which had charged progressively on the basis of property values) was deeply unpopular in Scotland, viewed as inegalitarian and above all illegitimate. It was soon clear that Scotland's Labour local authorities would implement the tax and pursue non-payers vigorously. By contrast, the SNP's 'Can't Pay, Won't Pay' campaign aimed to unite the claims of the poor with the ethos of social solidarity in civil disobedience linked to a single unpopular issue. It was of course easier for the SNP, as they only controlled one council, Angus, but the Tories and Labour together had nonetheless handed the Nationalists the moral leadership in the fight against the tax, one which they shared with the far Left (it was the issue which brought Tommy Sheridan to prominence), but which they were the only mainstream party to support. In any case, they were already enjoying the benefits of public disenchantment with the inefficacy of Labour's MPs, dubbed 'the feeble fifty' by Alex Salmond, who had won Banff and Buchan in 1987, and was to become leader in 1990. In the 1988 local elections, the SNP secured 21 per cent of the vote, and in the autumn Jim Sillars won Govan from Labour.

Labour were instantly alarmed, and moved to support the development of the new cross-party devolution campaign which had been founded on the basis of the 1988 Claim of Right, which in its turn arose from a Constitutional Steering Committee set up by the Campaign for a Scottish Assembly's Jim Ross at the end of 1987. In 1989 the Scottish Constitutional Convention convened, which, driven by the Labour Party, was nonetheless to provide the basis for Labour and Liberal Democrat coalition politics in the Holyrood Parliament that eventually developed from it. The Liberal Democrats gained the important principle that any new Scottish Assembly or Parliament would be elected on the basis of proportional representation, which – although it would prevent the SNP forming a government – would more immediately seriously diminish Labour's dominance in terms of seats.[20] Here, the limited impact of Labour's 50 current MPs gave the Lib Dems a propaganda advantage.

The SNP were allocated representation in the Convention, but withdrew in the spring of 1989, to near-universal vilification in the press. It was a brave decision, and some Nationalists left the party because of it, but in strategic terms it was surely the right move. In 1974–9, the SNP had become bound to and (as the party most committed to constitutional change) inevitably associated with a Labour policy which the Nationalists were expected to deliver on while the government made no moves to prevent the establishment of a Labour Says No campaign. The Constitutional Convention (which was not going to consider either federalism or independence as options) would inevitably place the SNP again in the position of providing the activists to deliver a policy which was a long way from what they wanted, but for any failure in which they would be blamed. It was true that Gordon Wilson had suggested a Constitutional Convention in the 1980s, but what was on offer in 1989 was the same as in 1974: a rattled Labour Party's plan to buy off the Nats by signing them up to a new Labour policy. It was true that the Convention drew on a much wider section of civil society than the Labour Party, and that Labour made more compromises within it than in the 1970s; it was equally true that when there were marches or rallies for a Scottish Parliament (as in Edinburgh in 1992), it was the Nationalists who turned out in force. Leaving the Convention still left the SNP in the position of being able to support its resolutions in any referendum (as it in fact did in 1997), while the 1989–97 era paradoxically witnessed public demonstrations of support for the Convention's plans being dominated by the Nationalists who had left it. In effect, the SNP supported devolution while not being bound by it, which was a far superior position to that it had found itself in fifteen years earlier.

It was also important that the SNP had developed its own alternative policy. In the 1975 EEC referendum, the Nationalists, still influenced by Scotland's loss of autonomy and economic status rather than its realistic prospects of independence, campaigned for a No vote. This position endured into the 1980s, with Norway rather than Ireland still being the comparator nation of choice for Scotland. Then, in 1988 the SNP – thanks largely to Jim Sillars – returned to the pro-European stance which had been more typical of the outlook of its leading lights up to the 1960s. The new Independence in Europe policy was repeatedly attacked, usually by those who claimed that independence would lead to Scotland being excluded from the EU and not re-admitted, or not readily re-admitted: but no sucker punch was ever landed on the policy. In 1989 the SNP gained 26 per cent of the vote (though still only one seat out of eight) at the European elections, and the policy remained successful, although it alienated a small number of uncompromising nationalists, who left the party in the pursuit of the art of the impossible, and thus out of serious politics. In a survey carried out in 1999, 46 per cent of Scots thought that the new Parliament at Holyrood would be the most important political arena in twenty years' time, 31 per cent the EU and only 8 per cent Westminster.[21] Clearly, the

SNP's idea of bypassing Westminster for Brussels or Strasbourg had lasting appeal.

In the space of two years, the Nationalists had taken the lead on a key domestic issue (the Poll Tax), had gained Govan at a by-election, developed a new international policy, and had not suffered electorally from their withdrawal from the Constitutional Convention. In 1990 the SNP gained a fifth MP with Dick Douglas's defection from Labour. As a consequence, the party went into the 1992 election with high hopes, only to suffer the major disappointment of losing Govan and coming within 1,000 votes of defeat in Angus, despite an overall 22 per cent of the vote. A good deal of the result was bad luck: with the same level of support in February 1974, the SNP had taken seven seats, a result which would have signified major progress in 1992. On the other hand, as in 1979, the SNP could not make way when both major parties were doing well. For much of the campaign, Labour looked as if they would win the UK General Election; in addition, they promised that 'A Scottish Parliament will be along in a tick' (i.e., if you vote Labour), while the Tories arrested their decline in votes, and even gained a seat: possibly rising support for a Scottish Parliament shored up the core Unionist vote. In the context of the bravado of the ridiculous – if unofficial – 'Free by '93' slogan, the SNP were badly damaged.

But the Tories won the UK election again. After George Younger moved to be Secretary of State for Defence in 1986, they had largely ceased to listen to views in Scotland which did not originate among their own supporters. The Poll Tax had been one consequence; now the resolute opposition to a Scottish Parliament – which, had they introduced it, would have had very limited powers and would have wrongfooted Labour for years – set the seal on Tory decline. The Prime Minister, John Major, talked about devolution as if it was a terrible threat, instead of a limited concession of local autonomy commonplace throughout the European Union. The absurdly inflated rhetoric used by the Tories in 1992–7 against devolution exceeded that of the 1970s: it was also increasingly seen, despite its cheerleaders in business, to be ridiculous and out of touch. In 1993 the Conservative 'Taking Stock' proposals offered only tokenistic reforms, none of which addressed the apparent 'democratic deficit' of Tory rule in Scotland, especially a rule so unconsultative as it had become. As in the 1970s, tinkering with local government was viewed as a possible way to defuse devolutionary sentiment: such tinkering was always a failure because the sentiment was national. The Conservatives abolished the regions and created 32 unitary local authorities in order to replace the functions of the regions and districts. In some cases, the boundaries were redrawn in a way which apparently maximized Conservative chances of gaining control: the subdivision of Ayrshire and the tiny East Renfrewshire authority were examples of this. Despite such moves, the new boundaries did not help the Tories, and in removing the regions the Conservatives weakened the objection to devolution as providing a redundant tier of government. In the context of government privatizations, the 97 per cent Yes vote in a 1994 referendum organized by Strathclyde Region to endorse public ownership of water showed how little real support was commanded by major Tory policies: Scottish water remained in public hands. In the mid-1990s local elections, the SNP gained 26–27 per cent of the vote, and it won Perth at a by-election, holding a by-election gain for the first time in the 1997 General Election, at which Galloway and North Tayside also fell to the Nationalists. The Constitutional Convention had published its proposals for self-government on 30 November 1995, St Andrew's Day;[22] the Tory Secretary of State, Michael Forsyth, responded by the empty gesture politics of returning the Stone of Destiny from Westminster to Scotland exactly a year later. But the time was by for such political theatre. In 1997, the Tories were heavily defeated, losing every seat in the country, even Foreign Secretary Malcolm Rifkind's seat in Edinburgh Pentlands.

The incoming Labour Government insisted on a referendum. Though there was no retreat from the need for a simple majority only, the quasi-nationalist stress on Scottish sovereignty in the Convention's thinking was placed definitively in the context of Westminster sovereignty in the devolution White Paper. The Convention had assumed equal opportunities were to be devolved, but this was not the case, and hard-line Unionists in the UK Cabinet were reported 'to have demanded the reservation of drug and firearm laws'. Broadcasting likewise remained at Westminster: a potentially very serious loss, given the metropolitanism of British TV in particular, but one surely driven by political considerations, as the response to a lively and well-supported campaign for a Scottish six o'clock news indicated. However, the proposed Parliament would extend the putative powers of the 1970s Assembly with authority over 'economic development, financial and other assistance to industry, universities, training, forestry, certain transport matters and the police and prosecution system', as well, as, potentially, the ability to vary the basic rate of tax by 3 per cent. In addition, 'further transfers from and to the list of reserved powers' could occur by mutual agreement. There was scope for inter-governmental cooperation on EU and other areas, and also 'overlapping competencies' and the prospect of some conflict through them at a future date (for example, the Scottish Parliament could in theory use its powers over local authorities to give differential treatment to asylum seekers even when immigration was a Westminster matter, or use planning powers to stymie UK energy policy). The Scotland Act of 1998, which followed the referendum, listed those powers reserved to Westminster, rather than, as in the 1970s, listing those powers to be devolved: an important shift. There were to be 129 Members of the Scottish Parliament (MSPs), with 73 returned by first past the post (Orkney was divided from Shetland to create one extra constituency) and 56 by the Additional Member System, in an important concession to proportional representation. The government was to comprise a 'separate Scottish Executive led by a First Minister', and the Parliament was to run on a four-year fixed-term basis, unless no First Minister could be chosen or MSPs voted for earlier dissolution by a two-thirds majority. Main finance was to continue through the block grant from Westminster, governed – though entirely reversibly – by the Barnett formula, introduced to bridge the gap between justifiable levels of Scottish public expenditure in a UK context and the excess spending identified by the 1979 Treasury review of 'needs and public spending across the UK'. There was, however, 'total freedom of allocation within the assigned budget' for the Scottish government.[23]

Despite losing every single seat at the General Election, the Conservatives and their allies put up a determined struggle in the referendum on a Scottish Parliament which followed Labour's 1997 General Election victory. Faced with complete electoral destruction,

Conservative supporters in Scotland (the party itself was quieter) insisted on campaigning as if nothing had happened, and as if the political circumstances of March 1979 remained unaltered. With the prescience which had led them to the dominant position in Scottish politics they now enjoyed, many on the Right predicted that it was possible that the No campaign could win. There were two questions on offer: the support for a Scottish Parliament in principle, and whether it should have the right to vary the standard rate of income tax were it to be established, up to a maximum of 3 per cent in either direction. On 11 September 1997, the 700th anniversary of William Wallace's victory over the forces of Edward I at Stirling Bridge, Scotland voted 74-26 in favour of a Parliament, and 64-36 in favour of its having tax-varying powers. Every local authority area voted Yes by a strong majority to the first question; only Galloway and Orkney voted No narrowly on the second count, though the Yes vote in Orkney and Shetland more than doubled from its 1979 figure. The highest Yes votes, of 84 and 85 per cent, were returned by Glasgow and West Dunbartonshire. Turnout was 60 per cent compared with 64 per cent in 1979, though this was of course in the context of declining rates of political participation more generally.[24]

In 1998 Labour introduced its second Scotland Act, which further reserved 'abortion and other issues where criminal law, medicine and morality' meet and confirmed the reservation of 'broadcasting, equal opportunities and monopolies and mergers'. It was just as well that implementation was imminent because the signs were that every time devolution was reviewed in Westminster, it faced further dilution. The Government was in large part of the opinion that devolution would undermine the SNP's appeal and render it increasingly irrelevant, so it was rather an unpleasant shock when the early polls suggested a lead for the Nationalists in the 1999 Holyrood elections (peaking at 14 per cent over Labour), polls which also made it clear that there would be significant differences in voting behaviour between Holyrood and Westminster elections.[25] In the event, the customary media onslaught, the SNP's ill-judged pledge to raise tax by 1 per cent and Alex Salmond's condemnation of NATO action in Kosovo in a campaign for a Parliament with no foreign policy responsibilities damaged Nationalist prospects. Nonetheless, the 28 per cent secured gave the SNP 7 first past the post and 28 list seats: 35 MSPs, by far their most successful electoral performance ever. Labour, with 56 seats, formed a coalition with the Liberal Democrats, a form of political settlement for which the Constitutional Convention had provided excellent practice.

The performance and legislation of the Holyrood Parliament is the subject of Chapter Six, but from the point of view of national self-confidence some of its early blunders (magnified by a hostile press) had a negative effect. A sense of disenchantment with the results of the Scottish project predictably damaged the SNP more than Labour, and when Labour moved towards the low-key managed politics at which they were experienced from 2001 on, the SNP suffered. In the General Election that year, they lost Galloway to the Tories (the latter's only gain); in 2003 the Nationalists took 24 per cent at Holyrood and lost eight seats; in the 2004 Euros they took only 20 per cent, and at the 2005 General Election 18 per cent, coming behind the Liberal Democrats in Scotland, though they held all five seats and won Na h-Eileanan an Iar/Western Isles from Labour. The 2003 Holyrood elections in particular saw the SNP shed votes and seats to the other pro-independence parties, the Greens and the Scottish Socialists: 38 per cent of the electorate voted for pro-independence parties, but only 24 per cent for the SNP. There was some recognition of shared goals across this changing political spectrum: in December 2005 the SNP held discussions about a possible coalition with the Greens, which were to bear some fruit two years later. In Scotland, as in England at the 2005 General Election, the Liberal Democrats were the main beneficiaries of the outrage at the Iraq war, but as the 2007 Holyrood elections approached, there were signs that the SNP might be the bigger beneficiaries of disenchantment with Labour in a Scottish context. In January 2007 the Nationalists were polling an average of 33 per cent across the list and constituency votes, with Labour on 29.5 per cent, the Tories on 14.5 per cent, the Liberals on 12.5 per cent, and the Greens on 6 per cent. The 2007 election itself is discussed in Chapter Six.[26]

Despite the high Nationalist vote at the time, the evidence from social science in the 1970s was that many Scots were happy to adopt an identity which was both Scottish and British, and that if forced to choose were almost as likely to adopt the latter as the former. By the late 1980s this had changed. In 1987, 69 per cent of Scots felt more Scottish than British or Scottish not British; in 1992, 59 per cent; in 1994, 64 per cent; in 1997, 61–63 per cent; in 2000, 68 per cent. Over 80 per cent of those in these categories voted Yes Yes in the 1997 referendum, which indicated that they were some 30 per cent more likely to do so than the average Scot: of course, by this time, they *were* in some ways the average Scot, so the result is even more striking. Those who identified primarily with Scotland were twice as likely to vote Yes Yes as those who were equally Scottish and British, and four times as likely to do so as those who saw themselves as British rather than Scottish. Whatever Westminster thought that devolution was, it was quite clear that in Scotland it was the restoration of a symbol of national sovereignty as Scots not Britons. There was a clear increase too, in support for independence, which now tended to be at around 30 per cent in the polls, twice its 1970s level, and much closer to the dimensions of the SNP vote than hitherto.[27]

The figures for those who were given a forced choice to define themselves in the last resort as Scottish or British, but not both, show a similar drift. In 1979, 57 per cent chose 'Scottish' as the answer to this question; in 1992 and 1997, 72 per cent; by 2000, 80 per cent: and this is in the context of greater migration into Scotland from elsewhere in the UK and indeed the world, though this may have caused the figure to plateau subsequently: it was 79 per cent in 2005 and 76 per cent in 2007. That this is the case could be reflected by figures which indicate that in 2005 only 14 per cent chose a British identity in a forced choice, compared with 25 per cent in 1992, showing an increase in the proportion opting for neither nationality from 3 per cent to 7 per cent. Movement at the extremes of identity has been rapid. Between 1992 and 2000 alone, the proportion of Scots declining any British identity even when free to admit it, doubled. There were parallel – though much milder – rises in the declaration of English identity south of the Border. At the same time, it remains true that some 64 per cent of Scots expressed some pride in Great Britain in 2007, though only 23 per cent felt this strongly, little more than half the English total. Combined with other evidence, it seems that Scots continue to be interested in a British social union, but are less engaged with the shape of the current political one: 'Scots, even those who say they are "Scottish not British" are not hostile to the idea of Britain, its history or its empire and are happy to think of it in culturally unifying terms"'.[28] Only a minority of Scots see themselves as a colony rather than a past or current partner in Great Britain: but respect for the British past is not incompatible with current demand for independence, many SNP voters also expressing some sympathy with Britishness.

In the 1999 *Economist* survey only 49 per cent of Scots identified with the Union Jack, 72 per cent primarily identified as Scottish as against 18 per cent who primarily identified as British, and 78 per cent stated that they had too little say over the way they were governed (though this figure was still 66 per cent in England, suggestive of the corrosive effect of centralizing government on political consent across Great Britain). Interestingly, four times as many English as Scots identified with the United States flag. In January 2007 a Channel 4 news poll suggested a 44–40 lead for independence among Scottish voters, which fell somewhat as more detailed questions were put, with 31 per cent supporting independence (of whom more than a quarter opposed EU membership), 37 per cent opting for more powers for Holyrood, 12 per cent supporting the 1999 devolution settlement and 10 per cent wanting to return to the pre-1999 status quo. These disaggregated figures are a normal pattern in such polls: typically, surveys which offer independence as the only alternative to the present arrangements return a higher figure (mostly around 40–45 per cent) in its support than those which offer a variety of choices, while those that use language to make one of these options stark ('a totally separate Scotland outside the UK' for example) minimize support for it. What is clear, however, is that far from the 1999 Parliament being 'the settled will of the Scottish people', there is a drift towards greater independence from Westminster. Perhaps this is in part due to decreasing confidence that the Parliament can act independently of Westminster on key issues: according to a September 2006 survey, 'only 27 per cent of Scots thought the parliament had more influence on the way Scotland was run than Westminster',[29] a clear loss of confidence from the 1999 *Economist* survey. Such a finding suggests that the habit of using Westminster heavyweights in Scottish Parliament election campaigns may be counter-productive, because it only reminds the electorate of the dependency of Holyrood on London.

What do Scots mean by 'Scottishness' when responding to questions of this kind? The 1992 British Election Survey suggested that the distinctive people (which also surely includes consideration of distinctive culture, institutions and the public sphere) and landscape were factors which were strongly cited in evaluations of pride in Scotland.[30] This is perhaps unsurprising. There has also been a tendency (which can be found as far back as the mediaeval period) to self-define in terms of being as different from the English as possible: the improving behaviour of Scottish football supporters in a context of increasing violence among their English counterparts in the 1980s and '90s is evidence of this in more recent years. But a search for essentialist criteria in nationality is always reduced to a mixture of provisionality and prejudice, the proportions varying in proportion to the intelligence of the investigator. More significant is the fact that Scotland, always a mixed polity ethnically and linguistically, grew to unified nationality through its institutions, its monarchy and its social practices. Most of these were protected by the 1707 Union, while British markets opened up badly-needed mercantile, professional and military opportunities. The 1960s saw domestic autonomy, long in decline, in crisis and imperial opportunities disappear. In this sense, the Scots were not so dissimilar from their ancestors: the withdrawal from Britishness was a sign that the pragmatic compact of 1707 was no longer acting unequivocally in Scotland's interests.

The rising profile of Scottish identity was matched after 1999 by signs of greater indifference to, and psychological detachment from, Scotland south of the Border. When David Cameron brought his shadow cabinet to Scotland to support the Holyrood election campaign in January 2007, Oliver Letwin commented that 'the nearest foreign country is on our own border, is Scotland'.[31] The clear, and – if marginal – rising resentment at the outcome of the West Lothian Question is an indication that the Union is no longer one – insofar as it ever was – of hearts and minds. First posed in its modern form by Tam Dalyell in 1977, and given its name by Enoch Powell, the West Lothian Question (initially raised with regard to Irish Home Rule in 1886) points up the fact that under a devolutionary settlement Scottish MPs will have the power to vote on English matters, but that authority will not be reciprocated.[32] The more extensive the devolution granted, the more pronounced this effect will be. Since 1999, more particularly since 2003, discontent in England has been growing in response to this question. This has become clearly marked as policy in London and Edinburgh diverges: in particular, the imposition of top-up fees on English universities was seen as a consequence of the votes of Scottish Labour MPs, while MSPs in Holyrood had voted not to have them in Scotland (see Chapter Six).

The West Lothian Question is arguably more psychological than a matter of principle, as has been claimed. For 50 years from 1921 the British government countenanced (indeed rather unfortunately ignored) the Stormont government in Belfast, introduced as a consequence of the 1920 Government of Ireland Act, while happily allowing Northern Irish MPs to vote on English issues: indeed, until the late 1960s, the Ulster Unionists were entirely aligned with the Conservative Party. There were fewer MPs from Northern Ireland, it is true: but notwithstanding this, the Question obviously admits of compromise. Whatever else the West Lothian Question is, it is not the enunciation of a constitutional principle. The fact that it nearly always seems to be applied to Scotland rather than Wales may be not so much a question of its origin, nor of the number of Scottish members, but rather indicative of a more deep-seated anxiety that on it in some way the Union depends.

So far, three answers have been provided to the Question. First, the number of MPs from Scotland has been reduced from 72 to 59 from the 2005 election onwards: this was the route that had been taken in Northern Ireland. Secondly, there has been a stuttering but persistent interest in the establishment of an English parliament, which the polling evidence suggests enjoys majority support, even in Scotland, though such figures – lacking all detail as to implementation, accommodation, cost and powers – should be treated with caution.[33] Thirdly, there has been stronger support (now mainstream in the Conservative Party) for restricting the issues on which Scottish MPs can vote. The first option is a classic British compromise, but the signs are that it is not enough to satisfy English objections, even with a further reduction to the 45 MPS guaranteed under the Union (although this would be a tempting short-term solution for the Conservatives, given their weakness in Scotland). The second option is a federal solution which would so alter the powers and function of the House of Commons that it would be almost unthinkable to the metropolitan and constitutionally conservative (witness the agony over the prospect of an elected Lords undermining the power of the Commons) ruling elite, though it might command popular support if it were seriously and carefully proposed. (In fact, an elected Lords could be an important dimension in a federal solution: but it is absolutely not clear – whether the Lords is elected or not – that English, and more particularly London opinion is ready for this.)

The third and currently most popular political solution, the creation of a second class of Scots MP – also first mooted in an Irish Home Rule context – is the most revealing and the most unstable option, although Sir Malcolm Rifkind's notion of an English-brand committee might well ameliorate its effects. Enthusiasm for it is evidence that devolution is still seen in England not as a fundamental change to the government of the UK, but as a sop to the Scots, and that any further developments must punish Scotland not reform England. It is arguable that Scottish MPS do not seem to have a great deal to do, but the issues at stake are much deeper than this. Making Scottish MPS second class would make it very difficult for anyone sitting for a Scottish constituency to hold cabinet or even ministerial rank, and would give backbenchers absolutely nothing to do except serve as lobby fodder for votes on topics such as the Budget and war, mostly foregone conclusions anyway. In addition, unless taxes raised on Scottish soil or on Scottish territorial waters were solely spent in Scotland, the question of taxation without representation would rear its head: as pointed out by Vernon Bogdanor in 1999, 'expenditure on a domestic service . . . in England, would have consequential effects on Scotland's block grant', if this remained the method of funding.[34] Able Scots politicians would either have to choose to go to Holyrood or to find an English constituency, which in many cases would (given the views animating such legislation in the first place) be presumably loth to give them a home. It is very doubtful if the Union could long continue in such circumstances, but this does not seem to be an issue in the Conservative Party, who now show signs of readying themselves to import their attitude to the Scottish question in the 1980s into Westminster. Ultimately, unless the UK is prepared to live with the West Lothian Question, federalism or independence are the only answers: there is no convincing middle way in which the current asymmetric arrangements can be altered in Westminster's favour without seriously damaging the Union, since true federalism is currently politically unthinkable to any British government. Labour's very half-hearted gestures towards unwanted regional devolution to the (largely factitious) regions of England was not a federal solution; nor is the Brown administration's handwaving gesture towards 'regional' ministerial responsibilities a response which can solve the issue. England remains psychologically deeply centralist and metropolitan in a way that federal states such as Germany, the USA and Canada are not: is Vancouver to Ottawa as Manchester to London, or Frankfurt to Berlin as Sheffield to the capital? Even the development of city-regions in England is hamstrung by a clear and continuing bias to the South-east in major capital and research expenditure: 80 per cent of NHS R & D, for instance. In turn, London complains that it contributes more tax revenue than it receives. It depends how it is counted, but the core fact is that England is a long way from embracing the need for a federal solution to the West Lothian Question.

Scottish nationality and nationalism have developed rapidly since 1960, and the political landscape of Scotland has changed out of all recognition. Scotland and England have diverged politically to an extent unrealized by many south of the Border, as was evident during the 1997-9 implementation of devolution, when there was widespread concern at the absence of debate on such major constitutional change in England – concern which was oblivious to the decades of discussion north of the Tweed. Since devolution, it is not so much that Scottish news goes unreported in England as that there is more news than ever, and no more is reported than if Scotland were Shropshire. The lack of understanding that the UK is a multinational polity is the key risk factor in the possibility of its future dissolution, and resentment of Scotland in England is fed by lack of understanding which is sustained by appallingly low news coverage from network (as opposed to opt-out) broadcasting: in the 2005 BBC General Election night programme, two minutes in the first five hours were spent in Scotland, less than in major English cities. Scotland and Scottishness are very different since 1945, thanks largely to changes in British policy and the British state. The signs are that unless the UK government considers the implications of the relationship between its different nations more carefully, the trajectory of British policy will continue to increase the intensity of Scottishness in the years to come.

Chapter 3

Scotland's Cities: Populations, Cultures and Economies

One of the major distinctions between the urban cultures of Scotland and England lies in the fact that Scotland's largest three cities five hundred years ago occupy the same position today. In England, by contrast, of the four largest cities of the late middle ages and early modern period (London, Bristol, Norwich, York) only London retains its outsize primacy, while of the others, only Bristol is of any size. Moreover, while in the England as in the Scotland of the past, these major cities were the economic leaders of distinct regions, the nineteenth century changed the balance, so that the large English cities often cluster together (Manchester/Liverpool, Leeds/Sheffield/Bradford, the Tyne-Tees conurbation). In Scotland, by contrast, distinct city-region cultures have persisted. The burgh records of Aberdeen survive from 1398: in them at an early date one can find evidence of anxieties about Aberdeen's status vis-a-vis Edinburgh and the south of Scotland which still resonate.

This chapter will principally deal with the three leading Scottish cities which enjoyed that status by virtue of population, function and ecclesiastical significance from an early date, and which remain the three leading cities today: Edinburgh, Glasgow and Aberdeen. The discussion which follows will also address the status and qualities of the three cities which have gained charter recognition as such in modern times: Dundee, Inverness and Stirling. The cities by bishopric alone (e.g. Brechin, Elgin, St Andrews) are not discussed in detail, as their significance was to a greater or lesser extent compromised by the Scottish Reformation and its legacy: St Andrews, perhaps as large as Canterbury in 1560, is now only one-sixth the size, despite remaining the most important of these cities by bishopric to the Scotland of today. Perth, a city by courtesy and a regional centre of importance, is briefly noted. Other large urban centres which are not cities (e.g. Dunfermline, Motherwell, Paisley, Falkirk, Greenock) are often tied to the economic pull of Edinburgh or Glasgow.

Edinburgh was not always the core site of royal power in Scotland, but it was the place where Scotland's distinctive institutions, in many ways the most important unifying features of Scottish nationality, developed their main powerbase in the early modern period. One of the most beautiful cities in Europe (central Edinburgh was declared a World Heritage Site by UNESCO in 1995), the original spine of the mediaeval town runs down the Royal Mile from the Castle to Holyrood, with narrow 'closes' or 'lands' opening off it to the north, and the broader, deeper Grassmarket and Cowgate to the south. More even than in London, every alleyway is littered with history and the signs of past greatness, from the Honours (crown jewels) of Scotland in the Castle to Holyroodhouse itself, by way of the old Spanish Ambassador's residence from pre-Union days, now Huntly House, the city museum. After 1707 Edinburgh retained a sense of itself as a capital city, and it was with the conscious aim of providing a northern metropolis which could be a rival to London that the New Town, the largest area of Georgian architecture in Great Britain, was planned and built between 1752 and 1832. In the eighteenth and even to an extent in the nineteenth centuries, the great professional organizations, the Faculty of Advocates, the Writers to the Signet, and above all the General Assembly of the Church of Scotland, retained some of the features of the parliament lost at the Union: indeed, the Advocates took over its building. When the Faculty gifted the bulk of its great library to the National Library of Scotland in 1925,[1] it was no doubt in consciousness of its own role, so different from that of the Bar in England, as a custodian of key aspects of the nationality of the country. Similarly, when the Church of Scotland divided at the Great Disruption of 1843, the strength of feeling and purpose involved was in some degree due to the fact that the Kirk saw itself as more than a religious organization: it was also the repository of a key part of the national sense of self. These were examples of the quality of national identity as embodied in professional identity, alluded to in Chapter One.

In the early modern period Edinburgh was a huge city (almost 65,000 including environs in 1755), nearly as dominant in Scotland's contracted economy as London was in England's prosperous one. It was the second largest city in Great Britain at the Union, but by the early nineteenth century it had been overtaken by Glasgow. In opening up imperial markets (which for much of the eighteenth century, were heavily North American, not least, sadly, because of the slave trade), the Union initiated a process which shifted the economic focus of Scotland from the Continental trade of the east coast ports to the imperial trade of the major west coast port, Glasgow. In the nineteenth century Edinburgh fell behind Glasgow in population and in commercial terms; but it remained the professional and financial centre of the country, and the home of major cultural developments, including the National Portrait Gallery in the 1880s and the National Library of Scotland in the 1920s. From the 1880s administrative devolution also began to restore to Edinburgh some of its capital status, and more and more Scottish 'national' functions came to be housed in the city in the century that followed. In 1920 it finally swallowed its port of Leith, long an important centre in its own right.[2]

After 1945 the development of the Edinburgh Festival was a major force in securing Edinburgh's international status: at the time of its launch in 1947 it was years if not decades ahead of a more general understanding of the culturally revivifying power of the arts, and it and its spin-off 'festivals' were to be great successes for the capital. The original Edinburgh International Festival, Fringe and Film Festivals (1947) were joined over the years by the TV (1977), Folk (1979), Jazz and Blues (1979), Book (1983), Science (1989) and Children's (1990) festivals, and from 1992 by the Hogmanay (New Year's Eve) party. These were not all equally successful, of course. While the Hogmanay party quickly moved up to the 300,000-ticket mark in 1995, with the International Science Festival having 200,000 in 1994 and the Book Festival a creditable 70,000 (1995), the Folk Festival (in keeping perhaps with the lack of interest evident in Scottish traditional culture among Edinburgh's elites) attracted only 8,000 as an audience in 1993: its presence and influence have been intermittent. All were dwarfed by the original Festival and its Fringe offshoot: the International Festival could count on around a third of a million and the Fringe an incredible million and a half sales. At Fringe time in August, the 460,000 population of Edinburgh virtually doubles. The cultural developments of the 1980s and '90s in the city were by no means all related to the Festival, but its success had helped to make culture important to the capital, where of course it had long had a significant role. The Traverse Theatre was opened in 1963 to ensure that the spirit of the Festival could have a permanent outlet: a new Traverse was opened in 1991. The refurbishment of the King's Theatre (1985) was followed by the opening of the Edinburgh Festival Theatre in 1994 as a rival to Glasgow's Theatre Royal, while the development after 1975 of the Fruitmarket Gallery and the City Art Centre, the opening of the Scottish National Gallery of Modern Art in 1984, together with the expansion of the city collections at Huntly House Museum and of the national ones by the opening of the Museum of Scotland in 1996, all served to confirm Edinburgh as the primary destination in Scotland for cultural and intellectual tourism. Such new developments all bespoke a seriousness of purpose which was by no means limited to, but was not uninspired by, the vast number of locations required for the success of the Festival and its Fringe and the tourist upsurge attendant on ticket sales, while Our Dynamic Earth (opened in 1999) reflected the interests of the Science Festival.

At the same time, the capital's more traditional attractions continued to draw in huge numbers of visitors. Although Edinburgh's football teams (Hearts and Hibernian) have nearly always played second fiddle to the Glasgow giants, the city is the home of Scottish rugby, which brings many thousands every year to Murrayfield to spend their money in the city. In 2006 Edinburgh had three of Scotland's top five tourist attractions: the Castle (1.2 million visitors, even at £11 admission), the National Gallery (943,000) and the National Museum (831,000). Edinburgh Zoo has over 500,000, and between 250,000 and 500,000 a year visit the Royal Scottish Museum, the Scottish National

Portrait Gallery and Holyroodhouse, out of a tourist total of at least 2 million. The 30-hectare Royal Botanic Garden is the UK's second oldest and (after Kew) second most visited botanical garden, and Edinburgh's other strengths include the National Portrait Gallery and the National Archives of Scotland. The capital's primacy in high art and culture is vigorously guarded: in the early 1990s, attempts to set up a national gallery of Scottish art in Glasgow were sabotaged at an early stage by the Edinburgh arts establishment, whose antipathy to their west coast rivals is well documented. While south of the Border, national museum collections have been set up outside London at Liverpool, Manchester and York, in Scotland there is little movement of expenditure on national collections outwith the capital, even though Kelvingrove Museum and Art Gallery in Glasgow has had much higher visitor numbers than the national museum for years, and on reopening in 2006 topped the poll of attractions in Scotland, with over 1.9 million visitors.[3]

Although the industrial and commercial infrastructure of Edinburgh, in common with other cities throughout the UK, was changing in the postwar era, the city showed significant entrepreneurial and commercial vigour in compensation. Tom Farmer's Kwik Fit business was founded in the city in 1971, and Murray International Metals began to trade there in 1974; Johnston Press moved there in 1994, although electricity privatization in 1992 saw what is now Scottish & Southern Energy move from Edinburgh to Perth. Despite being the 'home of the Digestive Biscuit', the city saw continuing decline in biscuit manufacture, and GEC-Marconi was only one of the major employers which shed jobs heavily in the 1990s. However, the financial sector remained resilient. The fifteen largest companies headquartered in Edinburgh in 1992 were Standard Life, the Royal Bank of Scotland, Scottish Widows, Bank of Scotland, Scottish & Newcastle, Scottish Equitable, John Menzies, United Distillers, Scottish Provident, Scottish Life, Christian Salvesen, Dawson textiles, TSB Scotland, the Miller Group and Kwik-Fit: fifteen years later, half of these had been taken over or significantly restructured: only Royal Bank of Scotland was really stronger in global terms, though Miller was the second richest individual in Scotland, with a fortune estimated to exceed £800M, while Sir David Murray and J. K. Rowling both had fortunes exceeding £500M.[4] Edinburgh remained the fifth or sixth largest financial centre in Europe with up to £350 billion under management. Ivory and Sime, Edinburgh Fund Managers and Baillie Gifford were all among those companies headquartered in Edinburgh at the onset of the 1990s, and although some of these were subsequently taken over, other fund management businesses, including Artemis and Franklin Templeton, moved significant operations to the capital, where new groups such as Noble Fund Managers and SVM also developed. The scale of Edinburgh's existing power in financial services and asset management has meant that it is less likely that asset management will be relocated when Edinburgh-based companies are taken over, or traded between multinational conglomerates.

Despite its extraordinary beauty, and wealth of seventeenth-, eighteenth- and nineteenth-century domestic architecture of the first rank (Glasgow, a worthy rival in domestic architecture, perhaps always had the edge in the design of its major public buildings), Edinburgh did not altogether escape the wanton redevelopment of the 1960s, two particularly appalling examples being the destruction of most of George Square to provide modern buildings for the University, and the retail development at the St James's Centre, completed in 1970. In a city where there was less industrial history and therefore less need for brownfield development (the 25-year redevelopment of the waterfront at Leith being an exception) the planning regime was able to preserve a more conservative outlook compared to that in Glasgow.[5] This helped spare Edinburgh the vast urban motorways which tore through central Glasgow at a time when the majority of its citizens did not possess a car: however, by the 1990s, major traffic and parking problems resulted in the capital struggling to come to terms with the need for an integrated transport policy. Outside London, the city was the first to suggest tolls on cars, but the inhabitants rejected this move in a plebiscite in 2006. Restrictions on the freedom to use a car are always unwelcome to motorists, but in Edinburgh's case the longstanding lack of effective planning for alternatives made the city council seem simply inimical to cars, and rendered the populace even less sympathetic than usual. A comparison of Edinburgh's Park and Ride system with that of a city such as Oxford provides an effective indication of the apparent poverty of purpose in Scotland's capital's authorities in this area over many years.

Edinburgh University (founded in 1583) had had major international standing as an institution since the eighteenth century, particularly in medicine, and it continued to remain Scotland's pre-eminent research university on most measures after 1960. Although one of the great universities of the world in arts and humanities research, Edinburgh's own international gaze as an institution lost it many opportunities to become a world centre for the study of Scotland's European and global influence and relations, as many of its staff discounted Scottish-led research as marginal and provincial: to its credit, the University addressed this in the 1990s with the establishment of a corporate affairs unit devoted to the University in Scotland. More unequivocal success came in Artificial Intelligence and Life Sciences where the University became a world leader, and major independent research units also contributed to the capital's success, most notably Roslin, where Dolly the Sheep was cloned in the 1990s; in 2007 a vast BioQuarter was planned for development round the new Royal Infirmary. In 1966 Edinburgh acquired a second university when Heriot-Watt College gained University status: it did not (unlike Strathclyde in Glasgow) attempt to compete with the older university across a full range of subjects, but focused – with considerable success – on a relatively narrow spectrum of scientific and professional degrees. Napier University followed in the 1990s and, in 2007, Edinburgh became the only city outside London to boast four universities, when Queen Margaret University College achieved that status. As befits a city with a strong higher education tradition, Edinburgh is the centre of Scottish publishing, with Edinburgh University Press, Canongate, Mainstream, Birlinn and Luath all headquartered in the capital.[6]

Since the Scottish Parliament was established in 1999, Edinburgh has more fully achieved the status of the capital city it has always partly been since 1707, while the magnet effect that political power exerts on economic power has contributed greatly to virtual boom conditions. However, its population is much less cosmopolitan than that of other capital cities, and indeed many major cities throughout the world, and research indicates that diverse populations can be major assets to economic growth and development. Although things are changing slowly, Edinburgh is (even by Scottish standards) a city dominated by white people of Scottish or English origin. It is, partly as a consequence, rather inward-looking. The enormous fuss generated by the Scottish Parliament's cost overruns on the Holyrood building project amounted to more than a genuine concern over the proper allocation of public monies; rather, it was a self-lacerating inwardness which took almost no account of the commonness of vast cost overruns elsewhere, or the evident limitations of government everywhere in managing such costs. In London the press and public are relaxed about things of this kind: it takes loss-making expenditure on the scale of the Millennium Dome or (in prospect) the Olympics to raise even a murmur of protest, and even so it is at much lower a volume than that which greeted Holyrood. Capital cities are at ease with themselves over such projects: if they cost too much, well then, they enhance the status and resources of the city. Edinburgh's unease to some extent reflected lukewarm support for devolution among its elites but, arguably also, it is part of a deeper-seated problem, one also evident in the degree of contempt shown towards Glasgow by many in the capital: evidence of a faintly ridiculous limited horizon in a global age. Now once again fully the capital of Scotland, Edinburgh is still struggling to escape defining itself as the preferred custodian of local autonomy for Scottish professions and institutions, the role it held between 1707 and 1960. The appointment in 2006 of Laura Gordon as 'Director of the Glasgow–Edinburgh Collaboration Project' marked a serious attempt to build on the joint global brand profiles of the two cities, but there is still a degree of scepticism surrounding such developments.[7]

Glasgow, since the early nineteenth century the largest city in Scotland, has a much longer history, dating back to the twelfth century, when it was a single street of houses stretching from the Cathedral to the Clyde, and drawing its water from the Molendinar Burn: in the thirteenth century, the city crossed the Clyde for the first time. A large part of that original spine is still visible: both the Cathedral and the fifteenth-century canon's house of Provand's Lordship have survived, while part of the old Archbishop's palace complex was rebuilt in the 1990s to become the St Mungo Museum of religion. Along this main thoroughfare a grammar school (which survives today as the High School of Glasgow) and – from 1451 – a university developed, though it was not until 1611 that Glasgow became a royal burgh: by 1670, it was the second trading city in Scotland. The Union benefited Glasgow enormously, opening the city to the imperial trade, particularly in tobacco, and the 'Merchant City' grew up contiguously with the original settlement. In the nineteenth century, ironworking, shipbuilding and engineering continued the city's remarkable growth, which had turned it into Scotland's largest city by the time of the 1821 census, when it had a population of 147,000.[8] Glasgow already had far higher levels of immigration than Edinburgh, with large numbers coming in from Ireland and the Gaidhealtachd: today, one in five of Scotland's Gaelic speakers lives in the city, which opened its first wholly Gaelic medium school in 2006.

The nineteenth and early twentieth centuries were the apogee of Glasgow's status as 'the second city of the Empire'. It grew enormous, with its greater urban area peaking at around 50 per cent of the Scottish population: in 1938 it hosted the last great Empire Exhibition, visited by over 12 million people. Nowhere in the developed world was a country and economy so dominated by a single metropolis, and Glasgow began to conceive of itself as a kind of city-state, transcending the country in which it was situated, yet in a way typifying it too. The idea that Glasgow stands for the whole of Scotland, and that what is not Glaswegian is inferior or provincial, has not entirely vanished even today: Edinburgh, hard to classify in exactly these terms even by the most civically chauvinist Glaswegian, is rather viewed as fancy, etiolated and anglified. Although many in the Edinburgh elites despise Glasgow more deeply than the sentiment is ever returned, equally only in Glasgow can you hear inhabitants of Aberdeen, Scotland's third city, described as 'teuchters' – country bumpkins. Glasgow recycles its professional classes more than any other Scottish city. Something over 50 per cent of Glasgow University students and over 70 per cent of Strathclyde students come to university from home, and the once common Scottish trend of growing up, being educated, working and raising a family all in the same urban regional centre is preserved in Glasgow better than anywhere else in the country. At the same time, the city has historically close relations with Ireland: many of its Catholic families have relatives in the island, while back-migration of Protestant Unionists of Scots descent from Northern Ireland has long been a feature of west central Scotland. In no other city in the country are you as likely to hear an Irish accent. The legacy of sectarianism which is visible at a number of levels in Glasgow is a product of generations of connection and tension between Ulster Unionist and Catholic nationalist traditions in the city. As a great imperial port city with a large Irish diaspora, Glasgow has been compared with Liverpool: but Belfast and Dublin are in many respects closer comparators, and support for Glasgow's giant football teams is itself quite widespread in Ireland. In 2007 concern was expressed by SDLP and Sinn Fein representatives that attendance at Celtic's Champion's League tie with AC Milan could cost them thousands of votes in the elections to the Northern Ireland Assembly.[9]

By 1962, the year its famous tramcars stopped running, Glasgow was a city in serious decline, despite the relative health of some of its major industries, such as shipbuilding, still benefiting from the fag-end of the postwar boom. Urban housing conditions, which had long been terrible in much of the inner city, were no longer compatible with modern standards. Peripheral estates and 'overspill' towns were absorbing an increasingly dispersed population, who in turn had less work in the city to go to. Nor were the new living conditions necessarily an improvement on the old in the longer term. The 1957 plan, with its 'ruthless and unimaginative . . . total clearance of the inner city', was followed by the implementation of a convenient, if unsightly, urban motorway network. Large swathes of the inner city, including many fine buildings, were destroyed, and it was not until the 1980s that reconditioning the tenement stock started to replace knocking it down as the default option. Glasgow was visibly shrinking in importance: its three evening papers in 1956 had become one by 1974; two of its four rail terminals were closed in 1966. Steamers stopped sailing from Bridge Wharf in 1969; 'by 1972 Glasgow's remaining docks had little more than 2 per cent of Britain's overseas trade'. In 1981 'unemployment in the city as a whole was 21 per cent'. The importance of Glasgow Airport, opened in the early 1960s, was vitiated by the political decision to make Prestwick the international hub.[10]

Glasgow had responsibility for major high-status facilities (e.g. the subway system, the only underground outside London in the UK) which were costly to fund and maintain: the entire system had to be closed down in 1977–9 for renovation, and it is clear that the new system itself is short of funds: in 2007 a £2.6 billion plan was launched for its further extension and redevelopment. Thrown back in on itself by economic change and the enormous problems it presented to many people, the city did not always make the best use of its resources. The Mitchell Library, the largest reference library in Europe, opened in 1911 as a fitting facility for the Empire's second city. When the National Library of Scotland was established and became a copyright library, the Mitchell lost the possibility of ascendancy, and for many years it seemed as if Glasgow no longer knew how to make the best use of it and similar resources. When the shipping magnate Sir William Burrell (1861–1958) died, leaving his vast collection of art (gifted in 1944) to the city on condition that it was not housed (due to pollution concerns) within its boundaries, it took until 1980 for a place to display the collection to be identified and work on it to begin: the Burrell Collection opened in Pollok Park and Country Estate, a 1,500-hectare gift from the Maxwell family to the city, in 1983.

The city's historic size and importance in the immediately preceding generations helped to make it the location for a number of 'capital city' functions and facilities. The Royal Scottish Academy of Music and Drama (RSAMD) was based in the city, as was (after a brief exodus to Edinburgh) BBC Scotland and (from 1960) Scottish Television. The Scottish Exhibition and Conference Centre (SECC) was opened on the Clyde in 1985, although thereafter effective major waterfront redevelopment stalled for almost twenty years, with the opening of the Science Centre in 2002 a useful marker of a new phase, which will include the re-siting of the BBC to Pacific Quay in 2008 and the Glasgow Harbour and Clydebank Rebuilt projects, among others. The delay between the partial modernization of the Clyde waterfront in the 1980s and its second phase was evidence of more general economic weakness, with the 1992 Atlantic Quay development under-utilized by incoming business. In the early 1990s Glasgow had 150,000 square metres 'of empty modern floorspace', as the city continued to suffer from high levels of unemployment ('one in three males aged between 16 and 49') and low levels of business formation.[11]

The development of the Third Eye Centre, the Hunterian Art Gallery and the Mackintosh house all took place in the late 1970s, a decade which perhaps saw the beginning of the iconic use of the architect Charles Rennie Mackintosh (1868–1928) as 'a central part . . . in the rebuilding of Glasgow's self-image': in 1994–5 one of Mackintosh's plans for an architectural competition was built as the House for an Art Lover on the south side of the city. In 1982 the old sixteenth-century Tron Kirk in the Trongate in the heart of the old city became the Tron Theatre, a development which proved to be the beginning of the ambitious transformation of the old rundown Merchant City into a glamorous and upmarket locale, a change that was virtually complete within a decade. In 1988–90 the Royal Concert Hall was 'built at the top of Buchanan Street . . . for use by the . . . Scottish National Orchestra, and the new City of Glasgow Philharmonic Orchestra, founded in 1988'.[12] In the 1990s the Royal Concert Hall became the principal home for a major new music festival, Celtic Connections, which speedily grew to be the second largest festival of Celtic music and culture in the world, with around 100,000 ticket sales every January. Traditional music degrees began at the RSAMD and Strathclyde University, while the National Piping Centre also played an increasingly key role in the city's leading global position in Scottish music. By the beginning of the 21st century the Young Traditional Musician of the Year, held at Celtic Connections, displayed through its high standards the strength in depth of Scottish traditional music. It speedily became a significant national event, being opened by Alex Salmond, leader of the SNP, in 2006, and by Jack McConnell, the First Minister, in 2007. During the 1990s Glasgow had made significant strides towards becoming by a distance the national music capital of Scotland. It was both at the cutting edge of classical music performance, with major events such as Scottish Opera's Ring Cycle ushering in the new millennium, and had a rapidly rising profile in traditional music. Moreover, in Cappella Nova, based at the University of Strathclyde, the city possessed a major innovative group for the identification and performance of Scottish music of the mediaeval and Renaissance periods.

Like Edinburgh, Glasgow had discovered that culture sold the city, and following the beginning of the 'Glasgow's Miles Better' campaign in 1983, which invited visitors to see for themselves the scale of improvement and regeneration in the city (at that time, in truth, only just getting started), the 1988 Garden Festival, though it was never repeated, made a huge impact on civic self-esteem, further buoyed by being voted European City of Culture in 1990. In 1999 Glasgow was UK City of Architecture and Design: the Lighthouse design centre opened in the city centre with a permanent exhibition on Mackintosh, and a sadly more temporary exhibition in honour of Alexander 'Greek' Thomson (1817–75), whose Victorian visions of Hellenic and Oriental splendour seemed particularly in keeping not only with the era of Glasgow's greatness, but also with the brash manner of its celebration, long part of the city's nature. Since then, the trajectory has continued, with the 2014 bid to host the Commonwealth Games being only the latest in a series of ambitious cultural plans for the city, intended to extend the benefits of regeneration from the waterfront to the east end. Glasgow has become a major tourist destination, while the homegrown appetite for culture is also large: in the first six months after it reopened following a major upgrading in 2006, the Kelvingrove Museum and Art Gallery attracted more visitors than the Victoria & Albert Museum in London.

However, it took a considerable time for many of these developments to begin to impact on the general economic well-being of the city, where deprivation still exceeds that found anywhere else in Scotland (Dundee is its closest rival by proportion if not head of population). Indeed, many on the radical Left (traditionally strong in Glasgow) derided events such as the Garden Festival and the Year of Culture as having no relevance for the realities of economic deprivation. Many of the major job announcements of the early 1990s were linked to call centres, and although Scottish Power was headquartered in the city following privatization in 1992, Abbey National's takeover of Scottish Mutual (1991) and the increasing 'branch economy' status of the Clydesdale Bank under National Australia ownership weakened

Glasgow's ability to compete in the rapidly expanding financial and investment marketplace, losing a third of its 2100 jobs in 1991. Glasgow Fund Managers carved out a successful investment trust business, but theirs was a relatively small-scale operation, though the development of Resolution Asset Management's business and the move of a number of JP Morgan jobs to the city has improved matters in recent years. Glasgow is also home to a number of successful (and huge) private companies, including Edrington Group (who bought out the publicly quoted Highland Distilleries at the end of the 1990s), and the giant Arnold Clark car dealers, whose annual turnover far exceeded £1 billion. By the end of the 1990s, there were clear signs of economic progress. Between 1997 and 2007, 'almost 80,000 jobs were created' in Glasgow, while between 1996 and 2005, the employment rate among adults resident in Glasgow city rose from 55 to 66 per cent.[13] Yet despite plans to develop a major financial district, progress was slow, and shopping became the latest route whereby the city hoped to recapture its former greatness: following the opening of the Buchanan Galleries at the end of the 1990s, Glasgow became the second retail centre (by mass) in the UK. When it was clear in 2006–7 that this position was under threat, a plan was swiftly unveiled to render the Buchanan Galleries even more gargantuan in an attempt to recapture lost ground. Glasgow still badly needs to be a second city.

It remains, however, difficult to overcome Glasgow's two major problems. First, the size of greater Glasgow reflects its importance in the lost political structure of the British Empire: in its heyday, it was bigger than any British city outside London, both in its urban core and in its metropolitan area. Glasgow thus retains aspects of the infrastructure of a city of 1.1 million (2.5 million in the greater urban area) for a population of 600,000 (1.5–2 million in the urban area, depending how you measure it),[14] while many of its more prosperous citizens live outside the city boundaries, artificially restricted due to local government reorganization. In keeping with the arguments of this book concerning imperial opportunity and domestic autonomy, Glasgow, once the most British of Scottish cities, has become more and more intensely Scottish as its significance as a world city has declined in tandem with its loss of control over its own industries.

Secondly, Glasgow benefited enormously from the British Empire because it switched the trading and commercial focus of Scotland (and indeed Great Britain) to the west. As Edinburgh ceased to wield political power and Scotland moved away from its old European trading partners towards imperial markets, the west flourished. Conversely, the establishment of the Scottish Parliament restored to an extent the political status quo ante as it had existed before 1707, and the European Union, together with the expansion in the number of European states after 1989, is reinforcing the movement in economic and political power to the east. Although the Scottish administration has re-sited civil service and associated jobs from Edinburgh to Glasgow, it is clear that there is widespread objection to this in Edinburgh itself, both from politicians and employees: indeed, the relocation of the capital's jobs was a major issue in the local authority elections in Edinburgh in 2007. While Glasgow's recent economic growth has helped to stave off Edinburgh Airport's overtaking of Glasgow's in terms of passenger numbers (8.8 million Glasgow, 8.6 million Edinburgh in 2006), this will surely happen, not least because of the political willingness of Holyrood to expend vast sums of public money on the capital's transport network, over £600M being pledged to improve access to Edinburgh airport for Scotland's population. It's amazing to think what benefits might accrue to any airport that has the good fortune to have politicians flying into it and from it on a regular basis: they are among the most generous of consumer groups in their willingness to contribute to upgrading facilities. Glasgow had long suffered from a different political imperative: the desire to make the relatively inaccessible Prestwick an international gateway airport. Although this was reversed in the 1990s, it was a further feature which disadvantaged the city in its efforts to compete as a hub.[15] Glasgow's recovery is encouraging, but the financial, political and research clout of the capital, combined with Glasgow's deteriorating structural position in an economy no longer driven by imperial markets but by European ones, represent hurdles which are extremely difficult to surmount.

'New' Aberdeen was a twelfth-century royal burgh, which was established on a hill between the harbour and the beach above the foot of the

Dee, where the now defunct castle was built: Castlehill, which opened onto Castlegate, the main market area of the town, and still extant. There was an older settlement already present at the mouth of the Don: the Aulton, Old Aberdeen, which became an ecclesiastical centre with the removal of the local bishopric there from Banffshire in the twelfth century, and an educational centre with the establishment of King's College in 1495. In 1560 the 'new' burgh of Aberdeen gained its own university, Marischal College. The two universities remained separate for 300 years, and the two burghs did not unite until 1891. Fish and hides were two of the staples of New Aberdeen's trade; the Aulton remained relatively sleepy and conservative. Aberdeen speedily became an important regional capital for northern Scotland. Isolated from the south by poor roads and the barrier of the Mounth, where the mountains almost reach the sea at Stonehaven, it was isolated to the west by mountains also. Vulnerable from the north (hence the attack fended off at Harlaw in 1411), it was nonetheless from early times a larger population centre than anywhere else north of Forth-Clyde. It dominated its hinterland, and enjoyed strong trading links with the Continent: the Elbe is as close to Aberdeen as the Thames, and in an age of bad roads, Aberdeen was in all respects that mattered closer to Germany and Scandinavia than England.

By the eighteenth century the city had begun to be constructed in its trademark granite, and in the nineteenth roads improved considerably. By 1850 many of the public buildings which still mark the central districts of the city had been built, mostly by Archibald Simpson. The sea remained essential to Aberdeen, and some of the last great sailing ships were built there, including the *Thermopylae*, whose average of almost fourteen knots over 24 hours remains after more than a century the record speed for a wind-powered ship. By 1868 there were 200 boats operating out of the harbour, more than half in pursuit of the 'Silver Darlings', herring. Aberdeen's prosperity continued into the twentieth century, when it became a tourist resort, and its beautiful if chilly beach was populated to an extent hard to credit today. But flying and foreign holidays became cheaper, and for this among many reasons the city's financial strength was failing by the late 1960s, when the Gaskin report revealed a stagnating economy. The Beeching rail cuts of the 1960s had left the city more isolated than before, without rail communication to its western hinterland. In addition, the granite industry was declining, and many local and regional commercial concerns were being swallowed up in Central Belt or English company headquarters. Aberdeen, however, remained a beautiful city for flowers, parks and gardens, winning Britain in Bloom so frequently that it was disqualified from continued participation in the competition.[16]

By 1970 it was clear that oil would have a major impact on the city. Although the influx of oil workers from outside was initially low – about 2,000 in a city of 200,000 – the economic impact was soon felt. Men coming off the rigs would have been cooped up for long periods on high wages: on shore, they would spend them. Skilled and risky jobs such as diving could lead to wages of over £20,000 a year by 1976; £150,000 in 2007 money. Communication with Shetland, where there were also large fields and the huge Sullom Voe terminal, was already provided for by a regular ferry service from Aberdeen; in 1979 a second ferry terminal was opened. By 1981 there were 'about 750 oil-related firms . . . and office space was growing at 6 per cent a year'; by 1990 there were 'about 49,000 people in oil-related jobs in the area'. The usual (indeed, probably worse than usual) shopping centres and commercial developments followed. Unemployment was low and the city's housing market showed a stronger link to the oil price than to housing conditions in the rest of Scotland and the UK. Commercial and economic confidence was visible in other fields too, with the development of Aberdeen Asset Management in 1983 (up to £76 billion under management), although the fishing industry continued to contract under commercial and EU pressures. Major heliport development was only one of the features that transformed Aberdeen Airport, opened in 1955, into an important international centre. In 1992 over 2 million passengers used the airport, and in 1993–4 it had the highest number of aircraft movements in the UK after Heathrow and Gatwick; by 1994 Bond Helicopters were 'probably the world's largest civilian helicopter operator'. In 2006 there were 2.7 million aircraft and 505,000 helicopter passengers passing through Aberdeen.[17] The environs of the city, more than usually well supplied with upmarket country house hotels, blossomed with business, and small towns like Banchory in Strathdee, a little over 25 km from Aberdeen, quin-tupled their population in little more than a generation as leisure and sporting activities boomed. Donald Trump's proposed development of a vast golf tourism venue in the next few years will represent another step-change in the broadening of the economic base of the city and its hinterland, though this broadening itself is one that oil, and the pros-perity it brought, have made possible in the first place.

Despite Aberdeen's major cultural assets such as the City Art Gallery and Marischal Museum, the city was relatively slow in exploiting the turn to culture evident elsewhere in Scotland. In particular, although Aberdeen stands in the heartland of traditional Scottish music and song, it was Glasgow that cornered that market: in Aberdeen, only the university really tried to promote it. Similarly, although a maritime museum opened in the heart of the city, its many famous sons and daughters are very poorly commemorated by comparison with Edinburgh. Lord Byron's statue stands outside the Grammar School where he was educated, but the many philosophers, writers, artists and scientists the city has produced remain largely uncommemorated in it. The major economic successes of the last 40 years have perhaps rendered such celebration unnecessary: but for whatever reason, although the city is and feels wealthier than most of Scotland, it has not put as much effort into civic culture. Little of Aberdeen's recent archi-tecture can be described as an improvement, while Marischal College, the second largest granite building in Europe, lay virtually vacant and abandoned for years before being at last divested by the university to form a new Council headquarters. Many other historic buildings – for example the Town House in the Aulton's High Street – were vacant and deteriorating for long periods. There have been welcome signs in very recent years of greater attention being paid to the preservation of Aberdeen's built environment, but the city, given its size and strategic functions as a regional capital, often underperforms in areas like drama and the arts. Scotland the What?, a group of local professionals posing in their role as comedians as sly peasants and ordinary Aberdonians, was very successful in the 1970s and '80s: but the dialect humour the group depended on was in the last resort part of the traditional furniture of Scottish music hall comedy, rather than being innovative in the manner of cultural developments elsewhere in the country.

The University of Aberdeen did not have the right research focus to extract maximum benefit from the arrival of the oil industry, and the Robert Gordon Institute of Technology (later Robert Gordon University) took advantage of this. Indeed, as more centralist education policies took hold, Aberdeen University was faced in 1981 with substantial funding cuts and the beginning of the strategic reallocation of its subject base to other institutions: the departments of Classics, Linguistics, History of Science, Music and Scandinavian Studies were all either closed or had their staff transferred to other universities by 1990. The erosion of Aberdeen's research base by policy conceived in London was substantial and severe, while the centralizing of entrance procedures – confirmed when the university joined UCCA in the 1980s – diluted student quality. Hitherto, the most highly qualified school-leavers in northern Scotland had applied to Aberdeen as their 'home' institution; in a British market, Aberdeen's perceived remoteness served to dilute its attractiveness, while its hold on its home base also weakened. Although the magnificent fund-raising campaign spear-headed by Principal Duncan Rice helped to start to turn things round in the early 21st century, Aberdeen University suffered a major relative loss of status at just the time when its home city was benefiting from an economic transformation.

Dundee was a sufficiently important settlement to be made a royal burgh by the end of the twelfth century, and was one of the four 'Great Towns' of Scotland known to Bruges merchants in the fourteenth. It grew throughout the ensuing centuries as a trading port: banking, linen and whaling developed in the eighteenth century, jute, jam and journalism (for which the city became famous) in the nineteenth, with shipbuilding supplementing these. Dundee's prosperity was built more on trade than on being a regional market centre: roads to the hinterland were not improved until relatively late in its history. In 1889, when it was 'chartered as a City', its population stood at around 150,000. After World War I it suffered severely economically: by 1932 'over 70 per cent of the 37,000 jute workers were unemployed'.[18]

In the 1960s Dundee, though suffering from the final contractions of the jute industry, was significantly redeveloped. As the population in its city centre declined, shopping centres came into the space in two distinct developments, the Overgate and the Wellgate, constructed in the 1960s and '70s respectively. Dundee had also had a university college of St Andrews since the end of the nineteenth century: in 1967 the expansion of higher education in the UK led to it gaining its independence as the University of Dundee. Critically for its future success, it retained the faculties of Law and Medicine. St Andrews continued to provide pre-clinical medical training, but it was expected by the policymakers of the late 1960s that this would eventually wither on the vine. It did no such thing: but instead of developing clinical placements at Dundee, St Andrews found them at Manchester. Meanwhile, as the integration of universities with the goals of the wider economy became more manifest in the 1980s and '90s, Dundee's strengths as a centre of education for the professions helped to improve the university's standing, and the development of world-class research in medicine and life sciences brought scientists of international renown to the city, together with a good deal of associated light industry. By 2005 Dundee was one of the top twenty universities in the UK by research income, with one of the highest proportions of students studying for professional degrees in the traditional university sector. In 1994 Dundee gained a second university when Dundee College of Technology became Abertay: with a population of 140,000–160,000 (depending where the city's boundaries are drawn), Dundee was the smallest city in the UK to have two universities.

However, despite the accolades being heaped on the city as a leading location for scientific research, structural problems remained. By their very nature, the new industries coming to the city employed fewer people than their predecessors, and major redundancy stories continued to hit the press. D. C. Thomson, the owner of *The Sunday Post, The Dundee Courier, The Beano, The Dandy, The Hotspur* and *The People's Friend*, found the Scotland of the 1980s and '90s less amenable to their style than previous generations had been, while in 1988 Keiller's jam business was finally broken up: 'marmalade production ceased, and jam production was moved to Manchester'.[19] The manufacture of sweets stopped, and in 1994 the only major independent Scottish supermarket chain, William Low, was taken over by Tesco, and Valentine's card production disappeared the same year. The takeover of Willie Low's was in some ways even more serious than it appeared, because the sourcing of Scottish produce was less likely from the English chains, and campaigns had to be launched to press them to do it.

The development of Alliance Trust, one of the giants of the investment trust industry, has been a significant boost to Dundee as a financial centre: in 2007 it continued that commitment by unveiling plans for a major new headquarters in the city. Through its subsidiary, Alliance Trust Savings (ATS), Alliance has pioneered low-cost investment plans, self-selected PEPS and ISAS and more recently Self-Invested Pension Plans. In 2007, it made a major appointment by capturing Katherine Garrett-Cox, the Chief Investment Officer of Morley Fund Management, though there were arguably signs that it lacked the R & D or fund management capacity in depth to expand successfully at the rate of its ambition, and the performance of its flagship fund deteriorated against its major rivals. In other fields, Dundee Technology Park became a significant success in the use of its Enterprise Zone status to secure major job relocations in the 1990s, and Dundee Airport began direct flights to London City at the end of the decade, though major job losses at Timex, NCR and other employers continued to cast a blight on the city's overall economic performance. Dundee's dockland did, however, benefit substantially in the 1990s from a £30M redevelopment which included the permanent berthing of the *Discovery* as a tourist attraction from 1996.[20]

Dundee's football teams – always something of a proxy for the overall success of a city – declined markedly in the 1990s. Dundee FC, who had reached the semi-finals of the European Cup in the 1960s, found themselves unable to hold down a Premierleague place, while Dundee United, European Cup semi-finalists in 1984 and UEFA cup finalists in 1987, declined from being (with Aberdeen FC) half of the so-called 'New Firm' of Scottish football to being merely a fairly weak also-ran in the top division. Although Dundee's centre continued to redevelop, with the Dundee Contemporary Art centre opening close to the university, following the latter's merger with the very successful Duncan of

Jordanstone College of Art, and the smart Dundee Repertory Theatre (1982) flourishes, many structural problems remain. The city is still struggling to place itself on an unequivocally upward trajectory. Dundee has had extraordinary success in reinventing itself since 1960, but the process is still continuing.

Stirling, with a population (including Bannockburn and Bridge of Allan) of c. 42,000, became Scotland's newest city in 2002, to mark the Queen's Golden Jubilee. For much of the mediaeval and early modern period the town was a key strategic asset, for the moss at Stirling, impassable by armies until it was drained in the late eighteenth century, effectively gave the settlement control over the route between northern and southern Scotland, and many battles were fought in its environs. An important royal centre, Stirling Castle, largely built under James V (r. 1513–42) has been extensively restored in recent years, while the Wallace Monument, erected in 1869 to honour William Wallace, and his major victory over the English at Stirling Bridge, has become even more of a major tourist attraction since *Braveheart* was released in 1995, while Bannockburn Visitor Centre is not far away. The old town of Stirling, in many respects a smaller version of Edinburgh's Royal Mile, which runs down the hill beneath the castle, is very attractive. At the foot of the hill can be found the Smith Art Gallery and Museum, and some of the most popular residential areas of the city. A small town, often dependent on outside companies for its business, though with a significant agricultural hinterland, Stirling was more successful than many in its clearance of substandard housing, and started to blossom as a tourist resort in 1963, when the army vacated the castle, and it began to be redeveloped as a visitor attraction: a move which gathered pace in the 1990s, with the opening of the Tolbooth, the Renaissance house of Argyll's Lodging, and extensive restoration of the castle apartments. A safari park also opened nearby. In 1967, the town became home to a University (which included the city's only theatre), that came to have broad strengths in the arts and more specifically in aquaculture and sport. The Gannochy Tennis Centre has been located there since 1990. Apart from Coleraine and Keele (which is of course very close to the large city of Stoke), no smaller town than Stirling was selected as the site of a new university, and the jobs it provided and the students it attracted made a significant impact. In 1975 Stirling became the head-quarters of the new Central Region, and in the mid-1980s Scottish Amicable relocated there from Glasgow, with 1400 jobs: it was taken over by Prudential in 1997, and in 2007 the jobs are under threat. In the 1990s, new industrial estates began to develop, while Bridge of Allan, close by the university, became a favoured commuter suburb: the motorway, which bypassed Stirling in 1973, is adjacent.[21] Stirling's modest scale ensured that these economic developments had a dispro-portionate impact, and although the city continues to have its problems, it is regarded by many as a beautiful and desirable place to live, with high house prices (especially in King's Park and Bridge of Allan), first-rate cultural amenities, and a large number of services considering its size.

Inverness (c. 60,000 including Smithton, Culloden and Balloch), a Royal Burgh since the twelfth century, has long been the 'capital of the Highlands': 170 km from Aberdeen and 260 km from Glasgow, it was an important centre for trade and commerce. However, in 1931 its population was only 22,500, and 30 years later, only about 30,000, even with the growth of the Loch Ness monster cult in the intervening years. Despite the employment brought in the 1960s by the Highlands and Islands Development Board headquarters and other policy initia-tives, it was not until the Kessock Bridge and the partially dualled A9 from Perth were opened in 1982 and the 1970s respectively, that communication improved rapidly and with it commerce: the Eden Court Theatre, built in 1976–8, became an important regional cultural resource, and a number of sports and recreation facilities, including the Aquadrome, were developed in the city. By the early 1990s much of the Black Isle peninsula north of the bridge was a dormitory for Inverness, and there was rapid expansion to the east also, with a largely newbuild suburb of Culloden being built below the historic battlefield, which itself was attracting up to 250,000 visitors a year (half paying to visit the centre, the other half simply walking freely on the battlefield). In 1993 Raigmore Hospital 'employed some 2,000 people and was the major health institution serving the Highlands', while in 1995 the marketing arm of the Scottish Tourist Board transferred from Edinburgh.[22] By the later 1990s the plan for a new federal University of the Highlands and Islands, based at Inverness, went some way to reverse what was arguably the misjudgement of not siting a new university there 30 years before, while Inverness Caledonian Thistle, an amalgamation of two of the city's football teams, were admitted to the Scottish league (1994), finally reaching the Premier league eight years later. In 2000 Inverness became a city as part of the Millennium celebrations.

Scotland's cities and some of its towns still retain something of their traditional role as regional capitals. The large hinterlands which they serve render the character of a settlement of 40,000, such as Perth, very different from the more marginal economic function towns of the same size would perform in much of England. Often (as in Perth and – though less so in more recent years – Aberdeen) the agricultural hinterland is evident; sometimes the legacy of seafaring, fishing or whaling. Yet more and more the homogenization of UK retail markets means that Dunfermline or Inverness look from their centres like Hereford or Worcester: middle-sized settlements with traces of historic importance marginalized by identical high streets. Perth, perhaps because of its distinctive country markets, is slightly more resistant to this trend. Nonetheless, however similar patterns of retail behaviour are evolving or being imposed across the UK, appearances can be deceptive, and not only the historical character, but also the current culture, of Scotland's cities diverge from the British norm – if, indeed, there is such a thing. This is true in the areas of the arts in general, in diversity and of course in government: the subjects of the latter three chapters of this book.

Chapter 4

Cultural Independence?

One of the most intriguing ideas to surface in the years following the devolution debacle in 1979 (though indeed the cultural commentator Cairns Craig had presciently suggested it the year before), was that somehow Scotland was achieving a form of cultural autonomy in the absence of its political equivalent: that Scottish identity was materially if not constitutionally becoming ever more manifest. To some extent, the redevelopment of Scottish culture which presaged the expected devolution of 1979 continued in its absence, and this, though initially small-scale, was one of the most intriguing developments of the 1980s, which, in their turn, built on changes already under way for a decade. The shift to culturalism after political defeat had been the road taken in Ireland for twenty years following the fall of Parnell in 1891, though there was little sign of self-conscious imitation of this in Scotland, where the SNP itself was frequently almost indifferent to cultural matters. Instead, the main impetus came from outwith the sphere of party politics.

Scotland had long had national arts companies – the history of the Royal Scottish National Orchestra dated back to 1891, for example – but the 1960s saw a new and rapid pace of change. Scottish Opera was established in 1962, and in 1975 found a permanent opera house home in the Theatre Royal in Glasgow; Scottish Ballet moved north from Bristol in 1969 and the Scottish Chamber Orchestra was founded in 1974. In 1971 the Association for Scottish Literary Studies (ASLS) was founded to promote the languages and literatures of Scotland; in 1977 the Scottish Youth Theatre was opened. In the same year, the Saltire Society, active in defending and promoting Scottish culture since the 1930s, 'held a conference . . . to consider the policies necessary in an autonomous Scotland for the encouragement of artistic and intellectual life'. The debate which followed from this was not halted by the referendum, and an Advisory Council for the Arts in Scotland (AdCAS) was established in 1981. It would be too much to say that it was a nationalist front, but nonetheless a number of those involved with it or sympathetic to its aims were nationalists. Nonetheless, AdCAS managed to make itself heard in government circles. A number of the six points pressed for by Paul Scott, ex-diplomat and the leading light in AdCAS, in 1987 were subsequently implemented, including a fully devolved Scottish Arts Council, a separate Scottish Higher Education Funding Council and a National Theatre. Two of these three were put in place under a Conservative government before devolution. Meanwhile, the Scottish Arts Council, 'created in place of the Scottish Committee of the Arts Council of Great Britain' in 1967, became a fully devolved body in 1994.[1]

Scotland has, of course, long had an independent cultural life. After the Union of 1707 the maintenance and development of the autonomy of the surviving national institutions created the space for a domestic public sphere, populated and patronized by an elite, but not restricted to them for its audience. In the eighteenth century vernacular Scots (an Anglophone language, but not in its full form easily comprehensible to speakers of standard English) maintained – particularly in poetry – a status consistent with its role as the expression of a national self, in the work of Allan Ramsay (1684–1758), Robert Fergusson (1750–1774) and above all Robert Burns (1759–1796). Writers like James Macpherson (1736–1796) and Sir Walter Scott (1771–1832) achieved a global reputation, while Gaelic literature also developed in the hands of poets like Sileas na Ceapaich (c. 1660 to c. 1729) and Alasdair MacMhaighstir Alasdair (c. 1695–1770). In the nineteenth and early twentieth centuries, writers like Robert Louis Stevenson (1850–1894), Sir James Barrie (1860–1937), Sir Arthur Conan Doyle (1859–1930) and John Buchan (Lord Tweedsmuir) (1875–1940) reflected on Scotland's role in the

British Empire as well as creating characters of world significance like Sherlock Holmes and Peter Pan. The cultural nationalists of the 1920s and '30s, including Hugh MacDiarmid (the pen-name of Christopher Grieve, 1892–1978), Neil Gunn (1891–1973) and Fionn MacColla (1906–1975) were the mainstays of a movement termed the 'Scottish Renaissance', which also included figures of somewhat divergent (though still radical) political views such as Lewis Grassic Gibbon (James Leslie Mitchell, 1901–1935), Edwin and Willa Muir (1887–1959 and 1890–1970 respectively) and Somhairle MacGill-Eain (1911–1996), who fused Gaelic writing with Modernist themes.

Some of these writers were still powerful figures in the 1960s, although only Norman MacCaig (1908–1995) among the older generation had his best work ahead of him as the decade began. Younger writers such as Edwin Morgan (b. 1920), George Mackay Brown (1921–1996) and Iain Crichton Smith (1928–1998) had not yet made much of an impact, although 1961 saw the publication of Muriel Spark's (1918–2006) *The Prime of Miss Jean Brodie*, which utilized the old Scottish fictional technique of the unreliable narrator who seems to be withdrawn from the action and yet affects it profoundly to attack that old target of Scottish literature, Calvinism. Robin Jenkins's (1912–2005) quiet but effective novels dealt with themes including social change and war: *The Cone Gatherers* (1955) is often thought to be his best, exploring as it does the etiolation of the Scottish aristocracy, and the perversity of a soured Presbyterianism. Unquestionably, though, it was the 1970s that saw the beginnings of a 'new wave' Renaissance in Scottish writing. William McIlvanney's (b. 1936) *Docherty* (1975) and *The Big Man* (1985) presented the masculine working-class life of the west coast in a way revisited profoundly in James Kelman's (b. 1946) *The Busconductor Hines* (1984), which depicted such masculinity as in crisis thanks to the changing policies of the British state, Thatcherite lower-middle class social aspiration, the destabilization of community and the emasculating purposelessness of a man doing a job soon to be rendered extinct by changes beyond his control. Rendered in Glasgow argot within a Joycean narrative framework, Kelman's fiction presented the isolation, misery, humour and cynicism of life on the economic margins in Scotland. The largely hostile reaction in the

London media to his 1994 Booker Prize win was an indication how far his themes were out of kilter with the priorities of modern 'British' fiction in general. What was 'completely inaccessible' about Kelman's work was in some respects its explicit and unapologetic Scottishness.[2]

Alasdair Gray's (b. 1934) *Lanark* (1981) continued the Joycean theme, though in a more surrealist mode. Gray's Glasgow is Unthank, a disguised version of Joyce's Dublin/Ireland as 'the sow that eats her own farrow' from *Portrait of the Artist*. Both Gray and McIlvanney openly supported the pursuit of a strong measure of Home Rule in the late 1980s and early '90s, with Gray publishing *Independence: Why Scots Should Rule Scotland* in the run-up to the 1992 election. By this time a whole slew of young writers who have gone on to define contemporary Scottish literature, such as Ian Rankin (b. 1960), Robert Crawford (b. 1959), A. L. Kennedy (b. 1965), Alan Warner (b. 1964) and James Robertson (b. 1958) were becoming active, often taking a more positive view of Scotland and its future than that found in Kelman's work. At the same time, other traditions persisted: Margaret Elphinstone's (b. 1948) 'capacity to re-imagine the densely mythopoeic otherness of ancient times' being 'reminiscent of Naomi Mitchison' (1897–1999), whose evocation of pagan consciousness owed much to Sir James Frazer's *Golden Bough*, the work of a Scot and very influential on Scottish literature. Iain Banks's (b. 1958) *The Wasp Factory* (1984) revisited the Gothic to present both an individual tragedy and the tragedy of Scotland itself, imprisoned in a madhouse of militarism, racked by its own violence, and reduced to finding meanings in the rituals of its own torment.[3]

Irvine Welsh's (b. 1958) *Trainspotting* (1993), which presented Edinburgh as just as drug-, vice- and sleaze-ridden as Glasgow was usually depicted, made a major impact in England and North America, especially after it was filmed in 1996. To some extent it seemed to pander to the traditional image of Scotland as masculinized, primitive and violent; but it also addressed – or appeared to address – the alienation of youth culture in a corporate age. That alienation was itself figured in the text through a long-used technique of Scottish literature: code-switching between Scots and Standard English, as depicted in the chapter 'Speedy Recruitment', which shows the comic and insincere attempts of the youths to gain employment by mimicking the language of corporate culture, both standard and alien. Welsh, who is highly commercially successful as a writer, has a mixed reputation in Scotland, being seen by some as playing on a stereotypal image of the country, and providing titillation for a middle-class audience by his egregiously horrible visions of drugs, sex and violence. Politically, Welsh identifies Scottish self-hatred as key to the problem of its enslavement within the British state, with its true identity 'patronised by Scotland's smug political and media class, often more British than Scottish in its orientations, sometimes augmented by southern white settlers who've made a killing on the housing market' as an article in *The Guardian* in 2005 put it. Read this way, the drugs, sex and violence in Welsh are forms of self-harm and dependence which are manifesta- tions of a wider self-hating dependency culture.[4]

The development of theatre in the period mirrored the more general turn to culture. In 1963 the first Traverse Theatre opened in Edinburgh; in the late 1960s major developments in theatre at Edinburgh's Royal Lyceum (under Clive Perry) and at Glasgow's Citizen's Theatre (under Giles Havergal) followed. A reinvigorated drama developed to match, with its major impact arguably deriving from outside Scotland, in John McGrath's (1935–2002) 7:84 Company (named in reference to 7 per cent of the population owning 84 per cent of the wealth). This company produced McGrath's *The Cheviot, The Stag and the Black, Black Oil* in 1973: a devastating attack on the Clearances, big business and the corruption of Highland landlordism presented through a form reminiscent of the music hall genre in which Scots and Scotland had been mocked, often by themselves. On tour in the autumn of 1973, *The Cheviot* undoubtedly played its part in feeding the SNP vote in 1974, although its own perspective was more socialist than nationalist. McGrath went on to write and direct a series of radical plays, some of which focused on the plight of the Gaidhealtachd (e.g. *Mairi Mhór*), some on the political condition of Scotland more generally (*Border Warfare*). The revisitation of Scottish history was a favourite topic for figures such as Ian Brown (b. 1945) and Stewart Conn (b. 1936). Other dramatists also engaged – if in less overtly radical mode – with the political problems of Scotland, including sectarianism (Liz Lochhead's (b. 1948) *Mary Queen of Scots got her Head Chopped Off* [1987]). Lochhead's terrific ear for language (e.g. in *Perfect Days* [1998]), particularly the Scots of her native west, was also a feature of the drama of John Byrne (b. 1940), whose *Tutti Frutti* (1987), a series about an ageing Scottish rock band's last hurrah, was a major television hit, and a rare example of the screening of Scottish literature and culture by British TV.[5]

Scottish publishing flourished in the 1970s, with firms such as the specialist history publisher John Donald being joined by Mainstream, Canongate, the Polygon imprint of Edinburgh University Press,[6] Scottish Academic Press, the Association for Scottish Literary Studies and Gaelic publishing such as Acair. However, the economic downturn of the 1980s combined with lack of discrimination in commissioning in some quarters combined to severely reduce capacity. In the 1990s although Canongate transformed its financial position onto a much sounder footing, its academic publishing side went under; and the successor to that, Tuckwell Press, also disappeared early in the new century. Aberdeen and Glasgow university presses, together with Scottish Academic Press, fell by the wayside in the last quarter of the twentieth century, Aberdeen's as a result of the collapse of the Maxwell empire, though there have been recent discussions aimed at reviving publishing at both universities. The situation was not helped by the more marginal role enjoyed by Scottish books in bookshops increasingly run by large chains outwith Scotland, and although new specialist publishers, such as Birlinn and Luath, developed, and Edinburgh University Press became much more committed to Scottish publishing, the market for serious books about Scotland was still in a delicate condition in the early years of the 21st century. John Menzies's divestment of its retail outlets to W. H. Smith, the retreat of John Smiths from general bookselling to university textbook supply, and the takeover of Bisset's in Aberdeen and (especially) Thins in Edinburgh by Blackwells, all took their toll on the domestic marketplace.

Before the 1960s Scotland's role in film was often a mixture of Walter Scottian Romanticism, Harry Lauder music hall nationality, and cringeworthy caricature. Film adaptation of Scottish classics contributed to 'the internationalisation of Scottish literature', but there was small understanding of their Scottishness.[7] There was little sensitivity to locality outwith depictions of landscape and the strangeness and feyness of the natives. In 1948 the film of the Jacobite Rising of 1745 had David Niven playing Charles Edward Stuart as a public schoolboy in pursuit of a frightfully dangerous prank; as late as 1971 Michael Caine could be cast as a cockney Allan Breck Stewart, the Gaelic-speaking Jacobite patriot hero of Stevenson's *Kidnapped*, while in 1973, Christopher Lee's Lord Summerisle in *The Wicker Man* used the manners of Dracula and the social organization of the Glastonbury Festival to depict – preposterously if cultishly – the rooted paganism of a remote Scottish island. Films such as *Brigadoon* (1954) portrayed the country as a Neverland without Barrie's irony, and even *Whisky Galore* (1949), regarded as a classic by many, was heavily drenched in stereotypes of the whisky-obsessed wily native from the sticks. In such an atmosphere, *Gregory's Girl* (1980), came as a breath of fresh air, with its almost unmatched charting of the difficulties of being a teenage boy in a comprehensive school in Cumbernauld: it was a pity that *Local Hero* (1983), which followed it, lapsed back into the lazy stereotypes of *Whisky Galore*. *Chariots of Fire* (1981) showed that the presentation of a distinctive Scottish temperament, outlook and nationality was being recognized outside Scotland.

The standing of film in Scotland received a major boost from Hollywood, in particular from *Rob Roy* (1994) and above all *Braveheart* (1995). Both these films took Scotland seriously as never before – the trashy stereotypes of *Highlander* (1986) were left behind. What was notable in both was a tendency to align Scottish and Irish experience, a postcolonial drift new to American film. In *Rob Roy*, an Irish actor (Liam Neeson) played the lead, as he was to do in *Michael Collins* only a couple of years later; in *Braveheart*, not only does William Wallace receive Irish support, but the plot of the film itself is almost exactly repeated in *The Patriot* (2000), where Mel Gibson again plays a nationalist (American, this time) forced into war by the violence of English troops against his family, in a plot which ultimately dates back to the first *Mad Max* film of 1979. *Braveheart* was a huge hit in Scotland, though many voices were raised critical of its historical accuracy which had been strangely silent over *Rob Roy*, a film that took even more liberties with the known facts, but was not explicitly nationalist.

Scottish actors or Scottish accents became increasingly common in major films after *Rob Roy* and *Braveheart*, being touchstones for honesty and plain straightforwardness in pictures as diverse as *Gosford Park* and the Jackson *Lord of the Rings* trilogy while, in *Finding Neverland* (2004), Johnny Depp accurately played Barrie as a Scot in a way that would have been highly unlikely twenty years before. Outside the Hollywood blockbuster market, there were signs of subtlety in short films and in the 1994 cult film *Shallow Grave*. Developments had moved on to a new level by the early 21st century, with sophisticated recent studies including the mercurial, oversexed and less than pleasant protagonist of *The Last King of Scotland* and the obsessive and disturbed misery of *Red Road* (both 2006). The latter's poisonous mixture of voyeurism, vengeance and sexual obsession took the depiction of the misery of urban living in Glasgow to new heights, though its plot was not a match for other aspects of its execution.

The 1950s and early '60s saw a decided revival in Scottish folk music and folk-linked protest music. Hamish Henderson (1919–2002) played a significant role in collecting and making known these traditions to a wide audience, with the pivotal moment perhaps being the appearance of Jeannie Roberson, a traditional singer whom Henderson did much to discover and promote, at the People's Festival in Edinburgh in 1953. There were also major commercial successes. Bill Smith, Roy Williamson and Ronnie Browne went up to Edinburgh College of Art in 1955, where they met: in 1962–3, *The Corrie Folk Trio and Paddie Bell* was formed, which made its TV debut in June of the latter year. By 1966 the group was down to Williamson and Browne, and was simply *The Corries*, a pair who were to become the most successful commercial folk group Scotland ever produced. In the year Williamson sadly died (1990), his 'Flower of Scotland', first recorded in 1966, was sung at Murrayfield for the first time as the national anthem for Scottish rugby: Scotland obliged by winning the Grand Slam. It is hard to overstate the impact of 'Flower of Scotland' in the 1970s and '80s, when it was widely sung, and it was far more likely that one would learn it by oral transmission than from reading the words. Williamson almost succeeded in creating a new national anthem, which there is reason to believe he set out to do: *The Corries* used to end their concerts with

'Flower' as a deliberate alternative to 'God Save the Queen'. Despite perhaps an inevitable reaction against the celebration of historic victory in 'Flower of Scotland' as an imperative to do something about the melancholy present, it remains a towering achievement: the ability to write a new song in the folk tradition which inserted itself at the head of that tradition in the late twentieth century was evidence enough of Williamson's extraordinary talent. In 2006 'Flower of Scotland' was still the top choice in the Royal Scottish National Opera poll to find the most popular national anthem for Scotland. More broadly, folk music became a significant part of the Scottish scene, with Glasgow alone producing bands like the Whistlebinkies, the Battlefield Band and Ossian, while Scottish dancing remained strong in the growth of social ceilidhs and elsewhere. Classical composers such as James MacMillan (b. 1959) remained strongly influenced by Scottish traditional music, in a continuation of a hybrid relationship between folk and classical traditions which stretched back to the eighteenth century. The rise of pop music saw the formation of many Scottish bands, including Nazareth, Simple Minds, The Proclaimers and Franz Ferdinand, while the Bay City Rollers, a saccharine and overblown pop act of the 1970s, may, as Cairns Craig has argued, have done much to make tartan a respectable statement of Scottish identity.[8]

The conceptual art of Ian Hamilton Finlay (1925–2006) was only one aspect of the strength of a distinctive tradition in the visual arts, also found in sculpture in the public work of Eduardo Paolozzi, which remains strong in a new generation in the unapologetic neo-classicism of Sandy Stoddart (b. 1959). Joan Eardley (1921–1963), who spent many years at Catterline near Stonehaven, produced powerful visions of the intersection of sky, land and sea in a manner not unlike that of Jack Butler Yeats (1871–1957) in Ireland: her 'influence remained strong among west coast painters'. John Bellany (b. 1942) interrogated both Scotland's (e.g. in Homage to John Knox [1969]) and his own personal history 'in a way that led more and more towards a private language', producing some disturbing pictures along the way. Ken Currie (b. 1960) and Peter Howson (b. 1958) both developed in painting the grandiose manliness of the west (Currie's work has been described as 'socialist realism'), but moved towards portraying human weakness and suffering. As

Rory Watson puts it, 'Howson . . . and Currie can be seen to be making their own very different contributions to a view of life that can also be found in the writing of James Kelman and Irvine Welsh'; and in a further different dimension, this is also true of the poet Tom Leonard's (b. 1944) interrogation of standard English's claims to speak on behalf of the Glasgow Scots speaker. Some figures such as Alasdair Gray worked in both prose and pictorial art, while painters such as Sandy Moffat (in *Poet's Pub* [1980]) mythologized the writers of the Renaissance era.[9]

One of the features of the creation of a Scottish cultural agenda after 1979 was a determination to rid the country of the historical cliches, inferiorism and misunderstandings which it was believed by some had held Scotland back from devolution. The cultural moment which typified this turn away from tartanry was Ian and Barbara Murray Grigor's 'Scotch Myths' exhibition of 1981 which was the visible expression of a school of belief 'that Scots have connived at the manufacture and peddling of clownish, contorted versions of their history and culture'.[10] 'Tartanry' in particular was a target for attack, and the demythologizers of the 1980s and '90s pursued the work of their Enlightenment predecessors, whom they saw themselves as transcending, in imposing moral categories on the Scottish past to justify a judgement on it. Tartanry was to be as inferior, false and misleading as Jacobitism once had been: and the supreme irony of these decades was that just as academics and cultural commentators lamented the meretriciousness of tartan and shortbread images of their country, the kilt and all its associated furniture of stereotype were being increasingly adopted by young people as a mark of vibrant, modern Scotland. In the 1970s and even the '80s, getting married or attending formal occasions in a kilt was far less common than it is today, and many who wore it wore it as a badge of belonging to a caste in society rather than simply the visible performance of being a Scot, which is what it has now become. While the academy practised postmodern theorizing combined with a naive allegiance to the 'facts' of Scottish history and culture, Scottish society was increasingly being performed by those able to revisit the past without irony in order to show their commitment to the present. We all have our myths, and it turned out that 'Scotch myths' are no worse than anyone else's.

Scots, an Anglophone language once significantly distinct from English in much of its vocabulary and the circumstances of its use, has been steadily absorbed into the standard since the sixteenth century. By the 1970s and '80s, Scots language enthusiasts all too often resorted to writing 'Scots' with the syntax and construction of English, letting the odd Scots word surface in a representation of difference largely composed of spelling variations rather than any feel for the Scots language itself. A full, rich Scots had almost ceased to be spoken, and those who did not speak it did not learn it either. Even a significant work such as W. L. Lorimer's *New Testament in Scots* (1983) seems to depend on the English of the Authorized Version more than nineteenth-century Scots translations of the Psalms did. On the other hand, despite the refusal to give it a census question in 2001, evidence from other surveys indicated that about a third of the population identified themselves as using functional Scots to some extent, with the highest and most consistent figure of around 60 per cent in north-east Scotland. However, although the formation of new Scots words is heavily driven by Glasgow usage, speakers in the west were more likely to perceive Scots as 'slang', while those in the north-east had 'a generally positive attitude'. Thus, although Scots is strong and vibrant in Glasgow, there is a tendency still to see it there as an urban *patois* rather than a national tongue. There is thus a lot of controversy over the status and nature of the language among its users, while its traditional vocabulary, figures of speech and formations continue to disappear rapidly. Both Scots and Gaelic have status as minority languages under 'the European Charter for Regional or Minority Languages', ratified by the British Government in 2001, but Scots has a lesser status within the charter. Despite the setting up of the Boord o Ulster-Scotch (in imitation of Bord na Gaidhlig) in 1999 as a sop to Scots speakers in the north of Ireland (who are mainly Protestant Unionists), this situation continues.[11]

The status of Gaelic in Scotland has long been more problematic even than the state of Scots. Its use in administration and government had declined by the end of the fourteenth century; the Reformers on the whole disliked it, using the term 'Erse' to describe it, and in so doing identifying Gaelic with the language of (Catholic) Ireland. Serious efforts were made to extirpate it from the seventeenth century on. In

1891 the language was spoken by over a quarter of a million people over 40 per cent of the country's land area. Lacking any support and subject to widespread ridicule among Anglophones, the number of speakers dropped to 88,000 in 1971 and less than 83,000 in 1981, before plunging to not much over 65,000 in 1991 and to around 58,500 in 2001, though there was some hope in the last-named census in that there was a slight increase in the number of users of Gaelic who knew some but were unable to speak the language. The percentage of 'Gaelic speakers' living 'in the traditional Highland counties' was only 55 per cent, indicating retention or learning of the language more widely throughout Scotland was proportionately increasing within the context of overall decline. The slide in Gaelic speaking was heaviest among the under-45s, and indeed the younger people were, the less likely they were to speak Gaelic. In 1991 Gaelic speakers were over 2 per cent of Scots over 75, but less than 1 per cent of those under 25. This was different from the situation in Wales, where although there was a decline among young adults and the middle-aged, it was nothing like as great, while under-16s were more likely to speak Welsh (almost 25 per cent of the age group) than over-65s. In the north of Ireland, Irish Gaelic, as the language of nationalist identity, was spoken by 9–12 per cent of those under 45, as opposed to fewer than 5 per cent of over-65s.[12]

Even if change was slow, a new-found respect for Gaelic as the ancestral tongue of the country was emerging in Scotland in the 1970s and '80s, although misunderstanding and prejudice continued. After the 1979 Referendum, the extension of some government support to Gaelic became a way of appeasing Scottish interests without political (or, indeed, many financial) implications. Gaelic was not solely associated with nationalist politics, although it was the Nationalist MP Donald Stewart who tried to introduce a bill to provide legal status for Gaelic in the present and former Gaidhealtachd in 1981. In 1982 the Highlands & Islands Development Board published a major development report, and a 'new Gaelic development body, Comunn Na Gaidhlig', was established in 1984, with priorities in developing 'Gaelic-medium education; the Gaelic arts; broadcasting; and business'. The 1980s saw bilingual signposting begin to appear in more Gaelic-speaking (or recently Gaelic-speaking) areas, while tentative moves were made towards more widespread education in Gaelic with the establishment of 'the first Gaelic playgroups' in 1981. Soon there were over a hundred such groups, with their own umbrella organization, Comhairle nan Sgoiltean Arach, though not until 1985 was there any proper Gaelic medium education, and not until 2006 did the first full Gaelic medium school (in Glasgow) develop from the 200 centres/ units which had grown up in the previous twenty years. In the 1970s and '80s, too, Gaelic publishing got under way, with Acair being founded in 1977, while the development of Sabhal Mor Ostaig in Skye provided – for the first time – the beginnings of Gaelic-medium higher education. Gaelic arts festivals for children began in Barra in 1982, again spawning an umbrella network, while 'the first Gaelic arts centre and art gallery, An Lanntair ("the Lamp") opened in Stornoway in 1985'. Gaelic rock emerged with bands such as the Skye band Runrig (1973), who sang in both Gaelic and English of the Scottish diaspora ('A Dance Called America' [1984] – cf. The Proclaimers' 'Letter from America') and the historic plight of the Gael: *Heartland*, their 1985 album, is typical of their concerns. There was a broad revival in Gaelic traditional music, symbolized by the success of bands like Capercaillie (1984): in 2007 a Gaelic singer won Young Scottish Traditional Musician of the Year for the first time. The devolved Scottish Arts Council commissioned a report on Gaelic arts in 1985, and in 1987 set up a Gaelic arts agency, Proiseact nan Ealan, 'with a national remit to identify new approaches to Gaelic arts development'. Arts Council funding of Gaelic arts multiplied six-fold in the next decade.[13]

In 1984 'there was very little Gaelic-medium radio programming, and only about seventy-five hours of Gaelic-medium television programming per year'. Five years later, Malcolm Rifkind, as Secretary of State for Scotland, 'announced there was to be a Gaelic Television Fund worth £8.5M'. The 1991 Broadcasting Act 'led to the Scottish commercial broadcasters having a legal obligation to broadcast 200 hours per year of Gaelic programming', and by 1998–9 there were 250 hours a year of Gaelic-medium TV 'offered over the two BBC services . . . Grampian Television, Scottish Television and Channel 4', while Radio nan Gaidheal broadcast 'about forty-four hours per week'. In this environment, much was expected of the Scottish Parliament in Gaelic policy after 1999, but despite some very positive early noises, when it came to a vote on 'the language's place in the Standards in Scotland's School Bill', the attempt to ensure that 'Gaelic-medium education' would be provided 'where there was reasonable demand' failed by 62 votes to 36. In the Meek Report, published in 2002, Professor Donald Meek concluded that Gaelic medium education was stalling in its effectiveness, and that a legal right should exist for parents to have their children educated in Gaelic. This was still, however, too bold a step for the Holyrood administration to take, and the Gaelic Language Act of 2005 merely 'requires, among other things, that all public bodies in Scotland develop Gaelic language plans if requested to do so'.[14]

However, despite fears that the Meek recommendations would peter out ineffectively, there were signs by 2006–7 that the awareness of Gaelic in Scottish society was reaching new levels, and that this was being recognized and encouraged by the Executive, spurred on by Bord na Gaidhlig, who had responsibility for enforcing the Language Act. In 2007 the Executive invested £12M in a new Gaelic TV channel: there was evidence that existing Gaelic programmes were attracting audiences of up to 100,000, which compared well with the figures for s4 Cymry in Wales, broadcasting to a much broader language base. Besides the increase in broadcasting and (with the opening of the Glasgow school) educational capacity, a 'National Plan for Gaelic' was unveiled in 2007, with a target of increasing the number of speakers to 100,000 by 2041, amid signs that numbers of speakers were 'beginning to stabilise'.[15]

In 1978 Radio Scotland was launched by the BBC, and by 1982 'it broadcast for 90 hours a week' compared to the eleven to twelve hours of BBC TV Scotland. As the 1980s progressed Radio Scotland made more and more cultural programmes, building on popular folk music revival slots like *MacGregor's Gathering* via the lunchtime and evening discussions of Colin Bell (who stood good comparison with Melvyn Bragg's *In Our Time*), and many other programmes, until by the time of winning the Sony National Station of the Year award (1994), Radio Scotland was in many respects a powerful combination of the best of Radio 2, 4 and 5 south of the Border. Presenters like Pat Kane and David Stenhouse clearly showed that new talent was coming through, and even lighthearted breakfast shows like those of Fred Macaulay often discussed at least one cultural topic. Literature, history, current affairs and the arts were all well served: in 1998 Magnus Magnusson's *Tales of a Grandfather* history of Scotland was evidence of the strength in depth of the station.

After devolution this changed, almost overnight. Only in music did Radio Scotland continue to offer a strong cultural programming base. There were tactical decisions made to pursue audience share and to stress vox pop encounters and opinions over in-depth coverage and analysis, as well as to expand football coverage to gargantuan proportions; but it was impossible for many to avoid the suspicion that some deep-seated strategic shift towards downgrading Radio Scotland to local radio existed deep within the BBC as part of the resistance to devolved broadcasting, which had come to the surface in a significant public debate in 1998–9 over whether there should be an independent six o'clock news broadcast from Glasgow, the so-called 'Scottish Six'. Certainly, the coverage of Scottish culture, politics and society offered by Radio Scotland has, in the view of a number of commentators, deteriorated markedly since 1999 for no apparently good reason. In December 2006, the Saltire Society attacked Radio Scotland's impoverished cultural coverage, and web comments, letters and newspaper articles suggest that the Society's view is quite widely held despite the 1.1 million audience Radio Scotland retains (itself possibly in some part a function of the declining coverage of Scottish football on Scottish television, due to commercial reasons).

One of the interesting features of BBC television in Scotland (touched on in the Introduction) was that in the 1980s only a tiny percentage of its programmes were networked compared with the proportion networked from English regional production in Manchester and Birmingham. It seems that, without admitting to it, BBC Scotland's limited programming was acting as a surrogate national broadcaster for Scotland, and it is interesting that in more recent years, as more of BBC Scotland's output is networked, that the increasing output and the networking are both of marginal importance to the national culture of Scotland, however much they may benefit the internal economy of the BBC. Instead of becoming more like a national station after devolution, BBC Scotland has become more like Pebble Mill or other English regional studios. BBC television in Scotland never offered the same level of coverage of culture and society as Radio Scotland, and has thus deteriorated less markedly: though even here, the high spots (Fiona Watson's outstanding television history of 2000, *In Search of Scotland*, and the 2001 programmes on Scotland's and Ireland's links, the 2003 programmes on Scotland's Empire) have been few and far between in comparison with the rather unimaginative and repetitive diet of Hogmanay and Burns Night programmes, which imply a false stasis in what is in fact a dynamic and developing culture. It is interesting and perhaps indicative in this context that the network opt-out *Newsnight Scotland*, which runs from 11–11.20 pm, opts back into the network again for *Newsnight Review* on Fridays, rather than addressing the powerful domestic literary and cultural agenda. Scottish Television (which took over the rather quaint Grampian and its continuity announcers in the 1990s) has been just as unimaginative (though it is interesting to see how its separate regional news bulletins within Scotland will develop),[16] while Border TV's attempts to promote a cross-Solway 'border culture' are very difficult to justify after devolution. Scottish culture has thus on the whole not been well-served by the electronic media, which, insofar as they are part of it, hinder rather than promote dialogues within it. The dilution of the 'regional' obligations of ITV, and the generally centralist and increasingly monopolist trend in modern broadcasting do not augur well for the future, though there are some small signs at STV that a recognition of their role as a Scottish national broadcaster is dawning. There was clear evidence at the time of devolution that the BBC in London – and some of its leading current affairs presenters – were less friendly to it than the mainstream of English centre-left public opinion, and it is hard to resist the conclusion that the overall response within public service broadcasting to constitutional change has been at best inadequate and at worst designing. There has been a national 'broadcasting council' for the BBC in Scotland since 1952, but only extensive lobbying by Scottish interests, up to and including the level of government, preserved 'a territorial dimension in the form of a Scottish Advisory Committee' to the new UK-wide Ofcom arrangements, which were a rare and disturbing reversal of the devolutionary process.[17] Nor is much of what passes as the 'devolution' of BBC broadcasting from London as a compensation for the greater centralism of broadcasting generally a solution if the programmes produced in Glasgow fail to reflect the significant political and cultural changes in the multinational polity of Great Britain. A truly federal BBC would have been a response that both educated all of the UK and let each country see something of the others. As it is, while London ignores Scottish or Welsh news more than ever, Glasgow drifts in much the same direction, even while London can proclaim that more is being spent north of the Border – on networked children's programmes rather than Scottish content, for which Gaelic-language broadcasting cannot act as a substitute. The situation in broadcasting is potentially serious because ignorance is the breeding ground for hostility, and all the home improvement programmes in the world do not make up for the lack of a serious multipart history of Islam or the networking of Scottish history and culture programmes – such as there are – to a UK audience, while in the domestic market there is reason to believe that some in the BBC are uncomfortable with Scottish culture, history and society per se. These limitations may affect democracy itself. In the 2007 Scottish elections, where over 140,000 votes were rejected and voters consequently disenfranchised, a complaint was raised that the media had done little to educate Scots about the new voting system in what the London BBC persisted in calling 'local' elections, a description that confused the issue in Scotland, where both council and national elections were taking place on the same day.

This process has led to what Adrian Turpin in the *Financial Times* assesses as 'the UK's cultural Balkanisation':

It was Neville Chamberlain who famously used the phrase 'a faraway country' populated with 'people of whom we know nothing'. The then prime minister was referring to Czechoslovakia. But increasingly his words seem an apt description of Scotland as seen from England.

Turpin then goes on to assess the new National Theatre of Scotland, which was established in 2006 after a long campaign, led in the main by Paul Scott, who as chair of the Advisory Council for the Arts in Scotland (AdCAS), tirelessly promoted the cause of a national theatre in the 1980s and '90s. Turpin points out in his article that the National Theatre's '28 shows in 62 locations' have reached an audience of 100,000, and that 'Quantity has been matched by quality' in this innovative national project, which operates as a commissioning agency rather than having a landmark building. The conclusion, that 'it pays to listen to what the neighbours have to say' is only too true,[18] for the National Theatre is inclusive and flexible in ways which represent an awareness within Scotland itself of the importance of moving away from centralizing metropolitan models rather than replicating them in Edinburgh or Glasgow. The National Theatre of Scotland is a sign that the nature of Scottish culture, not just the place where it happens, is different and increasingly divergent, as well as being poorly reflected in the media.

Traditionally, the distinctiveness of the Scottish education system rested on the opportunities it offered to the 'lad o' pairts', the working-class boy – and for most of the history of this concept, it was a boy – made good. Derided by some as a myth, in fact Aberdeen University had 16 per cent of its students from agricultural working backgrounds in 1860, rising to 20 per cent 50 years later, while Glasgow's proportion of 'students from manual working-class backgrounds' rose from 19 to 24 per cent in the same period.[19] These were proportions of the whole which bear favourable comparison with the modern era's claims of widening participation as a central British policy, and it is indeed arguable that the legendary superiority of Scottish education, once fact, now nearly fiction, has been severely damaged by British policy imperatives which have not allowed it to develop in a way consonant with its own strengths. Local university attendance and community engagement had been a part of Scottish higher education for centuries (some universities used to discount entry grades for local applicants) before the centralizing policies of the postwar era rendered Scottish higher education more like English, and it began to share the problems of a system it had once surpassed in its solutions. It is painful to anyone who knows the history of the Scottish universities to see that 'widening participation' was relatively better addressed a century ago than now: but one of the problems within the UK has always been England's reluctance to adopt Scottish models, whether or not they are superior: a reluctance not shared by the four-year degrees and generalist traditions of North America.

It remains true that – remarkably – Scottish history, literature, music and culture form only a marginal part of the school curriculum in Scotland, despite the best efforts of ASLS, AdCAS and other organizations. The situation as described by *The Scotsman* on 8 February 1979 ('in every country, except Scotland, it is taken for granted that national history and literature should be well taught in the schools') remains fundamentally unchanged 30 years later.[20] The school curriculum remains a major hindrance to the emergence of a proper understanding of Scotland by Scots themselves, in part because the interest in history in Scottish society – which is manifest and widespread – has a leaning towards conspiracy theory and anti-Englishness in part arguably because people have been deprived of their own history at school. To paraphrase Edwin Muir, rob people of their history and they will create a legend to take its place: the lack of Scottish history in Scottish schools does nothing to promote either national self-confidence or mutual understanding within the UK. Moreover, it leaves people ignorant of the many world-renowned figures Scotland has produced. As a departing US diplomat put it in 2006, 'A message for Scotland: stop beating yourself up and learn to love your country'.[21] Progress here has been painfully slow. Although Michael Forsyth, the last Conservative Secretary of State, suggested the introduction of 'a Scottish History Higher, his Scottish Parliamentary successors appear to want nothing to do with it'. The Scottish Consultative Committee on the Curriculum report of 1998 showed widespread support across Scottish schools and society for the teaching of Scottish culture, but these findings were shelved by government, being reformulated only as 'a ponderous declaration that politics, business education, and values are the true heart of what teachers should be doing about Scottish culture'. Such vague statements promised nothing and kept their promise.[22] A new campaign by ASLS to insert Scottish literature and culture into the curriculum began in 2006, but at present, as in broadcasting, the situation in school education lags the realities of the wider society badly.

Tourism supports 9 per cent of all employment in Scotland, and produces 11 per cent of GDP: large areas of the country are geared to it. Yet despite the fact that 'visiting historic buildings (castles, churches etc.) remains the most popular activity, with 83 per cent of overseas visitors doing this', Scottish development of cultural tourism long tended to be very poor. Whole areas – such as architectural tourism, or literature trails (e.g. for Rob Roy) – were marginalized or neglected, while small provincial tourist industries in England were squeezing the last drop from local traditions in domestic architecture, or the few historic moments small towns could boast. Scotland had history to burn and was wasting it, and it is hard not to put this down to the ignorance of the country's history and achievements created even among educated policymakers by the near-exclusion of these subjects from the educational system, an exclusion which thus has an economic as well as a social cost. This is not only true of Scottish subject-matter, but also of judgements about location: there was virtually no protest when the BBC filmed its 2005 *Kidnapped* production outside Scotland, despite the proven benefits to the economy from tourism arising from film location.[23]

There have been some signs of welcome change in the prioritization given to culture in Executive policy at Holyrood, although there is still too great a stress on culture as a means to personal, social and community improvement, rather than any balance between this worthy goal and the importance of culture as an end, necessary if any assessment of quality or international benchmarking is to be made. Encouragingly, however, the increasing profile of the Holyrood government in international affairs is strongly tied in with culture. The development of St Andrew's Day as a public holiday in 2006 was celebrated in 70 countries, with events including 'Slovenian businessmen reciting Burns'. The Year of Homecoming (2009), which is intended to bring Scots abroad back to work in Scotland or at least visit it, is strongly linked to the 250th anniversary of the birth of Robert Burns, whose global status among the Scottish diaspora is recognizably critical: 'one of the world's greatest cultural icons' in the words of the then Culture Minister, Patricia Ferguson. Burns was worth (according to research commissioned by David Stenhouse at the BBC) about £157.25M to the Scottish economy in the early 21st century, and there seems at last to have been a central political response to this. Burns documents were uploaded to the Internet in 2007 as a symbolic marker of the 'end of a process that began in 2001' to digitize all General Register Office for Scotland records, a process intended to facilitate the genealogical research so popular among diasporic Scots and those of Scots descent. Meanwhile, the struggling Burns birthplace museum received £5.5M from the Executive (part of an £11M package overall) for redevelopment as the Burns International Museum. Homecoming Scotland's aim, to produce a comprehensive database of diasporic Scots and Scottish organizations segmented by major areas of interest promises – even if it is in the end only partially realized – to transform Scottish culture's and Scottish tourism's global markets in the medium term.[24]

If Burns is the new spearhead of cultural branding internationally, within Scotland the Executive built on the recognition of Edwin Morgan as national poet (Makar) in 2004 (brought about by the ASLS and Alan Riach, among others), and the establishment of the National Theatre in 2006, by moving in 2006–7 towards a Culture Bill which would merge Scottish Screen and the Scottish Arts Council into a single national agency, Creative Scotland, as well as bringing Scottish Opera, Scottish Ballet, the Royal Scottish National Orchestra and the Scottish Chamber Orchestra under direct government control for the first time. Together with these developments, it was proposed to set up a new creative national academy, based loosely on the Irish Aosdana model, which would guarantee '£9,000 grants for the first three years' of membership. In contrast to other developments in cultural policy, this received a rather muted welcome, partly because Scotland has an existing national academy in the Royal Society of Edinburgh, and additionally has a natural cultural academy of sorts in the Royal Scottish Academy; partly because of the spectre of government control of the arts, which already loomed in other aspects of the Culture Bill. As Cairns Craig (again presciently) put it in 2003, 'Culture . . . has become the *medium* through which the social and economic aims of the Scottish Executive can be *managed* and *directed*'.[25] Controversy continues to surround these developments: the incoming SNP administration is backing off from the political control of culture.

What is clear, however, to anyone living in Scotland and engaged with one or more aspects of the cultural scene is the extent to which Scotland now marches to a different drum. Popular music is of course Anglo-American and international, but even here Scottish bands like The Proclaimers and the development of Gaelic rock provide significant national inflections, while piping and traditional music are becoming steadily more important. In classical music and even in theatre to some extent, Scottish culture often lies more in the domestic politics of Scottish organizations than in what they perform, but Scottish drama has become both stronger and more distinct since 1945, and the National Theatre seems to herald both a new burst of creativity and the creation of a truly distinctive institution to project it. Scottish literature has long enjoyed the status of a separate national literature: but its relation to Gaelic writing is now more developed than before, and Gaelic and to an extent Scots have increasing status in the public sphere in Scotland. Even the perceived problems in broadcasting and the schools system are sources of public debate rather than acquiescence. The claim of 'cultural independence' may be both too neat and too strong; but it is certainly the case that anyone with an interest in the arts moving from Scotland to England – or vice versa – will, except in those forms of popular culture now universal in the West, notice a number of differences. These differences have got larger in the space of 30 years, and the impact of the Homecoming agenda on tourism and culture generally is likely to be significant, as more and more Scots grasp for the first time the extent of interest in their culture across the globe. The future promises to be interesting.

Chapter 5

Who are the New Scots?

In the contemporary multicultural societies of the UK, Scotland, particularly as viewed from England, can seem monocultural. This may seem suspicious to some, especially in the context of an assumption that Scottish nationalism – or even nationality – is ethno-cultural and particularist to a degree unacceptable in modern Western societies. The paradigm for this attitude is itself paradoxically a legacy of the imperial era: that Scottishness is a local, and Britishness is an international identity: Scotland is culturally homogenous and colourful, while Britain is diverse, serious and global. On this reading, Britishness permits hybrid identities (Scottish/British, British Asian) but Scottishness does not, because it is itself a particularist term.

At the same time, some nationalists align the Scottish experience with a colonial one similar to that which pertained in Africa in the imperial age. English – particularly English middle-class – people who retire to Scotland or acquire assets there have been termed 'white settlers', as if they were Europeans colonizing the Kenyan not Scottish highlands. Scottish economy and society are sometimes viewed in similar colonial terms: Michael Hechter's *Internal Colonialism*, first published in 1975, is a foundational – if hotly contested – analysis of this kind. This point of view also is born out of the era of the British Empire; it also chooses to situate its analysis of contemporary Scotland within a colonial model.

Both analyses are incomplete. The first is based on a misunderstanding of Scotland's historical development and contemporary society; the second does not offer an account of the long and successful assimila-tionist tradition in Scotland within the agenda of Britishness. Scottish culture engaged in a complex relationship with English, where it was patronized, colonized, but also adopted, particularly in limited discourses such as those of the British Army. In general, being Scottish did not – after 1770 or so – provide grounds for discrimination within the British state, but performing Scottishness, being too overtly Scottish, was frowned on and might lead to discrimination. Assimilation was – as often – the price of integration, and just as Anglo-Irish Protestants and even native Irish converts to Protestantism took a full part in the UK, so did Scots. The fact that integration was sometimes on terms they them-selves had helped to define complicated the assimilative process: the rules of Britishness were in part, as Cairns Craig argues,[1] written by the Scottish Enlightenment, and sometimes Britishness was in part not that which absorbed Scots as outsiders but that which as insiders they had helped to create. Explicit Scottishness also retained an important role. Expatriate Scots associations and meetings provided locales in which to let off steam, and perform that Scottishness suppressed in daily dealings in the British sphere; on the other hand, the English understood such associations to be no political risk, and made no move to suppress them. The relationship was of course unequal: Scotland controlled much of its domestic sphere, and Scots could flourish beyond that sphere only if they weren't too Scottish about it, while Englishness was never confined to the area of its origin in the same way: one must not overlook the fact that even if Scots did contribute to the idea of Great Britain, that state's values remained predominantly – if understandably – those which had origi-nated in England. If in consequence there was a colonial relationship, it affected aspects of the personality rather than opportunities in public life, leading to repression rather than oppression, the self-policing of personality: the 'Scottish cringe' as it became known later in the twentieth century.

Scotland itself – far from being a unitary ethno-cultural society – has long been a place with high levels of immigration (and emigration) and cultural mixing. There has never been a time when one language was spoken within its borders. In the early centuries of the Christian era, present-day Scotland was occupied by distinct cultural (the term 'racial' is best avoided, despite its continuing use in non-discriminatory contexts) groups. Genetic particularities, which in any case cut across so-called 'races' and cultural groups, were much less relevant than distinctions in language, custom and social organization. Gaelic-speakers lived on the western coastlands and islands from at least the fifth century, and quite possibly earlier; Picts speaking some form of Brittonic Celtic speech lived in the centre and north; Britons also speaking Brittonic in the south-west, and from the sixth-century Anglophone speakers in the south-east: though the kings of the Angles might also speak Gaelic, just to confuse matters. In the eight and ninth centuries, Scotland was periodically unified under Pictish and eventually Gaelic overlordship, a process completed in the tenth century, by which time the Norse had also colonized the northern and western islands. Areas long defined as part of Northumbria fell under Scottish control, and with them came more Anglophone speakers, but Gaelic culture remained dominant. Social organization like that of Gaelic Ireland was extended across much of the country, but in the eleventh and particularly twelfth centuries this became hybridized with Norman-French models. Trade brought colonies of Flemings into the east coast ports, and while in the thirteenth century the Norse were displaced from everywhere but Orkney and Shetland, their influence remained: a form of Norse speech, Norn, endured in Shetland until the nineteenth century.

The kingdom of the Scots was thus a cultural and linguistic patchwork. Unity grew from the single monarchy and the patriotic defence of an independent Scottish Catholic church; later, major institutional innovation in the law, education and civic organization augmented this sense of a unity derived through institutions. The Reformation damaged the key link between Church and King, and Scotland became a much more unstable and vulnerable polity for the next two centuries in part as a result. However, the preservation of Scottish domestic institutions and the space for an autonomous Scottish public sphere after the Union continued to reinforce the domestic society of Scotland: only 56,000 English-born people lived in Scotland in 1861, about 1.5 per cent of the population.[2]

The major fear of immigration into Scotland in the nineteenth century was not of English but of Irish immigration, above all immigration from Catholic Ireland, although the – to some – alien quality of Orange Protestant back-migration from the north of Ireland was noted by a number of observers. The Reformation had gradually served to open up an increasing gulf between the basically not dissimilar societies of Scotland and Ireland, and Irish Catholics were viewed with a projected racial horror based in reality on their religious culture. It was notable that it was the Church of Scotland – most clearly in the infamous Church and Nation report of 1923 – who were among the institutions most prominent in identifying Irish culture as a threat. The 1923 report, 'The menace of the Irish race to our Scottish nationality' was a response to the incorporation of 'Catholic schools into the state system' in 1918, a move which continues to this day to attract anti-Irish and anti-Catholic feeling, so in that sense the 1923 report is current affairs, not history. The proximity of Ireland to Scotland and the back-migration of Orangemen of Scottish ancestry from the north, as well as the scale of Irish immigration itself, were all factors which led to bitter, hysterical and disgraceful responses from Scottish society towards Catholics of Irish background, particularly in west central Scotland, though there was successful integration also. It was notable that those of Irish Catholic stock who converted to Protestantism lost any supposed 'racial' stigma more or less overnight; it was also noteworthy that although Italian immigrants in the nineteenth and twentieth centuries (who came predominantly to Glasgow in the earlier period), Poles, Lithuanians and Ukrainians might suffer racial comments, their Catholicism was less of an issue.[3] Rangers FC, who did not sign Catholic footballers from the UK and Ireland until the 1980s, nonetheless saw no difficulty in signing the odd Continental Catholic earlier. There was an intriguing underpinning assumption here that the Irish were deliberately difficult and rebellious, because despite having the opportunity to taste the glories of Protestantism, they had eschewed it, while Italians could not help their Catholicism.

Anti-Irish sectarianism, 'Scotland's Shame', was arguably the most serious form of racism in Scotland for most of the twentieth century. For some – prominent among them the academic Joseph Bradley and the composer James MacMillan – it remains a corrosive problem. It is true that there is a reservoir of continuing bigotry and discrimination, and traditional anti-Catholicism has to an extent been reinforced by modern secularism to intensify a longstanding low-level war against Catholic-faith schools; in employment, however, it is likely, as David McCrone has argued, that many obstacles have been removed as local Protestant employers have been supplemented or replaced by 'large national or international firms or governmental organizations' using standardized 'bureaucratic methods of selection'.[4] In culture in general, and in sport in particular, Irishness and Catholicism are intermingled as if they are one category, not two, and a political category at that, not a cultural or national one, as the Rangers refrains 'We're up to our knees in Fenian blood' or 'Are you watching, Fenian scum?' indicate. In 2006 UEFA warned Rangers that exclusion from European competition could follow if its supporters continued to sing sectarian songs. Nor, in Scottish football, is the problem limited to Rangers fans: as research in the 1990s demonstrated, the Protestant anthem 'We are the Billy Boys' (which contains the phrase 'We're up to our knees in Fenian blood') has been sung by supporters of Hearts and Dundee (cities where there is another team of Catholic associations), but also by fans of Airdrie, Ayr United, Falkirk, Inverness Caledonian, Kilmarnock, Morton, Motherwell, Queen of the South, St Johnstone and St Mirren. Assaults on Catholics – including murder – for religious and cultural reasons continued to happen, even in the 1990s. On a broader cultural front, it is much more difficult to have a St Patrick's Day celebration or Irish festival in Glasgow than it would be in Manchester, let alone New York.[5]

On the other hand, it is fairly clear that the problem is on the wane; and it is also the case that it is less intense – or even absent – outwith west central Scotland, where both Irish immigration and back-migration of Protestants from the north of Ireland was heaviest. Catholics of Irish background are to be found in the most senior positions in Scottish society; anti-sectarian groups such as Nil By Mouth and Rangers' own policies which acknowledge the scale of the problem have started to make a significant difference to social attitudes, as did Jack MacConnell's praiseworthy high-profile opposition to sectarianism as First Minister. Irish music and culture are more acceptable to many, and the historic links between Ireland and Scotland are better and more widely acknowledged, appreciated and explored. Secularism, if it has maintained distaste for Catholic schools, has weakened other aspects of sectarian rivalry. The peace process in Northern Ireland has also helped, and it is certainly arguable that devolution has reinforced connexions between the two countries in a Scottish context also, by bringing into the open debates about the home society hitherto repressed in the cause of local management and party discipline. John Smith, from 1992 to his untimely death in 1994 the revered – and indeed distinguished – leader of the Labour Party, was MP for a constituency in Scotland which sat in the midst of some of the most rampant sectarianism in the country: but it was not a problem he seemed to acknowledge openly, far less address. Only a decade later, the situation was very different. It was a sign of the changing nature of Scottish society under devolution that it was a Westminster MP who sought to dissuade the Taoiseach of Ireland, Bertie Ahern, from visiting the national grotto at Carfin in 2001 to open a monument to those who died in the potato famine on the grounds that there were dangers of sectarian disorder, a view regarded with bemusement by much of Scottish civil society, as it slowly, painfully, but definitively, moved to close these ancient divisions, not exacerbate them.

Catholic anti-Protestantism is often regarded as the other side of the same coin: but in reality, things are rather different. Explicitly anti-Protestant songs and expressions are rare: it is more common for Protestant icons to be attacked ('F**k King Billy and John Knox') or for implicit or explicit support to be shown for the IRA. This is an irritant where songs of pre-1922 Ireland are concerned, but it was definitely a cause of significant offence to many Scots to find expressions of support for the Provisional IRA widespread during the Troubles of 1969–94, not least when they came from members of the 'Irish dias-pora' whose association with the home island was one more of remote bloodline than having family to visit in Derry. The conversion of cultural loyalties into political identification with the Provisionals (and not, for instance, the SDLP) meant that significant numbers of those with remote Irish background in Scotland were more radical in their Republicanism that the put-upon Irish Catholics of the north themselves, let alone their counterparts in the rapidly modern-izing Republic. To an extent, this over-identification with radical

Republicanism was a feature found in the Irish diaspora everywhere; to an extent, it was an understandable if unwelcome over-reaction to the discrimination suffered by Catholic Irish in Scotland. But it was also true that many people found such politics distasteful when Scottish soldiers – and English children – were dying in IRA attacks. Cultural identification sought its excuse in remote relation to the island of Ireland by blood, and justified its own identity by applauding the blood shed by others: 'Lord Mountbatten had a boat, and in that boat there was a bomb' (which continues in unprintable fashion) was only one of the unpleasant songs of the era, which jeered at the murder of Mountbatten off Sligo in 1979. Hardly sectarian in the classic meaning of the term, they were nonetheless highly offensive, and no doubt intensified demands that those of Irish extraction should acknowledge their Scottishness after several generations' residence. The difficulty, of course, remained what it had always been: that Catholicism was no more acceptable to many in west central Scotland whether or not a tricolour flew above it; for there was a UDA as well as an IRA tendency abroad. The imperfect integration of the Irish immigrant community in Scotland over 150 years is in reality a tale of two communities, one unaccepted and the other unaccepting, to the extent that the latter has sometimes converted the former into a version of itself. Large-scale immigration and associated cultural tensions are not unknown in Scotland historically: it is simply that one has to look in a different direction to see them.

By contrast, the numbers of English in Scotland were not an issue until the 1980s. In 1981 the total stood at around 5 per cent of the population (counting all English-born, an inexact measure), rising to c. 7.5 per cent over the next 25 years, although greater mobility in society at large has increasingly meant that the indicators of ancestry, place of birth and early socialization are present in different proportions in different cases. The large number of Scots with relatives in England (and vice-versa) means that although the nationalities are seen and felt to be real and distinct, they are more often hybridized than is admitted: it is easy to find Scots born in Barnet or Geneva, and as easy to find English born in Milngavie or Edinburgh. The same is true for Irish Scots to an extent, but in their case hybridity is more widely recognized. English immigration began to be seen as important because of the sense that Scotland was losing autonomous control of its own institutions and domestic society, a process discussed in the Introduction and Chapter One. Rising antagonism to the English – insofar as it existed, for it was exaggerated by magazines and newspapers who would typically have taken an anti-immigrant line in other contexts – was a product of the sense of collapsing control over Scottish civil society by Scots, as British policies and public institutions not unnaturally brought with them a British job market, and as general mobility and the buying of second homes in 'remote' areas increased. Concern focused on these questions in the early 1990s, with the 'Englishing of Scotland' a current phrase of the day (first found in the 1980s) intended to indicate the takeover of key positions in Scottish civil society by non-Scots. This was a particular source of irritation when it occurred in longstanding Scottish institutions, such as the universities: in 1996 it was possible to hear even deep-dyed Scottish Tories express surprise that a Scot had actually been appointed to a university chair. Sometimes the universities realized the perceived problem themselves: Edinburgh University set up a corporate affairs unit called the University in Scotland (headed in turn by Lindsay Paterson, the author and Cairns Craig) which mapped the university's commitment to the study of Scotland and worked to ensure good relations with the wider community.

After the 1992 General Election returned a fourth term of Tory government while Scotland voted Labour, the activities of groups such as Scottish Watch (which purported to chart English influence in Scottish civil society) and Settler Watch (which was designed to make English incomers to the Highlands feel uncomfortable, and occasionally intimidated) became briefly an area of concern to the media and politicians: but there was little sign that these groups commanded wide support. The SNP kept its distance both from the activity and the rhetoric of anti-Englishness, and in the formation of groups such as New Scots for Independence and Scots Asians for Independence (1995), moved to flag the commitment of both English and Asian (among other) incomers to Scotland to the cause of national self-determination. (The title 'New Scots' itself was derived from Bashir Maan's 1992 book *The New Scots: The Story of Asians in Scotland*. In 1970, Maan was elected the first Muslim councillor in the UK when he was returned for Glasgow Kingston.)

Nonetheless, English migration to Scotland remained a cause of unease to some, a phenomenon studied in part in Charles Jedrej and Mark Nuttall's book *White Settlers: The Impact of Rural Repopulation in Scotland* (1996). Jedrej and Nuttall argued that the manifest presence of English incomers in the Highlands often followed a predictable pattern, where the 'consumer of tourism looking for facilities' became the 'producer for other tourists . . . So guest houses, hotels, restaurants, inns, craft shops, boat charter businesses, and the like, come to be owned by people who previously used them, that is, tourists and holiday makers'. Such holidaymakers could find the facilities on offer inadequate, so settled there and improved them, all the while, however, wishing to retain a 'romantic' view of rural Scotland which clashed with local demands for economic improvement and change. Because the locals were viewed by the incomers as guarantors of the stability of a romantic environment of 'majestic glens, tremendous mountains, awesome cliffs, enchanting sea lochs . . . ancient legends of dark deeds and tragic heroism', the changes they wanted were often opposed by the incomers as betrayals of supposed authenticity, even to the extent of objecting to crofters driving taxis in the afternoon to make ends meet. Often uncomprehending of the contemporary dynamic of the society they had idealized, frustration with the apparent obduracy of the locals often led to fear, and a determination to repress the culture into which they had moved. Sensitivities to the Clearances were ignored in the Highlands, and one woman even claimed in the *Press and Journal* that 'the use of the Saltire was akin to the use of the Eire flag by the IRA'. Such attitudes only raised the level of tension between those who had sought to buy an unchanging rural paradise with capital acquired elsewhere, and those struggling to earn a living in a place that was to them home not Brigadoon, who were unable to afford the houses and businesses occupied by those who patronized them in their own locality. Where the English incomer was not wealthier than the local, the signs were – at least anecdotally – that the tension was much less. English nationality has always been inextricably mixed with wealth and snobbery in Scottish stereotyping.[6]

In the cities, the rise of identity politics was often marked by a stronger emphasis than before on a Scottish accent as a mark of nationality. As opportunities in the Empire and control over institutions waned, the bare evidence of belonging to the nation was to have its voice. Upper and even middle-class Scots spoke with English or near-English accents into the 1960s: it was a mark of assimilation to Britishness. More recently, although local accents became more acceptable throughout the UK, in Scotland they became a strong marker – much stronger than in Wales, where native speakers often speak English with little or no Welsh accent – of nationality. Occasional attacks on or baiting of people – children in particular – with an English accent took place, in an ugly display of sociolinguistic chauvinism. Sometimes (especially in Glasgow, which has both many strong accents and hypersensitivity to accent as a mark of origin), any upmarket sounding voice would be categorized as English: this soubriquet has – to the author's knowledge – been bestowed on life-long inhabitants of the west of Scotland whose voice appeared upmarket to their auditors. It would be unwise to exaggerate this: but there is certainly pressure of this kind in Scottish society. Once again, the indications are that a Geordie or northern English voice is less of a stigma than a southern one, even one with a marked accent: the north of England does not have the connotations of class, power and snobbery which are identified as 'English' to the same extent. The importance of accent as a mark of belonging is widely recognized among new Scots in general. It is of course (being almost as visible as skin colour) a dangerous premiss for stereotyping and assumptions about character.

And what of the incomers themselves, the English as a community in Scotland? Less work has been carried out here, but it would almost certainly be wrong to speak about a 'community' of English migrants. For one thing, the Scotland they experience is different. In Glasgow, there is a significant cultural pressure to integrate, while in Edinburgh in certain professional circles it is possible to be at social gatherings entirely composed of those from south of the Border. Where it is possible for social networks to be mainly or almost entirely composed of fellow-incomers, there may be little integration; otherwise many individuals acquire a real interest in Scotland and its culture, sometimes preferring it to England. In the rural areas, there are not always enough incoming English to provide self-sufficient social networks, but integration has historically been poorer because the gap in resources and culture between incomer and local has been larger. A retirement hobby of running a hotel with Scottish staff puts the hotel owner in a position of economic power as an employer, and is thus different from getting a job as a teacher in a Scottish school where one has to adjust to the expectations of others. There are nevertheless often cultural gaps which few manage to bridge: one is the middle-class (largely, but not exclusively southern) English habit of measuring people's importance by the volume of their voice, and talking over the conversation of others in public places in order to demonstrate one's social ascendancy. This is disliked in Scotland, and few who practise it understand this or read the signs right, for if they find nobody competing with them they presume, on the basis of the cultural language of their upbringing, that they are the most important person there. Meanwhile, Scottish society continues to communicate round them in its own relational and associational way, establishing its webs of connection in the manner typical of a small country, and – uneasily conscious that events are somehow passing them by – the loud conversationalist begins to apprehend the presence of what he or she sometimes calls a 'Scottish mafia', and is aggrieved that having demonstrated ascendancy by the standards of their own culture is not enough in a Britain they had thought a unitary state. It is important, however, to stress that the resulting social problems are usually minor ones: many English people who settle in Scotland grow to love the country, even if they do not quite understand it, and this feeling is more often mutual than some of the inflammatory tabloid language used to describe Anglo-Scottish relations would have us believe.

Since devolution in 1999, the signs are in any case that the level of tension between Scots and English incomers in both city and countryside has – in general terms at any rate – declined. The same things irritate on both sides, no doubt, but the restoration of a measure of domestic control to Scottish society has arguably made a significant difference to a situation which from the beginning was strongly associated with a lack or loss of control. According to work carried out by Asifa Hussain and Bill Miller, 62 per cent of the English in Scotland think relations have improved since devolution; on 3 September 2002, BBC News reported that 94 per cent of English migrants to Scotland don't think anti-Englishness is a problem. Devolution is an increasingly manifest marker of Scottish difference, and it was the failure to appreciate that difference which led to much anti-English feeling in the first place. The 2006 World Cup, where Scotland was – as normal – treated to coverage focused on English media hype, did lead to a resurgence of anti-English abuse and even on occasion violence which was ugly and dangerous; but the general jingoism of the occasion also led to attacks on Germans in England. It is hard to see this on either side of the Border as anything else but the fruit of irresponsibly chauvinistic media treatment, which has been thankfully absent in Scotland to the same degree since it received its nemesis in the gap between appearance and reality in the 1978 World Cup campaign.

This chapter has deliberately focused so far on the fact that multiculturalism in Scotland has historically related to the absorption of different white cultures (including the Jews, of whom there are 11,000 in Scotland, 9,000 in Glasgow) rather than groups from south and east Asia, Africa and the Caribbean and the African Asian group expelled from Uganda by Idi Amin. These black and minority ethnic (BME) groups formed a very low proportion of the population, even in the 1970s, mainly because they settled elsewhere in the UK: there were around 16,000 south and east Asians in Scotland in 1970, 0.3 per cent of the population. However, this has changed, and while much of Scotland remains clearly – to some eyes, disturbingly – white, there are significant areas of ethno-cultural mixing. The proportion of the Scottish population as a whole from these communities was 1.3 per cent in 1991, 2 per cent in 2001, with estimates now ranging up towards 4 per cent. Of Scotland's 50,000 Muslims, some 80 per cent live in Glasgow city, where Scotland's first Asian MP, Mohammed Sarwar, was elected in 1997. In the 2007 Holyrood elections Bashir Ahmad was elected top of the list in Glasgow for the SNP, and so became Scotland's first BME MSP: his role, and the importance of a diverse Scotland, was stressed by Alex Salmond in his acceptance speech as First Minister. The south Asian community in west central Scotland began in the 1990s to have a major impact on the national life, with entrepreneurs like Charan Gill becoming prominent, while among Scots of partly Iranian origin, Darius Danesh emerged as a celebrity pop singer at the turn of the 21st century. In the 2007 Holyrood elections there were eight BME candidates for Holyrood in Glasgow and environs.[7]

The identity of the south Asian group, and the east Asian ethnic minority group (there are over 20,000 people of Chinese origin in Scotland), was the subject of a Joseph Rowntree Foundation study of Scottish ethnic minority teenagers in 2006, which concluded that '80 per cent of the young people interviewed considered themselves to be Scottish', and that around a third of south Asians thought that a factor in their identity as Scots was a perception of cultural difference within Scotland compared to elsewhere in the UK. There was more likelihood of the adoption of a hybrid identity in Scotland than was the case south of the Border, and 'higher levels of self-esteem' resulted from the adoption of Scottish nationality, though this is stronger among the younger generation than first-generation migrants, for obvious reasons. It is possible to view community integration through rose-tinted spectacles: there are problems, particularly in Glasgow (where a Turkish asylum seeker was murdered in 2001) and the Lothians, reporting of racist incidents is on the rise, and there is the odd horrific or grossly insulting attack. Nonetheless, it is noteworthy that the Scottish press gives room for the hybrid New Scot groups to write and comment on their own experiences in Scotland in a way absent even from the pages of the *Guardian*. This is a practice not altogether unconnected with the relative lack of the cult of 'community leaders' or ethnic minority spokesmen and women in Scottish society, with the concomitant implication that the group so represented need to be interpreted to the wider society, rather than being members of it. A Londoner of south Asian origin married to a Birmingham lady of the same general background recently commented to me how welcoming their sojourn in a well-heeled (and very white) Scottish commuter town had been, and how much more friendly people were than they had been used to: anecdotal evidence, but with some backing in social science research and cultural practice. In 2007 the Commission for Racial Equality 'found a markedly more positive reception to new migrants' in Scotland, though there was 'little room for complacency'. According to polling evidence, Scots are significantly less likely to want to repatriate asylum seekers or to view themselves as racially prejudiced than is the population of the UK as a whole. Despite some racist incidents in the aftermath of the July terrorist attack at Glasgow Airport, the solidarity displayed between Scotland's government and community agencies and Muslim organizations was impressive, if not entirely unexpected.[8]

Scotland itself of course has had a history of emigration, which has contributed to long-term population decline and made immigration seem increasingly welcome as a means of protecting levels of population. In the sixteenth, seventeenth and eighteenth centuries, many Scots had left a country suffering declining wealth (possibly due to a combination of Little Ice Age climate change and internal conflict) to seek their fortune as soldiers, merchants and traders in Continental Europe, while many Scots professionals – particularly in Law and Medicine – were educated in the Low Countries. In the age of Empire, it is arguable that existing experiences of diaspora made Scots more flexible and successful within the imperial service; some may have left Scotland also due to their radical politics, as *The Scotsman* suggested in 1817. Scottish emigrants were often highly skilled, and this remained the case into the early twentieth century. During this period, permanent emigration was mainly to the USA, Canada and Australia.[9] Although often ruthless settlers, Scots were also associated (and associated themselves) abroad with native peoples and radical colonial causes; even senior imperial servants were often aware of their hybrid identity as Scots and British in a manner which influenced their outlook.[10]

Emigration to England was highest from the border counties: Dumfriesshire, Berwickshire, Kirkcudbrightshire, Roxburghshire and Wigtownshire all losing more than 10 per cent of their natives to

England in the early twentieth century, sometimes nearly 20 per cent. Both the Highlands and the Borders lost large proportions of their population, although Highlanders often tended to migrate within Scotland, for example to Glasgow. After 1960 opportunities for the less skilled in England began to diminish, and just at the time when Scotland's professional autonomies were being eroded, the opportunities for work elsewhere began to be principally open to the very groups whose assured position in Scottish professional life was under threat. This was of course part of the same process of globalization; but Scotland was no longer protected from such changes to any extent. Between 1976 and 1986 Scotland's population suffered 'a net loss of 152,000 people'. Some areas, notably west central Scotland – which would see most immigration in the years to come – were disproportionately hit. Many graduates were uncertain of getting work in Scotland.[11]

As a consequence of these developments, many Scots have relatives not only in England and Ireland, but also in North America and Australasia. There is a diasporic quality to the Scottish experience – particularly among the middle classes – which may be reflected in understanding of other emigrant groups. Scots also know what it is like to be stereotyped: positively, as the doctor, banker or engineer; negatively as the greedy, narrow and intolerant man on the make, or simply a picturesque drunk. Most Scottish stereotypes conferred by others are highly masculinized: Scotland has few women in the popular imagination of other countries. As the world at large became aware of political and cultural change in Scotland, Scottish experience began to be aligned with that of Ireland, particularly in North America; in England, by contrast, signs of recrudescent Scottish difference brought to the surface once more the old stereotypes of hairy, greedy place-seekers and complainers subsidized by English money, which had originated in the eighteenth century. Scottish emigration may be principally economic, and anti-Scottish prejudice may be very marginal in its importance, but the experiences of emigration and prejudice are alike not unknown to Scots. As Alan Taylor put it in *The Spectator* in 2002:

There are many Scotlands, but the majority of them are mythical, imagined by fevered, myopic commentators who write for publications such as this and who really ought to get out more. Scots, I read recently in a newspaper which used to boast that it was the nation's record-keeper, subsist on deep-fried pizza, deep-fried Mars bars and Irn Bru, a sweet, fizzy, rust-coloured drink said to be able magically to cure hangovers. I dare say there may be some Scots who enjoy such a diet, but I have yet to meet one.[12]

Poverty, greed, alcoholism, eating so wilfully unhealthy that it seems almost a deliberate burden on the health service and thus on the English taxpayer: these are very much contemporary, as well as eighteenth-century, stereotypes of the Scot.

In the early years of devolution Scotland's continuing relative population decline and the antipathy towards asylum seekers being shown by the British government led to political demands for different immigration regulations in Scotland, and a more facilitatory policy towards the settlement of those seeking asylum. As compared with England, 'Scotland's population growth has been slower in every decade for almost 200 years', and by the 1960s it was slower than Wales's as well: between 1971 and 2001, the population of Scotland dropped by 3.5 per cent. In this context, measures to reverse population decline began to be seen as a priority, and this had an impact on official policy, as well as drawing strength from a wider spectrum of Scottish social attitudes. There was widespread distaste in particular at the Home Office practice of 'dawn raids' on families, while the slow processing and pursuit of asylum applications meant that those who had effectively settled in Scotland were facing deportation. There was some popular support for more lenient measures from groups such as the 'Glasgow Girls', a group from Drumchapel High School who campaigned 'for an end to dawn raids and the detention of children', though it is also fair to say that opinion remains mixed, and many Scots shared the resentment of asylum seekers found south of the Border. Nonetheless, there was enough popular antagonism to the Home Office measures to press the governing administration at Holyrood to issue a muted challenge to Westminster on a reserved matter, and one of the most sensitive ones at that. The Executive first of all 'intervened in the issue of forced removals as part of their responsibility for the welfare of children' in 2005, but by 2007 were going further in urging the Home Office to take a 'sensible and pragmatic approach to reviewing' the cases of those who had effectively settled in Scotland.[13]

Even after a slight recovery in population projections in 2007, there was still estimated to be a need for 13,000 immigrants a year. The Fresh Talent initiative was launched in 2004 to encourage immigration to Scotland, and as the country now has 'one of the fastest-growing foreign-born populations in the UK', the initiative must be judged a success. As well as publicizing Scotland, the Executive also provided relocation and advice, and permitted (from 2005) any student from outside of the European Economic Area with an HND or degree from a Scottish university to stay on for two years without a work permit. 22 international studentships were created to encourage overseas students to study for master's degrees in Scotland.[14]

Homecoming Scotland can be seen as part of the second phase of this development. Its programme for 2009 shows a willingness on the Scottish Parliament's part to play a role on the global stage, one probably not predicted, and certainly not one sought, by Westminster. The aim of Homecoming, based on the 250th anniversary of Burns's birth in 2009, is to get as many of those who identify themselves as members of the Scottish diaspora (4.4 million in Canada alone, for instance) to return to work in Scotland, or at least visit it during that year. Cultural and trade links will be boosted, and cultural tourism, long a Cinderella dimension of the industry, looks as if it will be placed on a firm footing at last. The focus on the Scottish diaspora in north America is an obvious one, but it still appears to have made the British Government uncomfortable. This has been shown by the tensions over Tartan Week, the international fest of Scottishness in the United States set up to take advantage of the 1998 US Senate Resolution 155, which established Tartan Day on April 6 as a mark of the inferred but probable influence of the Declaration of Arbroath (1320) on the US Declaration of Independence (1776). Although the Executive invested substantially in Tartan Week, British ambassadors in the US have, it has been alleged, not always supported it with enthusiasm, and when the then First Minister, Henry McLeish, obtained 'a meeting with President George W. Bush in 2001', 'the sound of spitting from envious Westminster politicians became audible'.[15] London dislikes a number of aspects of the international projection of Scottishness practised by Holyrood, a sign of its functionality as a national rather than a regional parliament.

Between 2004 and 2006, over 27,000 workers came to Scotland 'from the new member states of the European Union', over 20,000 of them Poles, although the total number, including dependents, has been judged to be twice this. Polish-language recruitment websites began to appear, and flights were introduced between Scotland and Poland, such as the Ryanair Prestwick-Wroclaw flight, launched in 2006. Tourism from Poland into Scotland quintupled between 2001 and 2005, rising to some 53,000 visitors. Forty per cent of the Polish workforce were university graduates, and in the hope that some might settle in the country, the administration at Holyrood, as part of its Fresh Talent scheme to recruit immigrants to Scotland, 'launched a £120,000 campaign to produce Polish-language welcome packs and advertise a special information website on buses in four Polish cities, including the Warsaw underground'. This campaign generated 31,000 website hits and 17,000 enquiries in its first two months, so the chances are that at least some Polish expatriates will settle in Scotland in the longer term, and that trade and cultural exchanges between the two countries will intensify.[16]

Scotland has always been a hybrid society: this has sometimes been mythologized into an ethnic divide between Celts and Teutons, but it has a solid basis in fact. Scottish nationality has always been strongly marked by civic, institutional and associational practices. Scotland has also experienced waves of migrants, although not until recent years have many of these been from a black/minority ethnic background. These New Scots (the title of a 2006 exhibition at the National Library of Scotland, and a term by then in frequent use) are an important part of the formation and further development of contemporary Scottish identity. Relations between groups are not always good: it would be idle to deny it, and the Campaign for Racial Equality rightly warns against complacency, but there are many positive signs. The development of a BME presence in the Scottish Parliament will bring on further change. The fact that a Nationalist was the first BME MSP to be elected is a positive indication both of the difference and openness of Scottish society – which has itself contributed many New Britons, New Canadians and even New Russians to the world – to New Scots, even if there remains much more to be done.

Chapter 6

Devolving or Declining? Government and Society in Scotland since 1999

On the night of the referendum in 1997 a sense of expectation and hope was manifest in those interviewed by the media as the results came in. The Yes Yes (there were two questions, one on the establishment of the Parliament, the other on its tax-varying powers) campaign had been unified, unlike the fragmentary effort of 1979, fraught as it had been with bickering along party lines. The SNP had, despite their absence from the Constitutional Convention, been included in the campaign by the Labour Party, and this earnest of real support for devolution from Scottish Labour was reciprocated by the Nationalists, who did not use the campaign to press for independence. The Tories and their few allies had appeared isolated and out of touch. The breadth of interest in Scottish civic society represented in the Constitutional Convention, and the even broader front presented in the campaign by the participation of the SNP, helped create an atmosphere where politicians and celebrities alike queued up in front of the cameras to proclaim a new era of consensus in Scottish politics, far from the confrontationalism of Westminster.

In reality, of course, it was never going to be like that. It was not just the fact that Scotland, for decades in a state of relative decline, needed 'more consensus and conformity like it needs a hole in the head', as the composer James MacMillan put it. It was the fact that the Convention itself was in significant part 'a useful camouflage for the development of Labour Party ideas to which the Liberals would be bound'.[1] Neither independence nor federalism were even options on which discussion was allowed, let alone a vote proposed. The Labour Party's own goals were, however, increasingly compatible with a devolutionary agenda by the end of the 1980s. In Scotland, the party had moved towards supporting home rule in a more wholehearted way under the pressure of Thatcherism (and their own inability to resist it effectively without an alternative powerbase), while for the British Labour Party as a whole devolution ensured (since they presumed Labour would always hold power in a Scottish Parliament) that never again would the Tories ride roughshod over Labour's powerbases if and when they returned to government in Westminster. It was no accident that the Greater London Assembly was the only successful piece of English devolution: it was revenge for the abolition of the old Greater London Council by the Conservatives in the 1980s. It was no accident either that Ken Livingstone, leader of the old GLC, returned to power as London's elected mayor under the new dispensation. Many Westminster Labour MPs no doubt presumed that the Scottish Parliament would be like the GLA: a glorified local authority.

Every time legislation affecting the establishment of the Scottish Parliament came before Westminster in 1997–9, there seemed to be either the threat or the fact of diminution in its powers on the table (see chapter Two); and it seems likely that without committed supporters within Cabinet such as Donald Dewar the final product would have been a much instead of somewhat diluted version of the Convention's proposals: so much for consensus. This went largely unnoticed in the Scottish media, used as it was to printing Labour Party press releases as exclusives. What was noticed, however, was the colossal fuss over where the Parliament should be sited, a fuss that was to have lasting and expensive consequences.

The old Royal High School building, high in the east New Town of Edinburgh, had been the putative home for the Scottish Assembly proposed in the 1970s. Its chamber had even been prepared for the administration that never sat there. Since 1979 it had largely been redundant, but Edinburgh City Council bought it in the 1990s in preparation for a Labour Government that would introduce devolution. However, its security arrangements, accommodation and general space were not up to 1990s standards. More importantly, the Royal High School building's role as a focal point for nationalist protest since 1979 and its location as a place of a continuous home rule vigil since 1992 rendered it, in words attributed to Donald Dewar, a 'nationalist shibboleth' for Scottish Labour. Alternative sites were proposed at Haymarket (near a brewery and car showrooms), Leith (which would have suited the Scottish civil service, and helped with urban regeneration), and a development of St Andrew's House, opposite the Royal High School. The first two were seen as downgrading the role of the Parliament, and attracted little support outwith a nexus of politicians and civil servants; the last, which would develop existing accommodation to provide a debating chamber with panoramic views south over Salisbury Craigs and Arthur's Seat, was strongly supported by many architectural and cultural professionals within Edinburgh. However, it was virtually on the Royal High School site, which no doubt in due course it would have occupied: it was therefore unacceptable to Labour. A budget of between £10M and £40M was set for the Parliament building; the St Andrew's House option was budgeted at £65M. It is hard to imagine that in the end its cost would have approached that of the site eventually chosen.

That site, announced in early 1998, was beside Holyroodhouse, at the bottom of the Royal Mile. On the site of a former brewery, it had a footprint of 1.6 hectares and was to provide almost twice that in floorspace: the budget was £40M, neatly on the maximum allowed (and excluding various fees and costs), although once the 1999 elections were over, this figure rose almost at once (on 17 June) to £109M, and consent to the continuation of the project was only secured by a narrow majority. The Holyrood site had the advantage of a historic position and was adjacent to the official residence of the Crown, so its constitutional distinctiveness and constitutional subservience were alike symbolically preserved. A competition to design the new building was held, which was won by the Catalan architect Enrico Miralles, who sadly died before his adventurous new design could be completed in 2004, three years overdue. The Scottish Parliament began its official sitting in 1999 at the top of the Royal Mile, where the General Assembly of the Church of Scotland, so long a surrogate parliament to the nation, met every year. When the Assembly needed the debating chamber, the Parliament went on tour, sitting in the old Strathclyde Regional Council headquarters in Glasgow in 2000, for instance.

The trouble with Holyrood from the beginning was that it was almost certain (the initial agreeable budget figures not withstanding) to be more expensive than any conversion of St Andrew's House: it was completely new build on ground that had to be cleared, and there was a historic building on the site (Queensberry House) which could not simply be knocked down. Its eventual cost rose to £414M. Cost over-runs affect all projects of this type, but the arguments over Holyrood's massive increase in costs were to some extent driven by the very low estimate provided in the first instance, an estimate hard to justify in the context of similar-sized buildings erected elsewhere on expensive and confined urban sites, although the 2003–4 Fraser Inquiry into costs, launched by the Lab-Lib administration to clear the air, was relatively inconclusive in allocating responsibility.

However, in 1999, all that lay in the future. The May election returned a Labour-led coalition, supported by the Liberal Democrats, as foreshadowed by the discussions held in the Convention: these parties gained 56 and seventeen seats respectively. Donald Dewar became First Minister, and Jim Wallace, as Lib Dem leader, was his deputy and Justice Minister. The Liberals also gained a few other cabinet seats: their own whip, the deputy minister for Enterprise and Lifelong Learning and the Minister for Rural Affairs. The major portfolios were Justice, Enterprise and Lifelong Learning, Finance, Children and Education, Health, Rural Affairs, Social Inclusion with Local Government and Housing (Communities) and Transport and the Environment, with the Lord Advocate and Solicitor General (neither MSPs) also sitting in cabinet. The main change in the second parliamentary term was the upgrading of Tourism, Culture and Sport from a deputy's portfolio to full ministerial status, the separation of Transport from Environment and the latter's absorption of Rural Affairs, though some of the other titles also changed. The cabinet was slightly larger than expected, at 22 (21 by 2007, reduced to sixteen by the SNP Executive): the number of deputies gave the unfortunate impression of a political gravy train rather than an effective administration, as 30 per cent of the governing coalition were in the Executive.

There were also squabbles about office space and the relative standing of MSPs elected from a constituency on the Westminster model and those who were 'top ups' from the seats elected under the additional member system, where Labour gained only three of its 56 seats. Despite having voted on a bill which clearly introduced a partly proportional electoral system, a number of Labour MPs and even MSPs appeared taken aback that Labour had not won an outright majority, while the fact that 28 of the SNP's 35 seats – and all the eighteen Tory seats – came via the top-up list rather than being first past the post, led to grumblings about the 'second-class' nature of list MSPs. There were rather vague proposals that the status and powers of this group might be downgraded in some way or another: eventually these were quieted, if not entirely resolved, by the Reid Committee, which set guidelines for the conduct of constituency and regional business and emphasized the list MSPs' (of which George Reid was originally one) equality of status.[2] The fact that voters tended to be slightly more Nationalist in their Holyrood than in their Westminster voting behaviour, though predictable, also appears not to have been taken fully into account by Labour. The provision of the second ballot showed up some interesting elements in voter behaviour: 67 per cent of Labour voters on the first ballot voted Labour on the second (thus largely wasting their votes, particularly in west central Scotland), with the SNP the most likely alternative, and the figure for SNP voters was almost exactly the reverse of this. Liberal Democrats who switched on the second ballot were most likely to vote Labour, and Conservatives, Liberal. A significant number of Conservatives switched to the SNP, however, being a third more likely to do this than the Liberals, whose voters disliked the SNP more than any of the main Unionist parties.[3]

The Parliament opened in July 1999 to considerable fanfare and enthusiasm. The streets and open spaces in Edinburgh were packed, and school pupils came from all over Scotland to represent the youth of the country. The Queen received the Honours of Scotland (the crown jewels) from the Duke of Hamilton as Hereditary Keeper of Holyroodhouse, and she, Prince Philip and Charles, Duke of Rothesay and Prince of Wales, listened to Sheena Wellington sing the Burns republican anthem 'Is there, for honest Poverty': it made an interesting picture as Wellington's voice rang out with 'Ye see, yon birkie, ca'd a lord' and 'the rank is but the guinea stamp' among other egalitarian and republican sentiments. Donald Dewar, the new First Minister, that complex and interesting man, intellectual, artistic, naive, generous, statesmanlike and also at times a mean, crude machine politician, had approved Wellington's song. When he came to speak himself his sentiments were powerfully patriotic. Whatever his fellow Cabinet members might think of the Scottish Parliament, he clearly saw his role as a that of a national leader (he made no apparent protest at being received at head of state level in Dublin, for example). Yet he had seemed to discourage other Labour MPs from moving from Westminster to Holyrood (in the event, only half a dozen did so), and had appeared to actively block Dennis Canavan, a principled Socialist, from selection as a Labour candidate: Canavan won in Falkirk as an independent with a huge majority. The status and credibility of the Scottish Parliament seems at times to have been ultimately less important to Donald Dewar than his ability to control it: and on that paradox of power and status much of his character seemed to rest. He was a vulnerable man, and was at his most impressive when he thought he had least need to impress.

The Parliament's early years of operation were blighted by a succession of problems. Some were unavoidable: the sad death of Donald Dewar in 2000, for instance. The departure of Alex Salmond from the leadership of the SNP, and his replacement by the excellent organizer John Swinney was followed by weakness in the major opposition party. Other problems, such as the Holyrood costs overrun, were not altogether the Parliament's fault, though arguably it did not take sufficient responsibility for the onward management of the project. The negativity of much of the media was little short of appalling: those who had opposed devolution took revenge in as full measure as they could by criticizing everything it did. Everything about the parliamentarians – particularly their expenses and housing support costs – was subject to relentless scrutiny, and although it was an issue connected with his time as a Westminster MP which led to Henry McLeish's resignation as First Minister in 2001, the cynic might note that McLeish had made significant efforts to promote Holyrood as a national parliament which were unwelcome to some in the Labour Party, who were notably silent as he came under media pressure: in his own words, a 'small but damaging cabal' had formed against him.[4] Expenses which would hardly attract attention at Westminster were pored over at Holyrood, whose parliamentarians were seen as having to prove their usefulness, and the Tory leader David McLetchie became perhaps the most notable victim of an inquisitorial process – spurred by the Freedom of Information Act – which was in itself liberally laced with resentment: particularly in the context of how MSPs benefited from rising house prices in Edinburgh through use of their housing allowance. It was and is entirely appropriate that the use of public money should be accounted for: but the virulent pursuit of Scottish parliamentarians already subject (by comparison with other parliaments) to high degrees of transparency and disclosure by a journalistic profession whose own use of expenses might occasionally be called into question were there any watchdog to report on it, was unedifying in the extreme. The perception that MSPs were all 'on the fiddle' was almost certainly no more true – and quite probably less true – than could be said of many other legislative bodies, but combined with the gross cost overshoots of the Holyrood project, it was very damaging.

One of the results was that the 2003 election saw a determined turn away from the political establishment in the shape of the two major parties, with Labour losing six seats and the SNP eight, although the latter's share of constituency seats rose from 20 per cent to a third of their total haul of 27. Much of the vote that seeped away from Labour and the SNP did not seem to benefit either the Liberals or the Tories (although the latter won three constituency seats in their unchanged total of eighteen), but instead went to minor parties, with Tommy Sheridan's Scottish Socialists rising from one to six, and the Greens from one to seven seats. A senior citizens' candidate and an anti-hospital closure candidate were also elected, Dennis Canavan returned for a second term as an independent, and Margo MacDonald took revenge on her lowly ranking in the SNP's party list by winning as an independent nationalist in Lothian.

This disillusionment with the politics of government and opposition appears to have been very much conditioned by the negativity of the media and the disproportionate coverage given to the Holyrood project, by comparison for example with major public procurement cost over-runs on buildings in London. The idea that Holyrood's MSPs had done nothing but award themselves medals and expenses and authorize the building of an overblown 'politician's palace' next door to the Queen could be encountered even among otherwise educated and thoughtful people: it almost certainly played a part in the drop in turnout from 58 to 49 per cent between 1999 and 2003, though here wider factors, common to UK and US democracy in general, were in play.

The irony in this situation was that Holyrood initiated major and important legislation in its first term: arguably more so than in its second. The lesson learnt by the Labour Party under its new (from 2001) leader and First Minister, Jack McConnell, was to 'do less better'. The 'better' was a matter for debate; but it was sadly the case that when Holyrood attempted to do 'more', it came under assault from the media for taking the initiative, and was simultaneously castigated for its inaction while at its most active. The Abolition of Feudal Tenure Act (2000) brought an end to feudal superiority in Scotland (there being no leasehold or freehold in the English sense), which was often nugatory in its effects in the Lowlands, but carried a freight of bad memories (and sometimes continuing practice) in Highland landlordism. Following the Cubie Report on student funding (an achievement of the Liberal Democrats in coalition), the Education (Graduate Endowment Student Support) Act of 2001 replaced the student top-up fees that then existed with a graduate endowment, payable on graduation, and ensured a political consensus against the larger top-up fees which Westminster subsequently agreed for English universities. The Community Care and Health Act (2002) provided for free personal and nursing care for the elderly, while the Land Reform Act (2003) allowed crofting communities to buy land at any time, and gave rural communities in general the right to buy land when it came to market, thus eroding the grasp which private landlords continued to exert through the ownership of huge estates in northern and north-western Scotland. The Water Industry Act of 2002 confirmed the non-privatized status of Scottish water and merged the existing regional boards into a national authority, while the Abolition of Poinding and Warrant Sales Act (2001) showed the influence that backbench MSPs (in this case Tommy

Sheridan) could exert in getting a major piece of social legislation (which prevent the public roup or auction of a debtor's effects) on to the statute book.[5]

The Parliament itself worked on a different model from the adversarial one in place at Westminster. The chamber to be designed at Holyrood was to be semi-circular, as befitted coalition politics. Bills could be introduced by the Executive itself, as at Westminster, but also by a Parliamentary Committee or by a Member: although fewer than 10 per cent of bills in 2003–7 were introduced by 'individual members' or committee, these are still significant routes to legislation, especially under a minority government. Individual MSPs had more ability to introduce Private Member's legislation than was enjoyed by their counterparts at Westminster (the St Andrews Day Bank Holiday Act of 2006, introduced by Dennis Canavan, was a notable example, while the Smoking, Health and Social Care Act of 2005, which banned smoking in public places, also received significant pushes towards the statute book from individual MSPs). The Committees were given greater powers than their southern equivalents, and from the beginning formed a crucial part of Parliamentary outreach, meeting in different places in Scotland in an effort to offer public hearings inclusive of the whole country. In the Parliament itself, they were involved at two of the three major stages in the passing of any Bill. The 'composition of committees' was broadly in line with the strength of the different parties, and the governing coalition did not hog all the committee convenorships either. The committees' taking of evidence in support of developing legislation gave 'access and involvement' to pressure groups, and subsequent committee responsibilities included producing reports on each stage of a Bill and consideration of any amendments, as well as inquiries which might be connected to legislation. Explanatory memoranda were attached to bills summarizing their nature.[6] Sixteen committees (eight of them mandatory) were established at the discretion of the Parliament itself in June 1999: European, Equal Opportunities, Finance, Audit, Procedures, Standards, Public Petitions, Subordinate Legislation, Justice and Home Affairs, Education, Culture and Sport, Social Inclusion with Housing and the Voluntary Sector, Enterprise and Lifelong Learning, Health and Community Care, Transport and the Environment, Rural

Affairs and Local Government. Petitions to the Parliament from civil society at large were enshrined as a normal part of the conduct of business. The hours for which the Parliament sat were more suited to those with family responsibilities.

Ministerial policy outwith the realm of direct legislation helped to support the extension of a Scottish agenda in areas such as science policy and economic growth. In the latter – key – sphere, although the Executive had few powers, it benefited from the development of a more distinctive national consciousness in Scotland and a growing awareness of the importance of business and enterprise to the Scottish economy. Nonetheless, growth in Scotland consistently remained below the UK trend, passing it only briefly in 2005. The gap was not large: in six of the ten years from 1997, Scottish growth exceeded 2 per cent, but the overall cumulative lag was around 0.6 per cent per annum.[7] In addition, one of the problems for Labour is that they tend to resort to the argument that Scotland would be in a state of economic collapse if it voted for independence, in the process both talking the economy down and effectively criticizing their own stewardship of it. In 2007 the incoming SNP government moved to appoint an impressively international committee of economic advisors to help meet Scottish economic growth targets.

Dispersal of the civil service throughout Scotland was initiated, with '38 organisations, employing 3855 staff', subject to 'relocation reviews' between 1999 and 2007. As a consequence, over 2,500 jobs were moved out of Edinburgh in the Parliament's first eight years of operation, with just over half these posts going to Glasgow. Just as would be the case in England, there was a lot of foot-dragging and resistance to moving organizations out of the capital, and since this was also a costly process, it came under renewed attack when Holyrood's own Audit Committee 'concluded the policy has failed to deliver a true dispersal of jobs – and had been poor value for money'.[8] It was nonetheless – as were the moveable committee meetings – an important part of the Parliament's attempts to make devolution a nationwide rather than a metropolitan phenomenon. Resistance in Edinburgh to the idea of jobs going to Glasgow in particular had more to do with local rivalries and old autonomies than with the kind of project the Scottish Parliament was intended to be: besides, Edinburgh itself profited enormously, with huge rises in property values and the conversion of the Holyrood area from a marginal to a desirable part of the city centre, with both *The Scotsman* and the BBC relocating thither. As the Scottish Parliament became more and more of a national institution, there were signs from Edinburgh of the metropolitan argument that 'we produce the wealth and should consume it', so familiar from London in a British context. The new SNP administration in 2007 faced demands to spend billions on a new tram system, new airport link, and new Forth crossing, all intended primarily to benefit Edinburgh and its commuters.

Local rivalries were among the cultural difficulties in the administration of Scottish politics which the Parliament had to encounter, and one of the interesting features of its development was the way in which the Executive arguably perpetuated existing structures of managed local autonomy in tension with the rhetoric – and, to an extent, the reality – of the Parliament's status as an open democratic institution. For centuries – dating back to the era of Dundas in the eighteenth century, if not beyond – Scotland's domestic autonomy had been combined with an extensive network of government patronage to places and perquisites. Much of this power had aggregated in the hands of the Secretary of State, and from the Scottish Office these powers largely found their way to the Scottish Executive. In 1998 there were 3,652 appointments to national public bodies in Scotland available at the discretion of ministers.[9] Since 1999 the signs have been that instead of relaxing this control (whether through a 'bonfire of the quangos' or otherwise) it has in many aspects intensified, with political questions being asked in officially 'transparent' public applications for appointments to a wide variety of bodies, and a surprising number of talented people with the appropriate affiliations being found to fill them. The legislation enacted or proposed in the second session of Parliament (including the Culture Bill) increased the opportunities for political interference and a centralizing agenda. There was thus a tension between the greater democracy of the Scottish Parliament's structures as compared with Westminster, and the command and control politics of the Labour-led Executive, which sought on many issues, from law to the arts, to turn the autonomous organizations of Scottish civil society into policy functionaries of the state. This was more in keeping with the New Labour government in Westminster than with the vision of the Constitutional Convention, whose chair, Canon Kenyon Wright, pointed out in 2007 that the 'growing centralisation' of power ran against the spirit of devolution, and called for 'an open reaffirmation' of 'the Claim of Right, with its emphasis on the sovereign right of the Scottish people to determine how they will be governed'. Recognition grew that 'council wards and Holyrood lists are still carved up through a combination of nepotism and family dynasties' and that 'in politics the choices have got narrower, the products duller and the participation lower'. The management of Scotland by the McConnell administration rendered it in many people's eyes less 'national' than Rhodri Morgan's more feisty attitude towards London Labour in Wales: as McLeish put it, one of the problems with devolution in practice was that 'for Scots, the will of London still seems to prevail'. While in Wales the relatively powerless Assembly called itself a 'Government', in Scotland McConnell stuck rigidly to 'Executive', and was also criticized for a widespread use of 'Sewel motions', a constitutional shortcut which allowed Westminster to legislate for Holyrood in devolved areas. As a consequence, McConnell's administration was more secure than Henry McLeish's, but McConnell's own status – both with the electorate and arguably within the Labour Party – was not enhanced by his largely quiescent role as a junior cabinet minister managing a portfolio rather than a national leader running a government. Moves to introduce English New Labour legislation in the law and elsewhere were opposed by the SNP as not finessed enough for Scottish conditions.[10]

If there were tensions between the policies of the Labour-led Executive and the function of the Parliament as conceived by the Convention, and indeed by the more open structure legislated for by Westminster and further developed by MSPs after 1999, there were also tensions – as might have been expected – with London. Some of the greatest tensions were over foreign policy: McLeish's strong commitment to such a policy (evinced by what was thought to be his les-majesté in meeting George Bush, which infuriated senior UK Labour figures) and his insistence on his own position as that of 'leader of my nation' helped to make him short of friends when he came under media pressure. Peter Lynch stresses the helpful distinction between 'paradiplomacy', when a devolved or federal region/country uses foreign policy initiatives to enhance its global status (and perhaps buy off nationalism) and 'protodiplomacy' where such initiatives work in the interests of nationalism. The trouble with Holyrood's relationship to Westminster was that the British Government did not reliably seem able to distinguish the two.

The concordats governing Holyrood's relationship to Westminster left London with the last word, and moreover seemed to work rather informally and inexactly in practice. The much-vaunted 'Council of the Isles' which was to bring the devolved administrations together seemed to achieve little of note and the 'Joint Ministerial Committees . . . that were supposed to form a forum for ministers to share ideas and resolve disputes . . . hardly ever met': there was a distinct lack of preparation for the situation which would obtain when different parties governed in Edinburgh and London. The Scottish government established an office in Brussels, Scotland House, in 1999, and no doubt expected to have a significant say in formulating the UK line within the EU, especially where – as in fishing, where the country has 70 per cent of the UK fleet and 90 per cent of its fish farming – Scotland's role was out of all proportion to its population size. Scotland was always meant to have a minister included in EU fishing discussions, but it was awkward – as Michael Keating points out – if he/she had to keep details of UK negotiating strategy confidential from Scottish government colleagues, as sometimes happened. In fact, Whitehall frequently 'forgot' to inform the Executive of its discussions and decisions, sought to control Scottish access to EU Commissioners through the Foreign Office, and ignored Executive views on the whisky industry and fishing. Scottish ministers were often excluded from direct discussions, while officials were 'often asked to attend a meeting in London when it is too late to travel'. Little had changed in London since the 1970s, and the reservations over the Kilbrandon Report in a civil service often ignorant of Scottish difference: Whitehall 'appeared to be under the impression that their policy views and objectives were representative of the entire UK, rather than simply England'. In order to counter this impression, the McConnell administration sought to appear to take on Westminster over relatively small points of policy (though vital to those concerned), such as the exact details of the treatment of asylum seekers (the Home Office's substantive policy, though unpopular with many in Scotland, was not challenged) and the extension of 'any business tax concessions' offered to Northern Ireland to Scotland. In addition, the Executive sought through its relations with Malawi and through the Fresh Talent initiative and the Homecoming project to create a rhetoric, and perhaps even a slender reality, of a semi-autonomous Scottish foreign policy. On nuclear power, Trident and the alleged use of Prestwick Airport for US rendition flights the Scottish government was, however, silent in the face of Westminster, despite objections from Scottish civil society.[11]

The SNP's lacklustre performance in 2003, combined with a weak result in the 2004 European elections, led to John Swinney standing down as leader. The initial contest that resulted was disrupted when Alex Salmond, who had left Holyrood for Westminster, announced he would stand. Given his talents and the general feeling that the SNP had gone downhill since he left, he won easily, and a rather uneasy situation resulted, where Nicola Sturgeon led the party at Holyrood as the deputy for the 'king over the water' in London. Holyrood's second term in general witnessed a continuing decline in the number of ex-Westminster MPs and ministers, and the emergence of a more autonomous national politics in Scotland. In 2005 Jim Wallace, the first Liberal to hold peacetime ministerial office since the days of Lloyd George, stepped down to be replaced by Nicol Stephen, an MSP with a background in local politics in the north-east.

Even before the Parliament had been built, the visitors' gallery at the Mound between 1999 and 2004 had been well-frequented, and the BBC – at least on occasion – obtained surprisingly large viewing figures for *Holyrood Live*, up to 46,000 when First Minister's Questions had an afternoon slot. In the first six months after the Holyrood parliament opened in 2004, it received 250,000 visitors, a figure which rose to a million over the first three years of its operation. Concern over its operation and costs was to an extent quieted by the not unexpectedly inconclusive Fraser

Inquiry ('there was no single villain of the piece') and by the very fact of the Parliament's existence: the money had been spent, the building was built. Undoubtedly controversial, it was still sufficiently varied and exciting as an architectural departure to avoid widespread condemnation. Moreover, Holyrood was clearly a major visitor attraction, and 'feedback is around nine parts positive to one negative, particularly after people see inside the building'. After having been a major issue in the 2003 election, the 'critical acclaim' accorded to Holyrood has had a significant impact on perception: the Parliament has won 'eight major' architectural awards, including the 2005 Stirling prize.[12]

The second term of the Parliament saw – as indicated above – a slower pace of change: there were nonetheless some significant developments. The Further Education and Higher Education Act of 2005 built on the much more collaborative climate evident in Scottish HE and the strong articulation between HE and FE visible in the major cities, to set up a single Scottish Funding Council covering both sectors. The Planning Act of 2006 'greatly streamlined' the system and gave local residents 'more say' about new developments, though at the cost of denying them the right to object to major projects; minor domestic alterations were taken out of the planning process. The Gaelic Language Act (2005) has – as outlined in Chapter Four – arguably begun to have a significant effect on the status of Gaelic in Scotland, while the Transport Act (2005) began the process of creating a national transport policy, whose further development included the possible provision of direct rail access to Edinburgh and Glasgow airports. Rail network management became an additional power devolved from Westminster to Holyrood; the Skye Bridge Tolls were lifted in 2004, and the lineaments of the first fully integrated Scottish national transport policy began to emerge. The move in energy policy towards the use of renewables was driven from Westminster in many respects, but because of Scotland's major natural advantages in renewable energy – arguably greater than those of any other country in Europe – the Scottish government was able to set more ambitious targets and to develop an approach strongly inflected towards Scottish needs and concerns. Scotland's 2020 renewable electricity target was twice the UK's as a whole, and Scotland advanced more quickly to meet it. By

2007 over 1,000 MW of generation from onshore wind alone was occurring or in prospect, with 1200 MW of generation expected by the end of the year. It was estimated that the Executive's renewables target for electricity generation of 18 per cent by 2010 would be met in 2007, while the 40 per cent 2020 target was on course for 2015. Figures as high as 46 per cent were predicted for 2020, putting pressure on what some called 'the nuclear obsession gripping Whitehall'. After the 2007 elections, one of the first acts of the new government was to publicly state that whatever Westminster decided in terms of energy policy, no new nuclear power stations would be built in Scotland. On this, the SNP had Liberal and Green support, while even Labour was divided.[13]

In constitutional matters, the Executive was fairly radical, and the Liberal Democrats in coalition once again successfully pressed home a major change which ran against Labour's own interests by changing the election system for local authority elections. In 2007 the introduction of proportional representation (by Single Transferable Vote, not the Additional Member system used at Holyrood) for council elections was a critical reform which promised in the medium term to totally alter the political and patronage networks of town houses across Scotland. In the 2007 council elections, Labour retained outright control of Glasgow and North Lanarkshire alone, while the SNP doubled their seats to become the largest party across the country. Nationalists and Liberals occupied strong positions in Scotland's other three major cities, and more representative local agreements began to be negotiated almost at once, with Liberal-SNP coalitions emerging in Aberdeen and Edinburgh, as well as SNP-led or power-sharing administrations in previously core Labour areas such as East Lothian, West Dunbartonshire, Fife and Renfrewshire. Both major Highland councils gained SNP-led coalitions, and it was very clear that a new municipal politics had arrived overnight in Scotland. In a shrewd, if somewhat overbold, gesture to youth politics and the cult of the new, the SNP had an eighteen-year-old councillor nominated to be deputy Lord Provost of Aberdeen.[14]

Despite continuing rumblings among the press and some of the population about the Parliament's efficiency and the expenses claims of its members, the antipathy shown to it by many in the media declined after the Parliament building was completed. In 1999–2003,

some on the losing side in 1997 seem to have wished to create insta-
bility in the wistful hope that a Parliament established by popular
mandate might yet be withdrawn, abolished, or at least rendered an
object of such contempt that it could be bypassed. As year succeeded
year, this became evidently more and more unrealistic, and after
Holyrood opened in 2004, one of the major engines of complaint was
gone: moreover, the Executive moved more cautiously and made fewer
mistakes under Jack McConnell, who, though he might lag behind
Henry McLeish or Donald Dewar as a visionary, was usually better than
either of them at being a manager, and managing expectation in particular, making politics, in Ian Bell's words, 'low-grade, predictable,
almost reassuring', which was certainly the preferred option of a
strongly unionist media. McConnell also quieted internal opposition
by aligning himself more closely with Labour at Westminster than
Dewar or McLeish had done. In the short term this worked: in the
longer term it diluted the significance of his office, and rendered him
vulnerable to any downturn in support for the Labour Government.
McConnell did much to stabilize Holyrood in 2001–7, by managing
Scotland in the old style rather than confronting Westminster as often
happens in devolved or federal systems (for example, in Germany and
Spain). At least some of the ethos of his administration won support
and consent from across the political spectrum, which saw the need to
end the damaging stories about expenses and housing allowances once
and for all. In an attempt to spike any remaining concerns over these
issues, the retiring Presiding Officer, George Reid, suggested in March
2007 that 'we need a fairly radical look at the whole structure of
allowance', including the possibility of 'external evaluation' after the
May elections. Unfortunately, the aftermath of the 2007 election saw
foot-dragging from MSPs on the need for a truly independent review,
though it was evident that only this would clear the air.[15]
    As these elections approached, the constitutional faultline opened
up yet again in Scottish politics. In the late 1990s Catalonia had been a
favourite comparator for Scotland among Labour politicians and
sympathizers: it was, of course, a Catalan architect who had obtained
the Holyrood commission. Catalonia was held up as an example
because it was seen as a prosperous and successful autonomous region

of Spain with a long-lasting national tradition of its own. Moreover, it was widely thought that Catalan nationalism had been effectively disabled by the extension of regional autonomy in Spain. In contrast to Catalonia, however, where 74 per cent voted for a new and more powerful constitution in 2006, the demand for increased powers for Holyrood was repressed by the Labour Party, possibly to their electoral cost. Some senior figures in business, wooed by more business-friendly policies from the SNP and more impressed by the private sector experience of some of its leading figures, began to come out and support independence, while many more were silent, or far less definitive in their opposition than would once have been the case. Brian Souter of Stagecoach gave the Nationalists a large donation amounting to up to half a million pounds, while Sir Tom Farmer, the founder of Kwik-Fit, gave £100,000. The conflict, though, was not simply between Labour and the Nationalists, although the press, still used to a first past the post system, chose to portray it as such. Whichever of these parties 'won' would need to form a coalition to gain a majority, and although there was disappointment with the 1999–2007 coalition's performance in many quarters (a reason why the Tories went into the 2007 election refusing to consider a coalition, and why Labour – if they were strong enough – hinted that they might prefer to govern alone), such disappointment saw little sign of being turned into votes. In 1999 Labour and the SNP had captured 64 per cent of the vote between them; in 2003, 58 per cent. The additional member system had led to a growth in minor parties, and though due to inter-nal strife the Scottish Socialists had been weakened, new Christian parties such as the Scottish Christian Party and Christian People's Alliance emerged in 2007 onto an electoral stage which had already shown that not only minor parties but also independents (Dennis Canavan, Margo MacDonald) could be elected through the additional member lists. On this occasion, they were to be disappointed.

The 2007 elections were very hard-fought, and the battle between Labour and a resurgent SNP eclipsed the other campaigns, and in the end drove the minority parties (of whom there were an unprecedented number) and independents down to three seats: two Greens and Margo MacDonald, who argued for the transfer of eleven new powers to the Parliament. Labour's campaign was heavily influenced by Westminster, and focused on scaremongering about the Nationalists. The broadsheet media viewed this as counterproductive and, in a shift not seen since the 1970s, *The Scotsman, Scotland on Sunday, Sunday Times Scotland* and the *Sunday Herald* all came out in favour of an SNP-led coalition in the final week of the campaign. It was, however, by no means certain that Labour's negative campaigning lacked effectiveness in its core areas. *The Sun* surpassed itself by carrying the SNP's iconic thistle in the shape of a noose on the front page on polling day, and in its west of Scotland heartlands the Labour Party largely held off the Nationalists, losing only Glasgow Govan and Cunninghame North to the SNP, who failed to take seats where they had been only a few hundred votes behind. Elsewhere in Scotland, it was a somewhat different story, with the Nationalists winning heavily enough to be the largest party, with a historic 47 seats to Labour's 46. Labour won 28 out of 33 first past the post seats in Glasgow and west central Scotland including the Ayrshire and South Lanarkshire seats, nine out of 40 elsewhere. The Nationalists had four in Labour's heartlands, seventeen elsewhere, but won heavily on the list seats. Although it was pointed out that the SNP did not win a single constituency seat in the south, where they failed to oust the Tories in the western borders or the Liberals in the east, there were clearer signs of split voting in this region than anywhere else, with an incredible 52 per cent voting SNP on the lists, with the Conservatives at 10 per cent the next largest party. In the eight regions, the SNP were top of the lists in five, with an average vote of 33 per cent across lists and constituencies: in the councils, their vote was slightly lower. Labour gained an overall 32 per cent nationally, the Tories 16 per cent and the Liberal Democrats 14 per cent.[16] Although the margin of victory in the quest for a plurality of seats was slim, the SNP were clearly the more national party: without greater Glasgow Labour would have been a long way behind. In the early hours of 4 May, Alex Salmond made a speech which claimed that a 'wind of change' was blowing, a clear reference to Macmillan's decolonization rhetoric of 50 years before.

The election itself was seriously marred by the rejection of an unprecedented 142,000 votes (not 142,000 ballots, for some had one vote counted as spoilt, some another). Despite a wish to suggest that this was because a new council voting system had been introduced at the same time, early indications were that with only 2 per cent of council ballots spoilt, the high rejection rate had more to do with placing both votes for the Scottish Parliament (constituency and list) on the same paper rather than on different papers as previously. Machine scanning of the votes compounded the problem, as ballot papers had to be submitted unfolded, while they had always had to be folded under the old system. The convenience of the electoral authorities and the demand for quick results – the returning officers recommended not starting the count until the next morning – appeared to have been preferred to the interests of the electorate. Although it was not clear that discounted ballots would have influenced any of the results, when their total exceeded that of a winning majority some doubt could inevitably be cast on the outcome. Turnout was up marginally to around 51 per cent, but was in effect probably around 55 per cent given the unprecedented numbers of rejected ballots.

At first sight, the result was a mandate, albeit a narrow one in a pluralistic system, for the SNP. However, it is important to examine the details of the vote more closely. It is very likely that part of the SNP's vote in 2007 came from other pro-independence parties, with the Scottish Socialists disappearing, and the Greens down from seven to two seats. In 2003 the vote for pro-independence parties averaged 38 per cent on the lists (the Greens, for example, did not usually stand in constituencies); in 2007 it was 37 per cent in Glasgow, 37 per cent in Central, 41 per cent in Highlands and Islands, 36 per cent in the Lothians, 34 per cent in West of Scotland, 61 per cent (significantly, as we have seen, due to tactical voting) in the south, 45 per cent in the north-east and 39 per cent in Mid Scotland and Fife: in much of the country broadly in line with the 2003 figure, or at least only a little higher. Nonetheless, it was not the case, as the *Financial Times* argued, that 'two-thirds of voters still back the Union': if that might be true in an independence referendum, it was not so at the polls in 2007.[17]

Opinion polling certainly did indicate that there was strong support for increased powers for the Parliament, if not independence, and discussions began before the election with a view to setting up 'a new

Constitutional Convention'. Such development were seen as forming the basis for the next stage of devolution. The reality, however, of the parties' election manifestoes was that the SNP wanted a referendum on independence and the Liberal Democrats (who lost one seat to the Tories, gained one from Labour and lost two to the SNP) refused to discuss any arrangement with them in the aftermath of the election unless this manifesto commitment was abandoned as a precondition to any talks. The SNP were quite prepared to include the alternative of more powers on the ballot paper – and to make further concessions in negotiation – but the Liberals were intransigent. Both parties faced the possibility of being accused of reneging on a core part of their campaign if they backed down, so politically their stance was understandable, but opinion in Scotland – both in the newspapers and from the electorate – appeared to favour a coalition. Ironically, as the parties stalemated at Holyrood, across the country alliances were being forged on councils which transcended old party boundaries in the interests of excluding Labour, not the SNP, from office, in East Ayrshire in a tacit alliance (formal coalitions with the Tories are banned by the SNP) with the Conservative Party.[18]

At Holyrood, the sad fact was that while the electorate had delivered a result which indicated a desire for a more patriotic parliament that stood up for Scotland and sought extra powers, the only options on offer were independence or no change. It was the SNP which had argued that independence was a process, not an event: but the referendum commitment imprisoned the party in the logic of events, and this meant that unionists found it hard to share in any process of development for a Scottish parliament over which the shadow of imminent separation hung. It was of course not likely to be in the SNP's interest to hold a referendum on independence in the near future, as many commentators pointed out: but once again the Nationalists were impaled on the horns of the MacCormick dilemma of 60 years before: co-operate and lose your identity or stand up for independence and be opposed by everyone. The latter strategy had increased the level of nationalism in the other parties since the 1960s, but by no means enough to allow for agreeing a referendum on independence by 2010. An SNP alliance with the Liberal Democrats would reconfigure Scottish politics: but both of them were unwilling – or unable – to reconfigure it at the expense of their party interest, whatever the general verdict of the election might indicate. Instead, the SNP reached a provisional and limited agreement with the Greens, and prepared to enter on a minority administration where they would be under pressure to act and would have little power to do so. The potential for the 'new politics' the Parliament had promised seemed to have arrived at last, but it was doubtful if it would end in anything else but a series of ambushes on a minority SNP administration, leading to further disappointment among the electorate with the Parliament's achievements. This could, perhaps, only be avoided by a mixture of crossbench goodwill and Alex Salmond's political skills, which are on the whole of a higher order than those of any of his predecessors as First Minister. Certainly his election took British politics somewhat by surprise, and in taking the initiative he gained important ground, though whether his promise of consensus politics combined with a desire to implement an SNP programme will have staying power is another matter. Salmond certainly moved quickly on slimmed-down government, announcing a cabinet team of six ministers and ten deputies: Health, Education, Justice, Finance and Rural Affairs and the Environment were to be the five major portfolios, with the First Minister supported by deputies for parliamentary business, and – significantly – Europe, External Affairs, and Culture.[19] Swift action on populist measures such as abolishing bridge tolls and the graduate endowment payment followed, while there were also clear signs of pressure from Salmond's administration on the British Government to allow Scotland to take the lead in EU Fisheries negotiations.

The Parliament has certainly been an engine of change in Scotland in terms of the legislation it has introduced. But has it changed Scottish society since 1999? Issues such as sectarianism and the longstanding concern with alleged Scottish defeatism, 'the 'pessimistic thesis on modern Scottish society', have been discussed as never before in Scotland: arguably at the very time when the latter was actually going into decline. At first, the raising of these issues reinforced an atmosphere of negativity, but gradually more and more of those involved in the discussion came to realize that the frankness of the debate, the strength of grassroots activity and the pace of change were new and largely positive developments. There was a tangibly greater demand after 1999 for solutions to Scotland's problems, such as the severe deprivation, child poverty and poor health affecting many in the major urban areas, Glasgow above all. The level of demand for action rose: whether or not change occurred or was effective, it had support. Scottish society seemed to have a higher opinion of itself, its capabilities, what it could do and what needed to be done. At the same time its differences from England came more clearly to the surface in the context of its own national democratic institutions: for example, the greater importance of religion in Scotland than in English politics. In 2007, the two overtly Christian political parties, the Scottish Christian Party and the Christian Peoples' Alliance, gained 3 per cent on the Glasgow list between them, more than double the Scottish Socialist vote, 4 per cent in Central and the Highlands, 2.5 per cent in West of Scotland, 2 per cent in the South, 1 per cent in the North-East, Mid Scotland and Fife and the Lothians.[20]

Scottish and English domestic societies are steadily diverging on a range of issues, and the experience of living in the two countries is becoming increasingly different. The sense of renewal and possibility in Scottish life, more evident in the second term of the Parliament than in its first, opened up a range of options which themselves sometimes operated in tension with the traditional conservatism and local autonomies of Scottish society. Nevertheless, something was changing, and perhaps Scotland's greatest poet was a symbol of that change, just as his words had opened the Scottish Parliament in 1999. In 1996, on the 200th anniversary of Burns's death, three local councils in Ayrshire squabbled unproductively on how to celebrate it, there was little change in the tourism profile, and Burns's birthplace museum continued to deteriorate into a state of increasingly shabby dampness. In 2009, on the 250th anniversary of the poet's birth, a major national and international effort is being made by central government to use Burns as a figure of global as well as Scottish significance, making of him a cultural portal for the further development of the tourist industry in Scotland and a primary route of communication between the country and its diaspora. These developments, together with the renewal and redevelopment of the Burns birthplace museum, are being promoted by Scotland's government. It is a notable change. There is a clear sense of increasing desire to bring Scotland forward in the global marketplace as an independent brand: in food, tourism, sport, trade and finance among other areas. The Parliament's own self-consciously modern policies and processes have themselves been extensively scrutinized and complimented internationally.[21]

It is nonetheless important not to give too over-optimistic an assessment. The picture remains mixed, with many still having a low opinion of their country's possibility and potential, sometimes linked to a low opinion of themselves. In 2003, 26 per cent of eleven- to sixteen-year-olds and 29 per cent of seventeen- to 25-year-olds 'agreed that they would leave Scotland if they had the chance'; in 2005 these figures were 19 per cent and 28 per cent respectively: a drop, but still a worryingly high figure. Around 40 per cent across both age groups in 2005 thought that the Scottish Parliament had made at least a fair amount of difference to their lives, but 30 per cent thought it had made none or hardly any. It is possible that the London domination of the electronic media, so much more important than newspapers for this age group, has had a part to play here: an impression reinforced by the fact that a 'significantly' higher proportion of Scottish youth 'say that they know a fair amount or a great deal about what the Westminster parliament does' compared with their knowledge of Holyrood. In this context, it is interesting to note that almost two-thirds of fourteen- to 25-year-olds backed independence in a Scottish Youth Parliament poll in 2007.[22]

And what of Westminster in the governance of Scotland after devolution? In 1999, it was widely expected that the office of Secretary of State for Scotland would wither on the vine, since its surviving roles were to ensure 'that Scottish legislation did not conflict with Westminster's reserved powers' and to provide a voice for Scottish interests in Cabinet. It has, however, proved stubbornly resistant to final disappearance. The first holders of this post were John Reid (1999–2001) and Helen Liddell (2001–3). They appeared only occasionally to intervene in the Executive's business. Liddell was the last to try, though it was her positive intervention which helped to keep

Holyrood's constituency seats at 73, when the number of Westminster constituencies declined to 59: it had been presumed that Holyrood would follow suit. In 2003 the post appeared to be on the point of being abolished, before returning in part-time form as an adjunct of the Department of Transport, and as such held by Alistair Darling (2003-6) and Douglas Alexander (2006-7), whose Scotland Office had responsibility for the 2007 elections. This combined portfolio rather implied that neither post was of Cabinet rank on its own, an implication even more disturbingly present in the first Brown Cabinet, when Des Browne combined the Scottish Secretaryship with the Defence portfolio, at a time when the UK was at war in both Afghanistan and Iraq. In every way the position of the Scottish Secretary and his or her now rather threadbare Scotland Office looks redundant, and it would surely be better to have the First Minister or a Secretary of State for the Home Nations and Constitution present a view on reserved business where this is necessary. This is especially true because of the remaining tensions between the positions of First Minister and Scottish Secretary. When there can be no competition over who runs Scotland, the other part of the portfolio can act as its surrogate: of such a kind perhaps was the 2006 turf war over which bits of transport policy were Holyrood's and which Westminster's concern. Meanwhile, even the retention of the Scottish Secretaryship pending further steps in the revision of the UK constitution seems superfluous with the end of English regional devolution and the effective impasse over the nature of reform of the House of Lords. John Reid's proposed 2007 Home Office reforms saw the Department of Constitutional Affairs (which includes the Scotland Office) being subsumed under the Justice Ministry, rendering Scotland a third-tier concern of the subdivided Home Office. An SNP victory at Holyrood made this seem a rather premature decision: when different parties are in power in the different parliaments, a degree of greater constitutional formality will have to be developed in negotiating their differences, and the visit north of Jack Straw, Secretary of State for Justice and Lord Chancellor, to meet Alex Salmond in Edinburgh in July 2007 hardly appeared to be an indication that Scotland was in reality a third-tier issue. Extensive confusion remains in the treatment of constitutional affairs at

Westminster. While the Labour Government insists that in Scotland devolution is 'an event rather than a process', and is a final settlement, in Wales, Labour in coalition with Plaid Cymru is committed to campaigning for extended powers. In Scotland, fifteen new powers have been devolved since 1999, most recently (2007) the right of the Scottish Drug Enforcement Agency to carry out overseas surveillance on the authority of the Scottish government alone. Labour at Westminster was clearly fighting on three fronts in 2007: against the Tories who wanted English votes for English laws, against nationalism in all the devolved administrations, and even against their own MPs, who were beginning to complain of 'unfairness that Scots received more public money'.[23]

The popular response in England to devolution has been similarly mixed. Although earlier research indicated that English people were relaxed about devolution, since 2005, attitudes towards Scotland have certainly become more inflamed. The impact of Scottish Labour MPs in securing legislation affecting England or England and Wales only is a subject of growing resentment in the political context which followed the 2005 General Election, when Labour's popularity in England was clearly markedly reduced from 2001. Policy issues arising from Scottish legislation on nursing care and tuition fees are also an issue, and the fact that the Scottish Medicines Consortium (SMC) can – and does – approve drugs not approved by the National Institute for Clinical Excellence (NICE) is a sensitive point in the health service, where – as in education – Scottish facilities are often seen as the gift of English taxpayers.[24] Were it widely publicized, the fact that 'devolution halved' the workload of Scottish MPs would also be a cause of resentment. Even the reduction in Scottish parliamentary representation at Westminster from 72 to 59 was not enough to compensate for Scotland's over-representation in many eyes. Labour would have retained its overall majority without Scotland in 2005: but despite this there was a widespread view in England – where the Conservative Party had narrowly prevailed in the popular vote – that Scottish votes were keeping Labour in power. Slowly demand for an English Parliament began to grow, and the policy of excluding Scottish MPs from voting on English domestic matters (on which Labour's Frank

Field had advanced an unsuccessful Private Member's Bill in 2001) became Conservative Party policy. A *Daily Telegraph* poll in January 2007 suggested that 62 per cent in England wanted Scots MPs 'not to be able to vote on English bills', while 58 per cent supported an English Parliament. Senior Tory figures such as Boris Johnson argued that it would be a 'constitutional outrage' for a member sitting for a Scottish constituency to lead the UK, while Michael Portillo and former Scottish Office minister Allan Stewart were reported as supporting Scottish independence. For an analysis of the West Lothian Question in detail, see Chapter Two.[25]

Criticism of Scotland as a 'subsidy culture', a longstanding rumbling grumble in English politics since the 1980s, was given new force in the context of these constitutional anxieties, despite much of the logic of it having been undermined even before the oil boom by Gavin McCrone, who pointed out that it needed to be proved that public expenditure could be better deployed elsewhere (if spent in the south, an 'unsustainable boom' was a resultant risk).[26] Within Scotland, attacks on the country as a 'subsidy culture' began to be a source of public debate in the 1990s, not only in the somewhat sterile exchanges between Labour and the SNP, but also in a more open critique than was found elsewhere in the UK of the appropriation of non-identifiable government expenditure by London under the guise of national assets or initiatives. The Jubilee Line, the new British Library and of course the Dome all received criticism along these lines, while it was pointed out that the 2012 London Olympics would in fact swallow up a year's North Sea oil revenues in order to provide long-term benefits to London alone. This criticism was all the more inflamed by pressure on the autonomy of Scottish sport under the guise of creating a common effort for the Olympics, and by the apparent bullying – alas, probably the right word – of the Scottish football authorities to agree to a Great Britain team: a move made all the more offensive by recognition that this was not because some great Scottish player was required who would be a major asset, but simply to draw all British sport – or as much of it as possible – under the metropolitan control of the Olympics programme. Scottish scepticism of the 'subsidy culture' figures was no doubt reinforced by the disclosure that Labour ministers had suppressed the real value of Scottish oil in the 1970s in order to head off the SNP, and when a new generation of Labour ministers employed the 'subsidy culture' argument ahead of the 2007 Scottish election it seemed to no longer carry the resonance it once did. Indeed, the SNP attacked Scotland's relative economic decline, demanded why Labour were celebrating it as an electoral strategy, and promised to improve the Scottish growth rate to a rather ambitious – not to say unlikely – 4 per cent.[27]

Scotland has changed very markedly since 1960. The old Presbyterian Unionism of bygone generations has faded; the Empire and the domestic control of Scottish institutions which alike supported that Union at home and abroad has also faded. Devolution brought back some of that control to Scotland: in doing so through the mechanism of a national parliament, it gave the country more self-confidence and the ability to voice it. In 2007 the election issue was – as so often in the years since 1970 – the Union. In its aftermath, it is possible that nothing will be the same again. The SNP's victory means that competent performance in government will drain the nationalist bogeyman of the tabloids of any realistic threat, especially since independence is highly unlikely to be the outcome of a first term of Nationalist rule. Meanwhile, the new proportionally elected councils will erode Labour's patronage base. Will Scotland become independent? That probably depends on England, and whether there is the political will, not simply to reassert tired and outmoded concepts of Britishness, ineluctably tied to English manners, society, politics and culture, but to develop a multi-centred polity in these United Kingdoms. The exclusion of Scottish MPs from voting rights at Westminster will do nothing for the Union: but it is a real possibility, which would dismantle at a stroke the career structure of Scottish Labour. On the other hand, the diverse and inclusive Britishness promised by Labour will need to be diverse in point of political power, not merely colour and custom. It is arguable that this is less well understood in London than almost anywhere else: in the third of a century between the Kilbrandon Report and the present day, metropolitan attitudes have barely changed, while Scottish, Welsh and Northern Irish politics and culture have all shifted radically in their different ways. A loosely federated UK with clearly distinct locales for control of politics, culture and society and their representation through the media could be the most stable solution the Union can now enjoy: indeed, Ireland would probably still be in the UK had this begun to happen a century earlier. However, serious doubts must remain that this will be recognized by Westminster in time, or that English politics can change enough to accommodate a multinational polity. As this book was being prepared for press, the row over the British Government's failure to consult its Scottish counterpart over the Memorandum of Understanding with Libya which implied the transfer of the Lockerbie bomber, convicted under Scots law, from a Scottish gaol, and the suggested recrudescence of the old Empire Day as a national day for 'Britain', alike suggested that British government continues to act as if devolution had never happened. Critical change is necessary. While that remains doubtful, I trust that no one who has read this book to the end doubts the need to understand Scotland's separate history, as well as the things it shares with our wider world.

References

Introduction: Why Scotland?

1 See Tom Johnston's role as 'Scottish Regional Commissioner' in 1939 in Richard J. Finlay, *Independent and Free: Scottish Politics and the Origins of the Scottish National Party 1918–1945* (Edinburgh, 1994), p. 208.
2 David Stenhouse, *On the Make: How the Scots took over London* (Edinburgh and London, 2004), p. 16.
3 Kevin Schofield, 'Salmond to press Brown to hand over lead role in EU fish talks', *The Herald* (13 July 2007), p. 1.
4 James Mitchell, 'Contemporary Unionism', in *Unionist Scotland 1800–1997*, ed. Catriona MacDonald (Edinburgh, 1998), pp. 117–39 (pp. 122–3).
5 Lindsay Paterson, *The Autonomy of Modern Scotland* (Edinburgh, 1994), pp. 85, 99.
6 Murray Pittock, *A New History of Scotland* (Stroud, 2003), pp. 266–7, 290–2; Christopher Harvie, *No Gods and Precious Few Heroes: Scotland 1914–80* (London, 1981), pp. i, vii, viii, 17, 22, 24, 78.
7 Richard Finlay, 'Unionism and the Dependency Culture', in MacDonald, *Unionist Scotland*, pp. 100–16 (p. 105); James Mitchell, *Strategies for Self-Government: The Campaigns for a Scottish Parliament* (Edinburgh, 1996), p. 309; James G. Kellas, *The Scottish Political System* (1973; Cambridge, 1992), p. 262.
8 Murray Pittock, *Scottish Nationality* (Basingstoke, 2001), pp. 112–13; William L. Miller, *The End of British Politics?* (Oxford, 1981), p. 10.
9 Joyce M. Ellis, *The Georgian Town 1680–1840* (Basingstoke, 2001), pp. 148–51.
10 Miller, *End of British Politics?*, pp. 2, 4, 25; Pittock, *New History*, p. 268; Vernon Bogdanor, *Devolution in the United Kingdom* (Oxford, 1999), p. 112.
11 Richard J. Finlay, *Modern Scotland 1914–2000* (London, 2004), pp. 258–61; Pittock, *New History*, pp. 278, 292.
12 This argument on British policy during the Famine is cogently put in Cecil Woodham-Smith, *The Great Hunger: Ireland 1845–1849* (1962; London, 1991). With regard to outrage at Carson's reward of a Cabinet place for his threatened rebellion, see Donal Nevin, *James Connolly* (2005; Dublin, 2006), p. 593.
13 Montserrat Guibernau, *Nations without States: Political Communities in a Global Age* (1999; Cambridge, 2005), pp. 39–41; Paterson, *Autonomy*, pp. 91–2, 98.
14 Guibernau, *Nations without States*, pp. 39, 106.

15 Ibid., pp. 51, 57.
16 Angela Morris and Graeme Morton, *Locality, Community and Nation* (London, 1998), p. 80.
17 Pittock, *New History*, pp. 22, 24, 52–3, 122.

Chapter 1: Contacts and Corporatism: Scotland Since 1945

1 Keith Webb, *The Growth of Nationalism in Scotland* (Glasgow, 1977), p. 63; James G. Kellas, *The Scottish Political System*, 4th edn (1973; Cambridge, 1992), p. 106.
2 Jeremy Black, *The Making of Modern Britain* (Stroud 2001), p. 181 reproduces this poster.
3 Kellas, *Political System*, p. 2.
4 Black, *Modern Britain*, p. 199.
5 Jeremy Peat and Stephen Boyle, *An Illustrated Guide to the Scottish Economy* (London, 1999), p. 83; Christopher Harvie, *No Gods and Precious Few Heroes: Scotland 1914–1980* (London, 1981), pp. 57, 62.
6 Richard Saville, 'The Industrial Background to the Post-War Scottish Economy', in *The Economic Development of Modern Scotland 1950–1980*, ed. Saville (Edinburgh, 1985), pp. 1–46 (pp. 1, 2, 12, 24–5); Gavin McCrone and J. N. Randall, 'The Scottish Development Agency', in Saville, *Economic Development*, pp. 233–44 (pp. 233, 234, 242, 243); J. N. Randall, 'New Towns and New Industries' in Saville, *Economic Development*, pp. 245–69 (pp. 246, 268); Richard J. Finlay, *Modern Scotland 1914–2000* (London, 2004), pp. 244–5; Gavin McCrone, *Scotland's Future: The Economics of Nationalism* (Oxford, 1969), p. 38.
7 Saville, *Economic Development*, p. 34; Neil Buxton, 'The Scottish Economy, 1945–79: Performance, Structure and Problems', in Saville, *Economic Development*, pp. 47–78 (pp. 49, 69); Laurie Hunter, 'The Scottish Labour Market' in Saville, *Economic Development*, pp. 163–82 (p. 172); David McCrone, *Understanding Scotland: The Sociology of a Stateless Nation* (London, 1992), p. 122; John Foster, 'The Twentieth Century, 1914–1979', in *The New Penguin History of Scotland*, eds R. A. Houston and W.W.J. Knox (London, 2001), pp. 417–93 (p. 468); Harvie, *No Gods and Precious Few Heroes*, pp. 63, 143, 145.
8 Harvie, *No Gods and Precious Few Heroes*, 1; Buxton in *Economic Development*, pp. 51–3, 70, 73, 76.
9 Peter L. Payne, 'The Decline of the Scottish Heavy Industries, 1945–1983', in Saville, *Economic Development*, pp. 79–113 (pp. 79–83); Peat and Boyle, *Scottish Economy*, p. 55; Murray Pittock, *A New History of Scotland* (Stroud, 2003), p. 295.
10 Maxwell Gaskin, 'The Scottish Financial Sector, 1950–1980' in Saville, *Economic Development*, pp. 114–40 (pp. 114, 116, 118, 129).
11 Gaskin, 'The Scottish Financial Sector', pp. 131, 133–4.
12 Tom Nairn, *After Britain* (London, 2000), p. 241.
13 Jo Skailes, 'Sir Tom is Scotland's first homegrown billionaire', *The Herald* (20 April 2007), p. 10.
14 Peat and Boyle, *Scottish Economy*, pp. 57, 77; Ian Fraser, 'Big salaries draw accountants back to the old country', *The Herald* (12 February 2007), p. 28; 'Glasburgh would be miles better', *Sunday Herald* (11 February 2007), pp. 16–17.
15 Pittock, *New History*, pp. 297–8; Peat and Boyle, *Scottish Economy*, p. 117.
16 Finlay, *Modern Scotland*, pp. 253–4; Andrew Gibb and Duncan Maclennan, 'Policy and Process in Scottish Housing, 1950–1980' in Saville, *Economic Development*, pp. 270–91 (pp. 270, 272–3); Peat and Boyle, *Scottish Economy*,

p. 101; Richard Rodger, 'Urbanisation in Twentieth-Century Scotland', in *Scotland in the 20th Century*, eds T. M. Devine and Richard Finlay (1996; Edinburgh, 1997), pp. 122–52 (p. 140).

17 Murray Pittock, *The Invention of Scotland: The Stuart Myth and the Scottish Identity 1638 to the Present* (London, 1991) p. 131; Murray Pittock, *Scottish Nationality* (Basingstoke, 2001), pp. 130–2; *Football League Tables 1889 to the Present*, ed. Jim Mallory (Glasgow and London, 1977); *SkySports Football Yearbook 2006–2007*, eds Glenda and Jack Rollin (London, 2006), pp. 761–3, 769; Natasha Woods, 'Mighty Mouse League', *The Sunday Herald* (4 February 2007), p. 23.

18 'Scottish Daily Mail's price slash sparks rumours', *Sunday Herald* (25 February 2007), p. 10; Pittock, *New History*, p. 298; Kellas, *Scottish Political System*, pp. 198–9; Douglas Fraser, 'Leaders make final push to win over undecided', *The Herald* (3 May 2007), p. 6; I.G.C. Hutchinson, *Scottish Politics in the Twentieth Century* (Basingstoke, 2001), p. 101; Peter Lynch, *Scottish Government and Politics: an Introduction* (Edinburgh, 2001), p. 189; Michael Keating, *The Government of Scotland: Public Policy Making after Devolution* (Edinburgh, 2005), p. 89; Finlay, *Modern Scotland*, p. 371.

19 Steven Vass, '£21M commissions crisis at BBC Scotland', *Sunday Herald Business* (8 July 2007), p. 1; 'A Scottish Broadcasting Corporation: the answer to our media woes?', *Sunday Herald* (8 July 2007), p. 16.

20 Sandy Mullay, *The Edinburgh Encyclopedia* (Edinburgh, 1996), pp. 40–1; 'Television channels "ignoring the outside world"', *The Herald* (12 June 2006), p. 5; Steven Vass, '"Come to Scotland" workshop annoys local companies', *Sunday Herald* (20 August 2006), p. 11; Mediawatch, *Sunday Herald* (30 July 2006), p. 11.

21 Harvie, *No Gods and Precious Few Heroes*, pp. 138, 155; Irene Maver, 'The Catholic Community' in Devine and Finlay, *Scotland in the 20th Century*, pp. 269–84 (p. 281–2); *The Herald* (23 March 1992), p. 4; obituary for Ian Rodger, *The Herald* (12 February 2007), p. 21.

22 Pittock, *Scottish Nationality*, pp. 128, 135; David Ellis, in conversation, 11 May 2007.

23 Kellas, *Scottish Political System*, pp. 106–7.

Chapter 2: Scottish Politics and Identity

1 Andrew Murray Scott and Ian Macleay, *Britain's Secret War: Tartan Terrorism and the Anglo-American State* (Edinburgh, 1990), p. 82; *Scots Independent* IV, pp. 8, 100; James Mitchell, *Strategies for Self-Government: The Campaigns for a Scottish Parliament* (Edinburgh, 1996), pp. 115, 122, 144, 148, 149, 152, 155, 268; Keith Webb, *The Growth of Nationalism in Scotland* (Glasgow, 1977), p. 59; John M. MacCormick, *The Flag in the Wind: The Story of the National Movement in Scotland* (London, 1955), p. 197; Richard J. Finlay, *Independent and Free: Scottish Politics and the Origins of the Scottish National Party 1918–1945* (Edinburgh, 1994), p. 100.

2 MacCormick, *Flag in the Wind*, p. 217.

3 *Scots Independent* (11 November 1967), p. 1.

4 Richard J. Finlay, *Modern Scotland 1914–2000* (London, 2004), p. 321; Christopher Harvie, *Scotland and Nationalism*, 3rd edn (1977; London, 1998), p. 178; *Scots Independent* (27 January 1968; 2 March 1968), pp. 2, 4 (1 June 1968), p. 4; Vernon Bogdanor, *Devolution in the United Kingdom* (Oxford, 1999), p. 133; Mitchell, *Strategies for Self-Government*, p. 315.

5 Bogdanor, *Devolution*, pp. 134, 172–3; Murray Pittock, *Scottish Nationality* (Basingstoke, 2001), p. 122; Arnold Kemp, *The Hollow Drum* (Edinburgh, 1993), p. 118; James Mitchell, 'Evolution and Devolution: Citizenship, Institutions and Public Policy', *Publius* 36:1 (2006), pp. 153–68.

6 I.G.C. Hutchinson, 'Scottish Unionism Between the Two World Wars', in *Unionist Scotland 1800–1997*, ed. Catriona M. M. MacDonald (Edinburgh, 1998), pp. 73–99 (p. 80).

7 James G. Kellas, *The Scottish Political System*, 4th edn (1973; Cambridge, 1992), pp. 140–1, 264; David McCrone, 'We're a' Jock Tamson's Bairns: Social Class in Twentieth-Century Scotland' in *Scotland in the 20th Century*, eds T. M. Devine and Richard Finlay (Edinburgh, 1997 [1996]), pp. 102–21 (p. 119); Michael Keating, *The Government of Scotland: Public Policy Making after Devolution* (Edinburgh, 2005), p. 43. See also for comparison David McCrone, *Understanding Scotland: The Sociology of a Stateless Nation* (London, 1992), pp. 165–6 for voting behaviour at actual elections.

8 Joseph Bradley, *Ethnic and Religious Identity in Modern Scotland* (Aldershot, 1995), p. 148.

9 Christopher Harvie, *No Gods and Precious Few Heroes: Scotland 1914–1980* (London, 1981), p. 165; Donald Bain, 'The Brits, the Tartan Coolies and the Black, Black Oil', *Scots Independent*, Special Edition (Spring 2007), p. 1.

10 John Mercer, *Scotland: The Devolution of Power* (London, 1978), p. 223; Kellas, *Scottish Political System*, pp. 144, 148–50.

11 MacCormick, *Flag in the Wind*, p. 136; Hutchinson, 'Scottish Unionism' in *Unionist Scotland*, ed. MacDonald, p. 80.

12 Harvie, *No Gods and Precious Few Heroes*, p. 148; William L. Miller, *The End of British Politics?* (Oxford, 1981), p. 60; Pittock, *Scottish Nationality*, pp. 118–19; Richard Finlay, 'Unionism and the Dependency Culture', in *Unionist Scotland*, ed. MacDonald, pp. 100–16 (pp. 111, 112, 113).

13 James Mitchell, 'Contemporary Unionism', in *Unionist Scotland*, ed. MacDonald, pp. 117–39 (pp. 122, 136); Mitchell, *Strategies for Self-Government*, pp. 293–9.

14 Bogdanor, *Devolution*, pp. 180–5.

15 Harvie, *No Gods and Precious Few Heroes*, pp. 161–2.

16 *Hansard* 945 (2 March 1978); Mitchell, *Strategies for Self-Government*, pp. 320–1; Bogdanor, *Devolution*, p. 188.

17 Pittock, *Scottish Nationality*, p. 140; Mercer, *Scotland*, p. 238; Harvie, *No Gods and Precious Few Heroes*, p. 158.

18 Mitchell, *Strategies for Self-Government*, pp. 48, 100–01, 321–22; Pittock, *Scottish Nationality*, pp. 123–24, 140; Mercer, *Scotland*, p. 238; Kellas, *Scottish Political System*, pp. 158–9.

19 Scott and Macleay, *Britain's Secret War*, pp. 13, 49–54, 75, 82, 95, 117, 120, 124–5, 127.

20 Robert Maclean, 'A Brief History of Scottish Home Rule', in *A Guide to the Scottish Parliament*, ed. Gerry Hassan (Edinburgh, 1999), pp. 21–30 (p. 28).

21 Pittock, *Scottish Nationality*, p. 126; *The Economist* (6–12 November 1999),'Undoing Britain?' survey, p. 4.

22 *Sunday Herald Election 99* (4 April 1999), p. 11.

23 Andy Myles, 'Scotland's Parliament White Paper', in *A Guide to the Scottish Parliament*, ed. Hassan, pp. 31–5 (p. 32); Andrew Burns, 'The Powers of the Parliament', *A Guide*, pp. 43–8 (p. 43); Colin Mair and Barry McCloud, 'Financial

Arrangements', *A Guide*, pp. 73–80 (p. 75); Peter Lynch, *Scottish Government and Politics: an Introduction* (Edinburgh, 2001), pp. 20–2; Keating, *Government of Scotland*, pp. 20–1, 24, 156; Bogdanor, *Devolution*, p. 203.

24 Christopher Harvie, *No Gods and Precious Few Heroes*, 3rd edn (Edinburgh, 1998); Pittock, *Scottish Nationality*, p. 140.

25 Andy Myles, 'The Scotland Bill and Act', in *A Guide to the Scottish Parliament*, ed. Hassan, pp. 37–41 (p. 39); 'SNP set to be largest party at Holyrood', *The Herald* (6 July 1998), p. 1.

26 'How thistle and sunflower got together', *The Herald* (5 January 2006), p. 6; 'Poll predicts 3-party coalition', *The Herald* (10 January 2007), pp. 1–2.

27 Nicola McEwen, 'The Depoliticisation of National Identity? Territorial Politics after Devolution?', in *Ireland (Ulster) Scotland: Concepts, Contexts, Comparisons*, eds Edna Longley, Eamonn Hughes and Des O'Rawe (Belfast, 2003), pp. 11–27 (pp. 16–18); Angela Morris and Graeme Morton, *Locality, Community and Nation* (London, 1998), p. 98; Kellas, *Scottish Political System*, p. 267. See *Hansard* (23 November 1987) p. 30 for a quotation of the 1976 classic British devolutionary case resting on administrative convenience rather than national feeling.

28 Atsuko Ichijo, *Scottish Nationalism and the Idea of Europe* (London and New York, 2004), p. 145; 'Challenge for Brown as poll shows nationalism riding on crest of a wave', *The Herald* (January 24 2007), p. 4; 'Why Scots still like to think of themselves as British', *The Herald* (July 13 2007), p. 6.

29 *The Economist* (6–12 November 1999),'Undoing Britain?' survey, p. 4; Myles in 'The Scotland Bill and Act', in *A Guide to the Scottish Parliament*, ed. Hassan, p. 41; *The Herald* (10 January 2007), p. 1; 'Scots want more power for Holyrood', *The Herald* (22 September 2006), p. 1.

30 Ichijo, *Idea of Europe*, p. 20.

31 'How Letwin found that a "foreign country" could teach England a lesson', *The Herald* (19 January 2007), p. 7.

32 Bogdanor, *Devolution*, pp. 30–1, 33.

33 'New poll shows Scots support for separate English parliament', *The Herald* (16 January 2007), p. 1.

34 Bogdanor, *Devolution*, p. 230.

Chapter 3: Scotland's Cities: Populations, Cultures and Economies

1 Sandy Mullay, *The Edinburgh Encyclopedia* (Edinburgh, 1996), pp. 186, 231, 345.

2 Mullay, *Edinburgh Encyclopedia*, p. 262; Robin Smith, *The Making of Scotland* (Edinburgh, 2001), pp. 323, 590.

3 Martin Williams, 'Revamped Kelvingrove ousts capital castle', *The Herald* (3 May 2007), p. 3; Mullay, *Edinburgh Encyclopedia*, pp. 20, 31, 108, 338, 340, 345, 346; Smith, *Making of Scotland*, pp. 327–8.

4 Smith, ibid.; Mullay, *Edinburgh Encyclopedia*, p. 163; Jo Skailes, 'Sir Tom is Scotland's first homegrown billionaire', *The Herald* (April 30 2007), p. 10.

5 Gerry Braiden, 'Forging a future from the old ashes', *The Herald* (April 30, 2007), p. 11; 'Forth backs £5.5bn scheme to bring sunshine over Leith', *Sunday Herald Business* (25 March 2007), p. 1.

6 Calum Macdonald, 'Vast campus bid to halt brain drain', *The Herald* (May 8, 2007), p. 13; Mullay, *Edinburgh Encyclopedia*, p. 170.

7 'A tale of two cities', *Glasgow* (April–May 2007), pp. 12–13.

8 Smith, *Making of Scotland*, pp. 388-9, 393.
9 'Celtic face crucial clash . . . with assembly elections', *The Herald* (27 February 2007), p. 3.
10 Richard J. Finlay, *Modern Scotland 1914-2000* (London, 2004), p. 272; Smith, *Making of Scotland*, pp. 403-4.
11 Smith, ibid.; *The Herald* (April 30 2007), p. 11.
12 Duncan Macmillan, *Scottish Art in the Twentieth Century* (Edinburgh, 1994), p. 106; Smith, *Making of Scotland*, p. 405.
13 Smith, *Making of Scotland*, pp. 405-6; *Glasgow* (April-May 2007), p. 8; Gerry Braiden, 'A city ready to rise again', *The Herald* (March 21 2007), p. 11.
14 James G. Kellas, *The Scottish Political System*, 4th edn (1973; Cambridge, 1992), p. 11.
15 Smith, *Making of Scotland*, pp. 408-9.
16 John S. Smith, 'The Growth of the City', in *Aberdeen 1800-2000: A New History*, eds W. Hamish Fraser and Clive H. Lee (East Linton, 2000), pp. 22-46 (p. 25); Richard Perren, 'Survival and Decline: The Economy 1918-1970' in *Aberdeen 1800-2000*, pp. 99-125 (pp. 108-15); Smith, *Making of Scotland*, p. 7.
17 Smith, *Making of Scotland*, pp. 10, 12, 301; www.hesev.org.uk
18 Ibid., pp. 273, 279, 281.
19 Ibid., p. 282.
20 Thomas Mitchell, 'Foreword' to Lorn Macintyre and Peter Adamson, *Dundee: City of Discovery* (St Andrews, 1988), p. 5.
21 Smith, *Making of Scotland*, pp. 118, 861; Craig Mair, *Stirling: the Royal Burgh* (Edinburgh, 1990), p. 235.
22 Norman Newton, *The Life and Times of Inverness* (Edinburgh, 1996), pp. 166, 175; he places the economic growth trajectory as beginning in 1961. Smith, *Making of Scotland*, pp. 492-3.

Chapter 4: Cultural Independence?

1 Paul Scott, *Towards Independence* (Edinburgh, 1991), pp. 74, 154-6; David Christie, 'Theatre chief crowned woman of influence', *The Sunday Herald* (11 March 2007), p. 8; Duncan Macmillan, *Scottish Art in the Twentieth Century* (Edinburgh, 1994), p. 106.
2 Roderick Watson, *The Literature of Scotland*, 2 vols, 2nd edn (Basingstoke, 2007 [1984]), II: pp. 161, 172-3, 175; Richard Harris, '"Completely Inaccessible": James Kelman, the Booker Prize, and the Cultural Politics of Subaltern Representation', in *To the other shore: cross-currents in Irish and Scottish Studies*, eds Neil Alexander, Shane Murphy and Anne Oakman (Belfast, 2004), pp. 68-75 (p. 74).
3 James D. Young, *The Very Bastards of Creation* (Glasgow, n.d. [c. 1996]), pp. 302, 307, 311-12; Watson, *Literature of Scotland*, II: pp. 175, 267, 270.
4 Irvine Welsh, 'Scotland – capital of murder', *The Guardian G2* (20 October 2005), pp. 8-11 (p. 11).
5 John Mercer, *Scotland: The Devolution of Power* (London, 1978), p. 35; Eleanor Bell, 'Old Country, New Dreams: Scottish Poetry since the 1970s', in *The Edinburgh History of Scottish Literature*, eds Ian Brown, Thomas Clancy, Susan Manning and Murray Pittock, 3 vols (2006; Edinburgh, 2007), III: pp. 185-97 (p. 193); Ian Brown, 'Staging the Nation', *Edinburgh History*, III: pp. 283-94; Watson, *Literature of Scotland*, II: pp. 180-4.

6 Young, *Bastards of Creation*, p. 305.
7 Richard Butt, 'Literature and the Screen Media since 1908', in *The Edinburgh History* III: pp. 53–63 (p. 55).
8 *The Corries* (Edinburgh, 1989), *Corries* tour souvenir programme; Cairns Craig, in conversation, 13 March 2007.
9 Macmillan, *Scottish Art*, pp. 81, 115, 120, 122–3, 125, 128, 129, 140, 171; Watson, *Literature of Scotland*, II: pp. 198, 201–2, 296.
10 Craig Beveridge and Ronnie Turnbull, *Scotland After Enlightenment* (Edinburgh, 1997), p. 58.
11 Cf. P Hateley Waddell's *The Psalms: Frae Hebrew Intil Scottis* (1871), reprinted as *The Psalms in Scots*, intr. Graham Tulloch (Aberdeen, 1987); Scott, *Towards Independence*, p. 75; Caroline Macafee, 'The Demography of Scots: The Lessons of the Census Campaign', in *Scottish Language* 19 (2000), pp. 1–44 (pp. 9, 38); Wilson McLeod and Jeremy Smith, 'Resistance to Monolinguality: The Languages of Scotland since 1918', in *The Edinburgh History*, III: pp. 21–30 (p. 28).
12 Malcolm MacLean, 'Parallel Universes: Gaelic Arts Development in Scotland, 1985–2000', in *Aithne na nGael: Gaelic Identities*, eds Gordon McCoy with Maolcholaim Scott (Belfast, 2000), pp. 105–25 (p. 107); Robert Dunbar, 'Legal and Institutional Aspects of Gaelic Development', in *Aithne na nGael*, pp. 67–87 (p. 69); Kenneth MacKinnon, 'Neighbours in Persistence: Prospects for Gaelic Maintenance in a Globalising English World', in *Aithne na nGael*, pp. 144–55 (p. 153); McLeod and Smith in *Edinburgh History*, III: p. 23.
13 Mercer, *Scotland*, p. 59; MacLean in *Aithne na nGael*, pp. 105, 107–10, 112, 114; Tormod Caimbeul, 'The Politics of Gaelic Development in Scotland' in *Aithne nanGael*, pp. 53–66 (pp. 54–7).
14 Tormod Caimbeul, Robert Dunbar and Malcom MacLean in *Aithne na nGael*, pp. 60, 66, 67–8, 115; McLeod and Smith in *Edinburgh History*, III: p. 28.
15 David Ross, '"Symbolic milestone" as five-year plan for Gaelic is unveiled', *The Herald* (March 27, 2007), p. 3; Steven Vass, 'Cunningham defends £16 million spend on BBC Gaelic channel', *The Sunday Herald* (25 March 2007), p. 10.
16 James G. Kellas, *The Scottish Political System*, 4th edn (1973; Cambridge, 1992), pp. 8, 209; Steven Vass, 'Regionalised bulletins launch tomorrow', *Sunday Herald* Media (7 January 2007), p. 9.
17 Peter Lynch, *Scottish Government and Politics: An Introduction* (Edinburgh, 2001), pp. 197, 199; Michael Keating, *The Government of Scotland: Public Policy Making after Devolution* (Edinburgh, 2005), pp. 90, 93; Steven Vass, 'STV will not revive Scots poll coverage', *Sunday Herald* (27 May 2007), p. 4.
18 Adrian Turpin, 'Northern Lights', *FT Magazine* (February 17/18 2007), pp. 34–5.
19 David McCrone, *Scotland: The Sociology of a Stateless Nation* (London, 1992), p. 101.
20 Quoted in Scott, *Towards Independence*, p. 113.
21 *The Sunday Herald* (27 August 2006), p. 3.
22 Murray Pittock, *Scottish Nationality* (Basingstoke, 2001), pp. 145–6; *The Herald* (May 4 1999), p. 19. See also Alan Riach, 'In danger of losing the plot', *The Herald: Society* (March 13, 2007), p. 10.
23 Jennifer Cunningham, 'Selling Scotland: the great escape from a world of tartan tourism', *The Herald* (March 6, 2007), p. 15; adaptations of *Kidnapped* are discussed by Butt in *Edinburgh History* III: p. 59.
24 Tom Gordon, '70 countries to join in St Andrew's Day celebrations', *The Herald* (November 8, 2006), p. 5; Martyn McLaughlin, 'Poetic justice at last for the

bard' and 'Birth and marriage papers go online', in *The Herald* (25 January 2007), p. 11.

25 Ruth Wishart, 'The stage is set: but where next for the art and soul of a nation?', *The Herald* (February 21 2007), p. 17; Phil Miller, 'Academy honours stars of Scottish culture', *The Herald* (March 8, 2007), p. 9; Cairns Craig, 'Scotland: Culture after Devolution', in *Ireland (Ulster) Scotland: Concepts, Contexts, Comparisons*, eds Edna Longley, Eamonn Hughes and Des O'Rawe (Belfast, 2003), pp. 39–43 (p. 41).

Chapter 5: Who are the New Scots?

1 Cairns Craig, in conversation, 14 March 2007.
2 Dr John MacDonald, 'The English in Scotland', *Scots Independent* 4:8 (April 1939), p. 1.
3 T. M. Devine, *The Scottish Nation 1700–2000* (London, 1999), pp. 498–9, 507–12; Rory Williams and Patricia Walls, 'Going but not Gone: Catholic Disadvantage in Scotland', in *Scotland's Shame? Bigotry and Sectarianism in Modern Scotland*, ed. T. M. Devine (Edinburgh, 2000), pp. 231–52 (p. 233).
4 James MacMillan, 'Irish in Denial', *Scottish Review of Books* 2:3 (2006), p. 13; Williams and Walls in *Scotland's Shame?*, p. 247.
5 Joseph Bradley, *Ethnic and Religious Identity in Modern Scotland* (Aldershot, 1995), pp. x, 37, 41.
6 For Bashir Maan, see www.onescotland.com and www.theglasgowstory.com; Charles Jedrej and Mark Nuttall, *White Settlers: The Impact of Rural Repopulation in Scotland* (Luxembourg, 1996), pp. 3, 17, 24, 81n, 104.
7 Liam McDougall, 'Leading Jew sent hate mail amid spate of attacks', *Sunday Herald* (27 August 2006), p. 7; Devine, *The Scottish Nation*, p. 564; Lindsay Paterson, Frank Bechhofer and David McCrone, *Living in Scotland: Social and Economic Change since 1980* (Edinburgh, 2004), p. 55; Lucy Adams, 'Museums asked to create prayer rooms', *The Herald* (April 16 2007), p. 3; Emma Seith, 'Will it still be all-white in May?', *The Herald: Society* (March 27 2007), pp. 2–4 (pp. 2, 4).
8 Martin Williams, 'Why ethnic minorities feel more Scottish than whites', *The Herald* (August 8 2006), p. 5 (see the report on 'Young people's experiences of transition to adulthood' at www.jrf.org.uk); Neil Mackay and Jennifer Johnston, 'The New Scots: Immigrants' Stories', *The Sunday Herald* (27 August 2006), pp. 38–9; Rowena Arshad, 'Daring to be different: a new vision of equality', in *Tomorrow's Scotland*, eds Gerry Hassan and Chris Warhurst (London, 2002), pp. 207–21 (p. 216); Lucy Adams, 'Scots more welcoming to migrants, says race commission', *The Herald* (March 27 2007), pp. 1–2 (p. 1); Michael Keating, *The Government of Scotland: Public Policy Making after Devolution* (Edinburgh, 2005), p. 33.
9 T. M. Devine, 'The Paradox of Scottish Emigration', in *Scottish Emigration and Scottish Society*, ed. T. M. Devine (Edinburgh, 1992), pp. 1–15 (p. 3); Malcolm Gray, 'The Course of Scottish Emigration, 1750–1914: Enduring Influences and Changing Circumstances', in *Scottish Emigration and Scottish Society*, pp. 16–36 (p. 17); Michael E. Vance, 'The Politics of Emigration: Scotland and Assisted Emigration to Upper Canada, 1815–26', in *Scottish Emigration and Scottish Society* pp. 37–60 (p. 40).
10 See chapter Ten, 'Fratriotism: Empire and its Limits in the Scottish and Irish

Imagination, 1746–1837', in Murray Pittock, 'Scottish and Irish Romanticism' (Oxford, forthcoming).

11 Jeannette M. Brock, 'The Importance of Emigration in Scottish Regional Population Movement, 1861–1911', in *Scottish Emigration and Scottish Society*, pp. 104–34 (p. 114); Isobel Lindsay, 'Migration and Motivation: A Twentieth-Century Perspective', *Scottish Emigration and Scottish Society*, pp. 154–74 (pp. 157–8, 166–9).

12 Alan Taylor in *The Spectator* (August 17 2002): reproduced at http://findarticles.com (stereotypes of Scots).

13 Paterson, Bechhofer and McCrone, *Living in Scotland*, pp. 10–11; 'Executive will press Home Office to allow integrated families to stay in Scotland' and 'A special case for Scotland', *The Herald* (March 21 2007), pp. 1, 12.

14 Douglas Fraser, 'Wanted: 13,000 immigrants a year to revitalise Scotland', *The Herald* (March 13, 2007), p. 2; for details on Fresh Talent, see www.scotlandistheplace.com; Lucy Adams, 'A warm welcome to Scotland', *The Herald* (March 27 2007), p. 11.

15 Paul Hutcheon, 'Our man in the US puts Irish ahead of Scots', *Sunday Herald* (25 March 2007), p. 7; Jason Allardyce, 'McConnell urges expat Scots to return home', *Sunday Times* (October 2, 2005), News Section, p. 11.

16 'The Pole Position', *Sunday Herald Focus* (6 August 2006), pp. 12–13.

Chapter 6: Devolving or Declining? Government and Society in Scotland Since 1999

1 James Macmillan, 'Desire for reconciliation', *The Herald* (March 31 2000), p. 17; Murray Pittock, *Scottish Nationality* (Basingstoke, 2001), p. 127.

2 Michael Keating, *The Government of Scotland: Public Policy Making after Devolution* (Edinburgh, 2005), pp. 98–9; Peter Lynch, *Scottish Government and Politics: An Introduction* (Edinburgh, 2001), p. 56.

3 Malcolm Dickson, 'Scotland's First General Election: Breaking the Westminster Mould?', in *Synergy: Scotland's Devolved Government: How Different from Westminster?* (Glasgow, 1999).

4 Henry McLeish, *Scotland First: Truth and Consequences* (Edinburgh, 2004), p. 182.

5 For a summary of Scottish Parliament Legislation, see www.scottish.parliament.uk

6 Douglas Fraser, 'What the parliament has done', *The Herald* (30 March 2007), p. 13; Lynch, *Scottish Government and Politics*, pp. 72, 75, 90–1.

7 Ian McConnell, 'Banking on the future: a new view of Scotland', *The Herald* (17 April 2007), p. 11.

8. Robbie Dinwoodie, 'Civil service dispersal "a failure"', *The Herald* (2 March 2007), p. 2.

9 James Kellas, 'The New Scottish Political System: Consensus or Conflict?' and Brian Hogwood, 'Quangos and Other Bodies in Scotland: What are the Key Issues?' in *Synergy*.

10 Robbie Dinwoodie, 'Holyrood founder says it is a failure', *The Herald* (March 30, 2007), p. 6; Alan Smart, 'We are just a click away from better government', *Sunday Herald* (11 February 2007), p. 37; McLeish, *Scotland First*, p. 192; Paul Rogerson, 'SNP says "Tesco Law" is not suited to Scottish society', *The Herald* (April 30, 2007), p. 28.

11 Keating, *The Government of Scotland*, pp. 24, 131; Lynch, *Scottish Government and*

Politics, pp. 150, 159–60; McLeish, *Scotland First*, pp. 7, 199; Douglas Fraser, 'Prime Minister must "devise a way" to handle SNP clashes', *The Herald* (8 May 2007); Fraser, 'Scotland "frozen out of Brussels"', *The Herald* (22 January 2007), p. 1; 'Why Scottish MEPs are left "isolated and frustrated"', ibid., p. 2; Douglas Fraser, 'McConnell wades into business tax relief row with Whitehall' *The Herald* (17 November 2006), p. 25; Alf Young, 'It's the season to be jolly, unless you're a fisherman', *The Herald* (22 December 2006), p. 19.

12 Douglas Fraser, 'Counting the Cost of Holyrood' and 'Building a pearl beyond price, say visitors', *The Herald* (22 February 2007), p. 15.

13 Robbie Dinwoodie, 'A bulldozer approach to planning?', *The Herald* (17 November 2006), p. 15; see also 30 March 2007, p. 13; Antony Akilade, 'Is the Future of, Wind Power On the Up?', *Sunday Herald* (14 January 2007), pp. 12–13; Duncan McLaren, 'It's time to give us the power to decide on energy', *The Herald* (29 May 2007), p. 13.

14 Stewart Paterson, 'Nationalists control of trouble-torn council', *The Herald* (17 May 2007), p. 7; Graeme Smith, 'Student and Deputy Lord Provost . . . and just 18', *The Herald* (16 May 2007), p. 13.

15 Ian Bell, 'A history lesson from Holyrood', *The Herald* (30 March 2007), p. 13; Douglas Fraser, 'Call to scrutinise MSPs' expenses', *The Herald* (29 March 2007), p. 6.

16 Daniel Woolls, 'Catalonia says si to more powers', *The Herald* (19 June 2006), p. 13; 'MacDonald's list of 11 powers to be transferred to Scotland', *The Herald* (30 April 2007), p. 6; Mick Common, 'Scottish election lacks legitimacy', letter, *Sunday Herald* (3 June 2007), p. 40.

17 *The Herald Election 2007* (5 May); 'British politics is competitive again', Leader, *Financial Times* (5/6 May 2007), p. 10.

18 Robbie Dinwoodie, 'Famous names back commission on constitution', *The Herald* (30 April 2007), p. 7; Iain McWhirter, 'It is an illiberal party that denies the people a voice', *The Herald* (16 April 2007), p. 13; 'Why Scotland needs a new Constitutional Convention', *Sunday Herald* (13 May 2007), p. 43; 'The progressive forces in Scottish politics must come together. Democracy demands it', *Sunday Herald* (6 May 2007), p. 25; Stewart Paterson and Lucy Adams, 'SNP strikes deal to keep Labour out', *The Herald* (10 May 2007), p. 4.

19 'The Scottish Executive', *The Herald* (17 May 2007), p. 6.

20 Carol Craig, *The Scots' Crisis of Confidence* (2003; Glasgow, 2004) is an example of this, which provides a rather essentialist reading of Scottish character; *The Sunday Herald: Seven Days* (19 November 2006), p. 11; William Tinning, 'Catholic Church in row over gay adoptions', *The Herald* (24 January 2007), p. 3; Douglas Fraser, 'Christian soldier takes up arms as hustings near', *The Herald* (13 March 2007).

21 Calum MacDonald, 'Taskforce wants Scotland put on the worldwide map for foodies', *The Herald* (27 December 2006), p. 10; Angus Macleod, 'EU to follow Scotland's lead', *The Times* (21 March 2007), p. 2.

22 Stephen Naysmith, 'Third of young Scots want to leave', *The Herald: Society* (1 November 2005), pp. 2–5 (pp. 2, 4); Douglas Fraser, 'Young people "back independence"', *The Herald* (24 March 2007), p. 6.

23 Lynch, *Scottish Government and Politics*, p. 130; Michael Settle, 'Security czar role for Reid to tackle terrorism', *The Herald* (30 March 2007), p. 6; Douglas Fraser, 'Prime Minister must "devise a way" to handle SNP clashes', *The Herald* (8 May 2007); James Kirkup, 'Executive given new powers on surveillance', *The*

Scotsman (18 July 2007), p. 20; Michael Settle, 'Warning to Labour MPs over "wrecking the Union"', *The Herald* (9 July 2007), p. 1.

24 Douglas Fraser, 'Why the English think Scotland is better', *The Herald* (31 August 2005); Vicky Shaw, 'Concern as cancer drug only given approval in Scotland', *The Herald* (9 May 2007), 10.

25 Lynch (2001), 135, 143; Iain MacWhirter, '"He'll be haunted by the West Lothian question"', *Sunday Herald*, 14 January 2007, p. 3; Douglas Fraser, 'Portillo backs separate Scotland because England "no longer needs it"', *The Herald*, 19 June 2006, 6; Douglas Fraser, 'Stewart urges Tories to back independence', *The Herald*, 2 September 2006.

26 Gavin McCrone, *Scotland's Future: The Economics of Nationalism* (Oxford: Blackwell, 1969), pp. 53–66 ('The Budgetary Position'); Murray Pittock, *Scottish Nationality* (Basingstoke: Palgrave/Macmillan, 2001), p. 120.

27 Joan McAlpine, 'Why there will only be one real winner in 2012', *The Herald*, 19 June 2006, p. 15; Douglas Fraser, 'Revealed: True oil wealth was hidden to stop independence', *The Herald*, 12 September 2005, p. 1; Angus Macleod, 'SNP pledges to grow economy by £19bn as tax policy attacked', *The Times*, 21 March 2007, p. 2.

Further Reading

Bogdanor, Vernon, *Devolution in the United Kingdom* (Oxford, 1999)
Bradley, Joseph, *Ethnic and Religious Identity in Modern Scotland* (Aldershot, 1995)
Brown, Ian, et al., eds, *The Edinburgh History of Scottish Literature*, 3 vols
    (Edinburgh, 2007)
Devine, T. M, ed., *Scotland's Shame? Bigotry and Sectarianism in Modern Scotland*
    (Edinburgh, 2000)
Devine, T. M. and Finlay, Richard, eds, *Scotland in the 20th Century* (1996;
    Edinburgh, 1997)
Edwards, Owen Dudley, ed., *A Claim of Right for Scotland* (Edinburgh, 1989)
Finlay, Richard J., *Modern Scotland 1914–2000* (London, 2004)
Guibernau, Montserrat, *Nations without States: Political Communities in a Global
    Age* (1999; Cambridge, 2005)
Harvie, Christopher, *No Gods and Precious Few Heroes*, 2nd edn (1981; Edinburgh,
    1993)
—, *Scotland and Nationalism*, 3rd edn (1977; London, 1998)
Hechter, Michael, *Internal Colonialism* (London, 1975)
Ichijo, Atsuko, *Scottish Nationalism and the Idea of Europe* (London, 2004)
Keating, Michael, *The Government of Scotland: Public Policy Making After Devolution*
    (Edinburgh, 2005)
Lynch, Peter, *Scottish Government and Politics: An Introduction* (Edinburgh, 2001)
—, *SNP: The History of the Scottish National Party* (Cardiff, 2002)
MacCormick, John, *The Flag in the Wind: The Story of the National Movement in
    Scotland* (London, 1955)
McCrone, David, *Understanding Scotland: The Sociology of a Stateless Nation*
    (London, 1992)
MacDonald, Catriona, ed., *Unionist Scotland 1800–1997* (Edinburgh, 1998)
Macmillan, Duncan, *Scottish Art in the Twentieth Century* (Edinburgh, 1994)
Mitchell, James, *Strategies for Self-Government: The Campaigns for a Scottish
    Parliament* (Edinburgh, 1996)
Nairn, Tom, *After Britain* (London, 2000)
Paterson, Lindsay, *The Autonomy of Modern Scotland* (Edinburgh, 1994)
Pittock, Murray, *Scottish Nationality* (Basingstoke, 2001)
—, *A New History of Scotland* (Stroud, 2003)

Smith, Robin, *The Making of Scotland* (Edinburgh, 2001)
Stenhouse, David, *On the Make: How the Scots Took Over London* (Edinburgh and London, 2004)

Acknowledgements

This book is in one dimension a study of Scotland over my own lifetime, and the many changes I have seen as a child in Aberdeen, a student in Glasgow, and an academic in all three of Scotland's largest cities. My own life has at times touched on the very concerns with culture and identity discussed in Chapters One and Four. But this book is principally an academic study, drawing on my own work over many years in the study of literature, culture, history and politics, addressed also in previous books such as *Celtic Identity and the British Image* (1999) and *Scottish Nationality* (2001). Scotland is, like any culture, a complex subject, and it has been an immense privilege to study it for so long while living in it: the two in fact cannot be separated.

The same is the case for my debts, which are many. I have had the privilege of long conversations with some of the most acute commentators on today's Scotland, others actively engaged in creating it, and others who analyse current affairs as their hobby or their daily bread. Douglas Carson, David Ellis, Clark McGinn and the late Ross Mackenzie have discussed nationalist and Tory politics with me for almost 30 years; and I also owe debts to my conversations with Charles Kennedy and Liam Fox, John Morrison, Michael Gove and Boris Johnson among my university contemporaries who went into politics. In academic life, I am indebted to the conversations and published work of Jeremy Black, Alexander Broadie, Jonathan Clark, Ted Cowan, Cairns Craig, Tom Devine, Owen Dudley Edwards, Richard Finlay, Chris Harvie MSP, Atsuko Ichijo, Joep Leerssen, David McCrone, Frank McLynn, James Mitchell and Lindsay Paterson, and to the committees associated with the University in Scotland initiative at Edinburgh and the Glasgow-Strathclyde School of Scottish Studies, as well as the Irish-Scottish Studies Research Group at Manchester. In politics and the media, I have talked to and learnt from the conversations of Colin Bell, Pat Kane, Paul Scott and David Stenhouse. My last and greatest debt is, as always, to my wife Anne and daughters, Lexie and Davina, who have seen so many hours that could have been theirs slip away in writing about this country. Any faults that follow are my own.

This book is dedicated to Sir Neil MacCormick, famous son of a famous father, and one of the deepest thinkers about the constitution of Scotland and Europe of the last 50 years. It has been a privilege to know him for more than half of them.

Index